Success and Failure in Analysis

Success and Failure in Analysis

The Proceedings of
The Fifth International Congress
For Analytical Psychology

GERHARD ADLER, Editor

PUBLISHED BY
G. P. Putnam's Sons, New York
FOR THE C. G. JUNG FOUNDATION
FOR ANALYTICAL PSYCHOLOGY

Published on the same day in the Dominion of Canada
by Longmans Canada Limited, Toronto.

Printed in the United States of America
Library of Congress Catalog Card Number 73–76973
ISBN 0–913430–21–8

Acknowledgment is made to Harcourt Brace Jovanovich, Inc., New York, for per-
mission to quote from T. S. Eliot's "East Coker" in the paper by Robert F. Hobson,
and to Princeton University Press and Routledge & Kegan Paul Ltd. for quotations
from the *Collected Works of C. G. Jung*.

Preface

The Fifth Congress for Analytical Psychology took place in London from 1 to 8 September 1971. Its subject was "Success and Failure in Analysis (with special reference to the shadow and creativity)."

Every analyst is aware of the almost insurmountable difficulty of assessing the results of analytical treatment by the criteria of success and failure. The results are generally too complex; too many subjective or imponderable factors come into play. Is the disappearance of a symptom to be regarded as proof of a successful treatment—indeed, is it the aim of analysis? Is the persistence of a symptom to be regarded as proof of failure, though the analysis has led to an enrichment of the patient's life? What is to be regarded as gain or loss, as enrichment or frustration?

These and similar questions were in the mind of most contributors. It was a healthy sign that the problems of failure in analysis and of the shortcomings of the analyst stood in the center of the discussion—a sign of a salutary self-searching and absence of complacency, far removed from the euphoria with which analysts so often embark on their careers. Here the problem of the "shadow" of the analyst was brought into the open, tapping new creative sources.

Another question frequently posed was that of the influence of the contemporary scene on the analyst's work. It becomes more and more apparent that the analyst cannot keep aloof from the social, political, and in general the cultural problems of his time—this may be in his work with the young generation, often so deeply involved in these conflicts, or with marriage partners whose conventional relationship is shaken by the new permissiveness, or by the change in the role and consciousness of women. Another problem arising from the new social situation is the need felt by some analysts to go beyond the confines of the two-persons situation into confrontation within a group.

All in all, the Congress showed a healthy skepticism about the value of orthodoxy, a constructive self-criticism, and an openness to new ideas manifesting the resources and vitality of analytical psychology.

London, November 1972   Gerhard Adler

Contents

Success and Failure in Analysis

1

Can We Evaluate Analysis in Terms of Success and Failure?

GUSTAV DREIFUSS, *Haifa*

My first spontaneous reaction to the words "success and failure" in connection with analysis, as they appear in the theme of our Congress, was definitely affective. Can one, I asked myself, evaluate the work of analysis, which occupies itself with the human soul, according to the notions of success and failure? I tried to explain this affect to myself, with the following results:

1. Does not the theme of the Congress, so clearly formulated, conceal a tendency to stress the scientific-medical direction in Jungian psychology and so to leave the soul out of consideration? True, the addition "Shadow and Aspects of Creativity" to the main title "Success and Failure" softens this impression. And yet I think there is a danger in using the terms success and failure undifferentiatedly: the danger of a too superficial and schematic estimation of the analytical relationship, which is an encounter of two individuals with their consciousness and

3

their unconscious together and with the problems of feeling-relationship (transference and countertransference).

2. The main reason for my affect is surely my own feeling function, for as I turned the problem over in my mind, I came to see how problematic the judgment and evaluation of analytical achievements really are. For I noticed my tendency to exclude all failure from analytical therapy! I felt that in almost every analytical relationship, even be it one that lasts no more than one hour, something dynamic and creative happens, which can be the beginning of a new development, even if we cannot notice an immediate and striking success or failure.

In order to clarify the complex of problems, I would like to discuss the subject from the following points of view:

(1) Evaluation by the patient.
(2) Evaluation by the environment (family, society).
(3) Evaluation by the therapist.

(1) EVALUATION OF ANALYSIS BY THE PATIENT

The evaluation of analysis by the patient is as varied as one individual varies from another, i.e., absolutely subjective. An important factor is the reason why a person comes to treatment. From your own experience you know how different these reasons can be. One man comes because his wife, his mother-in-law, or his mother has sent him, another because a friend told him about his own successful treatment, etc. A short time ago an elderly woman came to me and asked me to confirm that her mind was all right, that she was not crazy, as her brother had claimed, after they had quarreled. As a result of my confirmation, the consultation was a success for her, although she had been depressive for several years but did not admit this and consequently did not go to treatment for it.

Or a young man comes with his wife because of sexual difficulties for as many as three months after the marriage and because the doctor had advised consulting an analyst. I discuss the problem with both of them, first separately and then together, all within one hour, and a week later I get a telephone call saying that everything is "all right" now. Both of them were satisfied with the consultation (was that a treatment?) and they felt it to be a success.

Such one-hour consultations or short therapies have often a humorous note, and every analyst surely has had these experiences.

In analyses that lead to the healing of symptoms, evaluation is clear.

For instance, a patient who suffers from functional heart disturbances and is freed from them through psychotherapy will call this a success, which is right objectively, even if little has been reached from the analytical point of view, i.e., in the sense of development of personality.

But in a long-lasting analysis, the question of evaluation becomes much more difficult. This problem interested me especially, and therefore I turned to several analysands and ex-analysands who had had at least one hundred hours of treatment, and I posed them the question whether they evaluated their analyses as a success or a failure. I quote here only the essence of the replies:

A young woman, mother of two children, whose analysis was broken off, because of her departure, after three years and approximately 150 hours, writes: "I do not consider myself as recovered, and I cannot believe that I shall ever be healthy, nevertheless I cannot talk about failure here. On the contrary—the analytical work helped me to live my life in a simpler way. Moreover, I was enriched and freed from inhibitions, and all this expressed itself in a strong urge towards creativity. So I can say that there is success, but not complete recovery."

A woman of forty, who resumed her analysis after an interval of several years, following an interest in the inner process, thinks that the question demands an absolute answer, and continues: "This does not seem to me to be a healthy attitude, considering the fundamental meaning of Jungian psychology, for whoever wants to be faithful to the process is not allowed to have any preconceived opinions on success."

Another woman analysand declares that the patient has the right to be completely subjective in the evaluation. She may say that on the one hand she feels that treatment was a success, and in this she has achieved something. On the other hand she evaluates the treatment as a failure, as she feels that she was unable to live up to all its demands.

One analysand answers my question as follows: "In my opinion it is not possible to measure analysis by the standard of success and failure." He then brings up two factors that are of great importance for the estimation of analysis: "(1) Has the analysand reached the profound feeling that one cannot evade difficult situations (crises) and that there is no solution but to take up the battle against them in an honest and courageous way, notwithstanding the anguish connected with this confrontation (the way of the Hero)? And (2), does the analysand feel with his whole soul that not all the threads are in his hands? That although time may make us a little wiser, there are things that happen in the depths of the unconscious, over which man has no influence?"

We can say for certain that his analysis has touched this patient to the quick! In general, one could say that evaluation of analysis depends on the structure of the analysand's personality. I shall go deeper into this problem when I come to evaluation by the analyst.

A woman patient whom I treated for one year, a long time ago, and whom I turned over to a colleague because of her departure, answers my question in the following way: "I can say for sure that without your help the world would not have opened its doors to me and I would not have been able to manage by myself any longer. There is no doubt about that. But I am no less certain that a decisive part must be ascribed to the persistence of my *self*, which mercilessly spurred me on to development.. . . . I *had* to choose the way of development, for if not, I would have been lost. . . . But I would also call the work with your colleague successful. Most of the time I had the impression that I needed you both. It was as if one was complementary to the other. Seen in the light of the self, we might even think of an arrangement of that which I needed. — But be this as it may, I certainly belong to the lucky ones who went through a good therapy. I could unfold myself and grow out of problems in a manner which once I would not have thought possible. — And in spite of all this, in my case too, I would prefer not to speak of success, but to say that therapy has helped me to find my own way and to develop my faculties. Therapy was not for nothing, it was meaningful, and I could say it supported my own true will. Added to that, there were external conditions which made further development possible."

This analysand had been sent to me in a very critical life situation, which is often a favorable condition for analysis. In such a case, progress in treatment is—understandably enough—felt as success.

These statements show clearly that evaluation must be differentiated as soon as we have longer analyses. Somehow the analytical process then becomes more important than its evaluation; the twin ideas of success and failure are, in a way, overcome.

(2) EVALUATION OF THE ANALYSIS BY THE PATIENT'S ENVIRONMENT

The patient's environment takes it as a sign of success when he functions better or with less friction in external reality, in his relations with his fellow men, and in his family and profession.

In general, in the treatment of adults, we have only the conscious and unconscious material of the patient by which to learn about improvement in his relationship with the environment. Only now and then are there exceptions to this rule, when for certain reasons we have contact with members of the patient's family; for instance, when he is physically ill. Also, we may receive spontaneous information from husbands, wives, or children of patients about improvement or worsening. In Israel we have a unique situation in the kibbutz system, through which we receive information about the condition of the patient from the health committee of the kibbutz. On such occasions I often find out that the community of the patient sees a positive change, which otherwise I would not have known of. When I discuss this with the patient, I learn that the reason may be a feeling of anxiety or insecurity in him, because he believes that an improvement could lead to a breaking off of treatment, or he cannot yet believe in a real improvement or change of his personality.

The conclusion is that the analyst must be careful of that which he hears or does not hear from the patient about a change in his relationships.

(3) EVALUATION BY THE ANALYST

The problem of evaluation is connected with the general problem of diagnosis. For example, I remember a woman patient, an artist, who was sent to me by a psychiatrist with the indications: lesbian, alcoholic. In the course of treatment, after having talked about her relationship to her parents (the father, a Christian, had stayed in Poland in 1939, when mother and daughter had fled to Israel through Russia), she painted a picture that showed the two worlds, father and mother, as a world globe, split in the middle. During treatment, the alcoholism diminished considerably, though with many relapses; her general condition improved. Treatment was stopped after two years. Catamnesis: after three years of stationary condition, no worsening of the alcoholism. Success or failure?

The psychiatrist who had sent her to me and who examined the patient after one year and again after two years of treatment considered the analysis a success as, according to his opinion, without a successful analysis the patient might have had to be hospitalized for an outbreak of schizophrenia. I myself was not satisfied with the result, because I had believed or hoped that a heterosexual relationship, which had begun during treatment, would develop positively; this did not happen.

We can see that estimation of success and failure is closely bound up with the diagnosis and with the evaluation of the therapist. Was the psychiatrist too pessimistic? Was I too optimistic in the way I saw the case? This young woman was my second patient after I had finished my studies at the Jung Institute. So I was still fresh and relatively un-burdened in the practice of the analytical profession. According to Jung (1960, par. 539) enthusiasm is the secret of success in psycho-therapy. In my enthusiasm, did I overlook the profound disturbance in the patient? Was the psychiatrist's diagnosis right? What would have happened to the patient if she had gone to another analyst or if she had not undertaken treatment? Idle questions without clear answers.

So evaluation of treatment is also dependent on diagnosis, and here we have all kinds of experience in our practice. With slight exaggera-tion we could say that everyone independently, i.e., without being acquainted with the previously diagnosing psychiatrist or psychologist, comes to his own diagnosis. I remember one analysand whom I could only see two months after the first contact by telephone because of excessive work, and who managed in these two months to see three different therapists and was diagnosed in three ways:

1) Schizophrenia camouflaged by compulsion neurosis with tendency to depression;
2) Character neurosis;
3) Slightly hysterical personality with profound anxiety.

About four weeks after starting treatment I met a woman psychiatrist who had seen the patient once, and I received an astonished look of admiration when I told her that the patient had not made any at-tempts at suicide and that he was still going to work. In the two months during which he visited the different therapists, the patient was in an acute condition of stress because of external circumstances. When he came to me, a slight tranquillization had already begun, but com-pulsion symptoms and depressive tendencies were still present.

This example shows not only how different appraisals by different therapists can be, but also the influence of the moment in time of the appraisal. A colleague with whom I discussed the case—she too had made a diagnosis—made no fuss over it and stated simply that the other colleagues never could diagnose! An easy solution to the problem!

Towards all diagnoses, especially my own, I am very critical. I prefer to relate to the sufferer and to carefully follow up changes in the conscious attitude and transformations in the unconscious.

And yet, as Bleuler (1955, p. 138) says in his discussion about the causes of psychical disturbances, we must accord to the diagnosis its due importance, even when keeping in mind the "uniqueness of every human personality."

In the foregoing, I talked about the subjective evaluation by the patient and its unlimited individual variation span. It seems to me that the same goes for evaluation by the analyst. The *Weltanschauung* of the analyst, his personality, his inner and outer experiences, his maturity and his age are all determinants in evaluation.

Riemann (1968), for instance, examines the influence of the analyst's personality structure on the course of treatment. He divides analysts into four groups: compulsive, hysterical, depressive, and schizoid. The depressive analyst, for instance, is devoted and willing to sacrifice himself; he is inclined to underestimate his own contribution to the analysis and to see everything that goes wrong as his own mistake. If we apply this example to the problem of evaluation, we could say that the depressive analyst is inclined to ascribe successes to the analysand's efforts or to good fate, and failure mainly to his own insufficiency. The other examples of Riemann can be applied accordingly.

The analyst's psychological type also influences evaluation of analysis. Meier (1971) has discussed the problem of analysis and psychological type. For our theme one could say that the analyst's psychological type influences the evaluation the more so when the analyst is insufficiently aware of his unconscious attitude and his inferior functions.

It seems to me that a precondition for an approximately correct evaluation of his own work is that the analyst constantly works on himself in order to keep himself conscious. For this the analyst must especially be conscious of his shadow, as Guggenbühl (1968, 1970) has pointed out. For instance, there is the danger of the analyst feeding his analysand with amplification material which he himself is working on or is interested in. Then a participation may be brought about: the analyst wants to "make pupils," and the analysand will, for a longer or shorter period, remain stuck in inflation. But, on the other hand, the archetypal relationship of master-pupil can also be meant synchronistically and lead to a fruitful, creative development. Here too, evaluation must be differentiated: through paying careful attention to the conscious and unconscious material of analysand and analyst we have to check again and again both whether the analyst is not dominated by a power-devil who wants to assure him of more influence by making pupils and whether the analysand is not kept infantile by this.

Another danger of succumbing to the shadow lies in the "careful selection" of patients, which can easily camouflage a wish for success and for increase of power. One turns an analysand down or sends him away after a short time and reasons to oneself that the patient does not have the necessary intelligence for analytical treatment. Of course, such a thing exists, just as there are patients who need medical treatment and ones with whom one cannot establish contact. The crucial point, however, is whether the analyst is conscious of his own motivation.

It seems to me, furthermore, that often we speak too disdainfully about supportive therapy in cases of chronic psychical sickness. These patients would—in a way—correspond in somatic medicine to the diabetics or to people with chronic heart disease. This happens when we view our work too strongly under the aspect of the "striking success." And yet such cases can be meaningful if we regard their treatment as "mental care," according to Jung (1958, passim). With people who had been through the Nazi persecutions—cases in which therapy is mostly supportive—the demands on the analyst's capacity for empathy with the patient's suffering are extraordinarily great. Supportive cases help the analyst to keep the limiting external reality in mind and to remain conscious of his own limits in "healing" ability. And when the therapist produces enough patience, then we can see how even in these cases a positive turn can sometimes be experienced or endured.

When it happens that the analyst registers an obvious success, again the shadow may turn up. We can observe this when the analyst talks about *his* success, instead of saying that success has occurred. Conversely, if the treatment is without positive result, we must ask the question, does there exist, or still exist, in the psyche of the analysand a tendency towards healing? Does a certain analysis stand "under a good star," under the "Deo concedente"? Who can judge that with certainty? Who knows if, in a seemingly positive analysis, the unconscious will not suddenly break through, destroying all that has been gained? And on the other hand, who did not yet see an unexpected positive turn in a seemingly hopeless case? Who decides whether a case is "hopeless"? Or is there always hope? And who knows if and when a man must die? (Hillman, 1964.)

CONCLUSION

The purpose of my paper was to show the difficulties that come up in the evaluation of analysis. I wanted to point out the dangers we run into when we look at the work of analysis from a scientific and objective point of view. All the same, we must try to do this again and again, in order to be able to exchange our experiences—and in constant awareness of the fact that in the final judgment only a differentiated evaluation of analysis can do justice to the problems of the individual, for it is clear that in many cases there is simply no "either/or" in connection with success and failure.

The analyst himself is likewise a patient in so far as, according to the process of individuation, he not only creates but also suffers his own fate in the never-ceasing confrontation with the unconscious. To the extent that the analyst continually works on himself, the possibility exists that the encounter with the analysand really will occur in the spirit of Jungian psychology.

Translated from the German by Channa Hoffman and Malka Katz

REFERENCES

BLEULER, E. (1955). *Lehrbuch der Psychiatrie.* 9th edn., revised by Manfred Bleuler. Berlin, Springer.

GUGGENBÜHL-CRAIG, A. (1968). "Der Schatten des Psychotherapeuten," in *The reality of the psyche,* ed. J. B. Wheelwright. New York, Putnam.

—— (1970). "Must analysis fail through its destructive aspect?" in *Spring 1970.* New York, Spring Publications.

HILLMAN, J. (1964). *Suicide and the soul.* New York, Harper and Row; London, Hodder and Stoughton.

JUNG, C. G. (1958). "Psychoanalysis and the cure of souls" (1928), *C.W.* 11.

—— (1960). "On the psychogenesis of schizophrenia" (1939), *C.W.* 3.

MEIER, C. A. (1971). "Psychological types and individualism," in *The analytic process, aims, analysis, training,* ed. J. B. Wheelwright. New York, Putnam.

RIEMANN, F. (1968). "The personality structure of the analyst and its influence on the course of treatment," *Amer. J. Psychoanal.* **28,** 69–79.

2

Hat Analyse als therapeutisches Instrument versagt?
Analytische Erstarrung und Ritual

ADOLF GUGGENBÜHL-CRAIG, *Zurich*

Der Sinn und das Ziel von Therapie ist die Heilung von Krankheiten. Uns interessieren seelisch bedingte oder teilweise seelisch verursachte Störungen der Gesundheit.

Es ist schwierig, den Begriff der Krankheit so zu fassen, dass alles, was wir damit meinen, umschlossen wird. Beeinträchtigen Störungen des physischen oder psychischen Instrumentariums das körperliche und seelische Wohl, das Heil und die sozialen Entfaltungsmöglichkeiten, so dürfen wir von Krankheit sprechen. Was in der landläufigen medizinischen Sprache als Psychosen und Neurosen oder neurotische Störungen verstanden wird, fällt zum grössten Teil unter den Begriff der Krankheit.

Die Behandlung der *Psychosen* hat in den letzten Jahrzehnten sehr grosse Fortschritte gemacht. Dies verdanken wir aber zu einem grossen Teil den neuen Medikamenten und der Neugestaltung der Heilanstalten, und nicht der analytischen Psychologie. Nur ein kleiner Prozentsatz von Menschen, die an Psychosen erkranken, wird eindeutig durch analytische Behandlung geheilt oder gebessert.

Die wichtigsten Arbeitsgebiete des analytischen Therapeuten sind die *Neurosen* und die *psychosomatischen Beschwerden*. Die Heilerfolge der analytischen Therapie sind auch hier nicht völlig befriedigend. Viele Neurosen bessern sich ohne analytische Therapie, ja ohne jede Therapie. Der Prozentsatz der Neurosen und psychosomatischen Leiden, welche eindeutig durch eine analytische Therapie geheilt oder gebessert werden, oder deren Verlauf doch verkürzt wird, ist auf alle Fälle relativ klein. Vielleicht hat die analytische Therapie einen entscheidenden Einfluss bei 10%, vielleicht bei 40% der behandelten Fälle. Wie dem auch sei: Die Resultate unserer therapeutischen Bemühungen sind ungenügend. Ungenügend und unbefriedigend— vom medizinisch-therapeutischen Gesichtspunkt aus—in zweifacher Hinsicht: Wir heilen erstens nicht 80–100% der von uns behandelten Kranken, und zweitens ist die Behandlung in zeitlicher und finanzieller Hinsicht sehr aufwendig. Auch noch zu erwähnen ist: Die jungianische Schule scheint weder grössere noch kleinere therapeutische Erfolge zu haben als andere psychologische Schulen.

Um die Jahrhundertwende begannen Freud, C. G. Jung, und andere grosse Mediziner und Psychologen Neurosen und psychosomatische Leiden mit Analyse zu behandeln. Wenig oder nichts deutet darauf hin, dass die Erfolge unserer heutigen therapeutischen Bemühungen besser sind als vor 50 Jahren. Heute stehen wir praktisch am selben Ort wie unsere Vorgänger vor vielen Jahrzehnten, ausser dass die Behandlung wahrscheinlich noch aufwendiger wurde.

Betrachten wir die Resultate der analytischen Therapie auf dem Hintergrund des allgemeinen medizinischen Fortschrittes, so bleibt uns nichts anderes übrig als festzustellen, dass die analytische Therapie, welche am Anfang sehr erfolgversprechend war, stagnierte und therapeutisch den medizinisch Orientierten enttäuschte. Wir analytischen Psychotherapeuten können heute nicht sehr grosse und kaum mehr oder schnellere Heilungserfolge aufweisen, als dies vor 50 Jahren der Fall war.

Was unternimmt in der Regel ein Mediziner in einer solch unbefriedigenden Situation? Er sucht nach neuen Methoden, Techniken, Medikamenten und allgemeinen Einsichten, um den Prozentsatz der Heilungen und Besserungen zu vergrössern, und die Aufwendigkeit der Therapie zu verringern.

Was tun wir Analytiker in derselben Lage? Wir verfeinern die bestehenden Methoden und Techniken und verbessern unsere Ausbildung im Sinne von grösserer Aufwendigkeit. Wir versuchen auch im Detail neue Erkenntnisse zu gewinnen, lassen aber grundsätzlich Theorie und Praxis unverändert.

Wir Analytiker machen also nicht nur therapeutisch keine entscheidenden Fortschritte, sondern wir haben uns auch noch dazu entwickelt oder uns so ausgebildet, dass wir das Ungenügen unserer psychologischen Techniken, Methoden und Einsichten annehmen.

Trotzdem wir uns in einer Lage befinden, die uns dazu treiben sollte, alles zu tun, um weiter zu kommen, stellen wir selten entscheidende grundsätzliche Fragen. Ein Beispiel: Wahrscheinlich ist das wirksame Instrument der analytischen Therapie nicht nur unsere psychologische Kenntnis, unser Verständnis der Psyche und unsere Technik, sondern auch wir selber, wir, die behandelnden Analytiker. Mit Recht wird deshalb nicht nur der theoretischen und wissensmässigen Ausbildung des Analytikers grosse Aufmerksamkeit geschenkt, sondern wir beschäftigen uns auch mit der Auswahl, und namentlich auch mit der persönlichen Entwicklung, des Analytikers. Vielhundertstündige Lehranalyse wird als Voraussetzung unserer Arbeit verlangt. Wir verfeinern und komplizieren unsere Bestimmungen zur Ausbildung und gestalten sie immer aufwendiger, länger und teurer und hoffen, so eine optimale Entwicklung und Entfaltung der therapeutischen Fähigkeiten zu fördern.

Ist aber je wirklich bewiesen worden, dass fast 400 Stunden Analyse die therapeutischen Fähigkeiten tatsächlich vergrössern? Wurde je überzeugend gezeigt, dass unser Ausbildungssystem, welches sich auf akademischen Qualifikationen und persönlicher, sich über viele Jahre erstreckender Analyse, wenn möglich bei einem Mann und bei einer Frau, aufbaut, erstens wirklich therapeutisch begabte Menschen anzieht, und zweitens die therapeutischen Fähigkeiten des Ausbildungskandidaten vergrössert? Oder schrecken wir vielleicht sogar therapeutisch Begabte ab, und vermindern wir durch unsere Ausbildung die therapeutische Begabung? Gibt es andere, bessere Methoden der Auswahl und Ausbildung? Dies wie gesagt nur als Beispiel.

Oft hört man, das Problem der Heilungen und Besserungen in der analytischen Arbeit sei zu subtil, als dass man es wirklich präzis in den Griff bekommen könnte. Was heisst bei Neurotikern und bei an psychosomatischen Leiden Erkrankten das Wort "Heilung" schon genau? Wir brauchen uns deshalb, so wird angenommen, durch scheinbar unbefriedigende Resultate bei allgemeinen Übersichten über Heilerfolge in unserem Gebiet keine Sorgen zu machen. Sicher ist es richtig, dass es in unserem Gebiet schwieriger ist als in andern Gebieten der Medizin, Heilungen und Besserungen exakt festzustellen. Genaue statistische Messungen sind nicht leicht, da das zu messende Phänomen sich einer genauen Erfassung entzieht.

Verschanzen können wir uns aber hinter dieser Schwierigkeit nicht, denn die Befreiung von neurotischen und psychosomatischen Symptomen, das persönliche Wohlbefinden und die mögliche soziale Entfaltung können doch, wenn auch nur sehr ungenau, einigermassen festgestellt werden. Durchschlagende Erfolge könnten sogar statistisch einigermassen bewiesen werden. Wie man auch immer die Resultate unserer heilenden Bemühungen beurteilt, welche Kriterien auch immer dafür gebraucht werden, gleichgültig ob wir von der Erfahrung des einzelnen Analytikers oder von allgemeinen Übersichten ausgehen: Wir kommen nicht darum herum festzustellen, dass unsere Erfolge ungenügend sind.

Unsere Lage ist bedrückend. Einige von uns reduzieren deshalb ihre therapeutischen Interessen und befassen sich vor allem mit Ethnographie, Mythologie, Religionsgeschichte, Literatur, Kunst usw. und leisten mit ihren psychologischen Kenntnissen in diesen Gebieten Grossartiges. Das ist für die Betreffenden eine Lösung der unbefriedigenden therapeutischen Situation, ändert aber nichts an der Tatsache, dass den psychisch Leidenden nicht genügend geholfen wird.

Andere wiederum werden in dieser schwierigen Situation von allem Klinisch-Medizinischen übermässig fasziniert. Der vor allem mit Medikamenten, Drogen und Operationen arbeitende Arzt wird offen oder geheim zum Leitbild; die Psychologie verliert an Wichtigkeit.

Ein anderer Ausweg ist es, die analytische Psychotherapie vor allem als Individuationslehrgang zu verstehen, den nur einige wenige Auserwählte, Begabte durchlaufen können, nicht aber der gewöhnliche, schwer leidende Neurotiker. Bald nähern wir uns dann dem alten Konzept: Krankheit ist Sünde; ein gewisser "Christian Science Mythos" taucht auf, der mir suspekt erscheint. Individuation und Heilung von Neurosen ist nicht dasselbe. So unerlässlich es für den therapeutischen Psychologen ist, die Realität der Individuation zu erfassen, so fraglich ist es, psychische Leiden vor allem als Mangel an Individuation im Jungschen Sinne verstehen zu wollen. Schwere Neurotiker können dem Sinn, dem Inhalt des Lebens, nahe kommen, "individuiert" werden, psychisch Gesunde haben anderseits oft keinerlei Beziehung zu dem göttlichen Funken in uns, und umgekehrt.

Oft scheint es mir, als ob wir modernen analytischen Psychologen uns ähnlich verhalten wie einst Geistliche: Wir verfeinern unsere Theorien und Methoden, stellen aber selten grundsätzliche Fragen; wir komplizieren und verschärfen Rituale, fragen aber zu wenig, ob sie grundsätzlich wirkungsvoll sein können. Wir gleichen mittelalterlichen Theologen, nicht etwa modernen; diese stellen nämlich alle ihre Grundlagen in Frage. Sie ringen mit Fragen wie: Gibt es überhaupt einen Gott? Ist Erlösung ein sinnvoller Begriff? Ist Christus wirklich als Gottessohn zu uns gekommen? usw. Stellen wir Analytiker uns häufig Fragen wie "Gibt es überhaupt ein Unbewusstes? Sind Interpretation, Amplifikation usw. therapeutisch wirksam? Ist es therapeutisch nützlich, den Patienten regelmässig eine Stunde zu sehen? Ist die Analyse, so wie wir sie heute betreiben, wirklich das bestmögliche Instrument, um das zu erreichen, was wir erreichen möchten?" usw.

Ich beschränke mich in meinen Ausführungen auf die klinischen Aspekte der Analyse. Aehnliche Fragen sind aber auch in einem grösseren Rahmen berechtigt, z.B. in bezug auf die Individuation, und auch dann, wenn der Sinn und das Ziel der Analyse im gesamten von verschiedenen Analytikern etwas anders gesehen wird. Es geht also ganz allgemein nicht nur darum zu fragen, ob die Analyse in einem bestimmten Falle ein von uns gesetztes Ziel erreicht, sondern ob die Analyse in der heutigen Form wirklich die beste Methode sei, alle oder einige der gestellten Ziele zu erreichen.

Interessanterweise sind alle klassischen psychoanalytischen Schulen in einer ähnlichen Verfassung wie wir jungianischen Analytiker. Auch die Freudianer und die Existenzialisten können z.B. wenig entscheidende therapeutische Fortschritte aufweisen. Dennoch stellen die Angehörigen des inneren Kreises auch weniger grundsätzliche Fragen, als man es bei der unbefriedigenden therapeutischen Situation erwarten könnte.

*

Ich glaube, ich habe auf die Frage, ob die analytische Psychologie als therapeutisches Instrument wenigstens zum Teil versagt habe, geantwortet, und ich könnte nun meine Ausführungen beenden. Es ist sicher wertvoll, eine problematische Situation darzustellen, auch ohne zu zeigen, wie eine Aenderung möglich ist. Ich kann aber dennoch nicht in diesem pessimistischen Geiste schliessen, da analytische Therapie mein Lebensinhalt ist, und fahre deshalb fort.

Lässt sich ein Ausweg aus unserer unbefriedigenden therapeutischen Lage vielleicht mit der Devise "Macht auf das Tor, macht auf die Tür" finden? Lasst uns in jeder Hinsicht vorurteilslos forschen und experimentieren. Unsere theoretischen Einsichten, unsere therapeutischen Verfahren, unsere Ausbildung, alles muss neu durchexperimentiert und durchgedacht werden. Jede Therapieform soll versucht werden, ob sie uns in das Konzept passt oder nicht, spielt keine Rolle, wenn wir nur helfen, heilen können.

Es gibt nun allerdings unter den analytischen Psychologen und auch unter Anhängern anderer psychologischen Schulen einige wenige unternehmungslustige Analytiker, die mutig immer wieder neues versuchen, Familientherapie, Gruppentherapie, Marathonsitzungen, LSD, mehr Beziehung und weniger Übertragung usw.

Auffällig ist, dass es bis heute den Anschein hat, diese mutigen Polyexperimentatoren hätten wenig neue bahnbrechende theoretische Erkenntnisse erarbeitet, und vor allem: Viel grössere therapeutische Erfolge als den klassischen Analytikern sind ihnen bis jetzt nicht gegeben worden. Der Ausweg "Macht auf das Tor, macht auf die Tür" bringt uns offenbar nicht eindeutig weiter. Und rein persönlich-intuitiv—nicht basierend auf genauen Untersuchungen—glaube ich sogar ein Paradoxon zu bemerken: Die Konservativen unter den Analytikern, welche ihre analytischen Erkenntnisse als unumstösslich erwiesene Tatsachen verstehen, die orthodoxen Ritualisten und Dogmatiker, machen in gewisser Hinsicht einen ernsteren, ergriffeneren Eindruck als die Polyexperimentatoren. Ja mehr noch—wiederum allerdings eine subjektive Behauptung: Oft scheint es mir, dass die Dogmatiker und Ritualisten ein grösseres Interesse für die Psyche haben, und dass ihr therapeutischer Einfluss sogar sehr beachtlich ist.

Allerdings habe ich mich jetzt wieder in eine Sackgasse hineinmanövriert. Einerseits wundere ich mich über die Stagnation, den Dogmatismus und Ritualismus, und anderseits zeige ich dann wieder keine grosse Begeisterung für die Polyexperimentatoren, die doch einen Ausweg aus unserer Lage zeigen könnten. Ich muss deshalb meine Gedanken weiter spielen lassen: In der analytischen Arbeit scheint etwas einigermassen sicher zu sein: Heilung und Besserung neurotischer und psychosomatischer Beschwerden, insofern sie durch analytische Therapie erfolgt, beruht zum Teil auf der Beziehung zwischen Analytiker und Patient, auf der Übertragung, auf irgendeinem Phänomen, das sich zwischen Patient und Analytiker abspielt und in seiner Wirkung stark vom letzteren abhängt. Weiter: Dogma und Ritual gehören teilweise zum Priesterlichen, und dass mit dem Priesterlichen im psychologischen Sinne vielleicht heilende Kräfte zusammenhängen, ist keine neue Vermutung. Hat vielleicht unser dogmatisches, rituelles Verhalten doch irgendwie eine Existenzberechtigung? Fördert unser priesterliches Verhalten vielleicht Heilung?

Der Patient ist verzweifelt, leidend und lebt in einem psychischen Chaos. Er sucht einen Heiler auf, von dem angenommen wird, er kenne sich im Irrgarten der Seele und der Krankheit aus. Die Legitimation zum Heilen ist für den Kranken am offensichtlichsten, wenn der Heiler folgende Qualifikationen zeigt:

1. Er hat einen bestimmten Lehrgang durchlaufen, gewisse Initiationsrituale hinter sich, z.B. einen akademischen Grad, so und soviele Lehranalysestunden usw.

2. Er kennt gewisse Techniken—oder sollen wir sagen Rituale und Zeremonien?—welche die Heilung konstellieren, z.B. sieht er den Patienten dreimal pro Woche, lässt ihn seine Träume aufschreiben und anderes mehr.

3. Der rituelle Lehrgang des Heilers und die Ausübung bestimmter Heilungsrituale und Zeremonien helfen dem Heiler, Kontakt zu bekommen mit den Tiefen der Seele und heilende Kräfte zu mobilisieren. Ist unsere heilende Wirkung zwar nicht sehr gross, aber doch nur deshalb möglich, da wir eine moderne Abart des Priesters sind mit seinen Dogmen, Ritualen und vielleicht sogar magischen Praktiken?

*

Müssen wir entweder Zyniker sein oder sektiererische Illusionisten, wie dies die Gegner jeglicher Analyse behaupten? Nein, wir müssen nur C. G. Jungs Betrachtungsweise uns mehr zu eigen machen. Seine Art des Verständnisses des Psychischen kann uns und auch andern psychologischen Schulen helfen. Namentlich seine Auffassung des Symbolischen, des lebenden Symbols, das etwas ausdrückt, das intellektuell nicht formuliert werden kann, das aber auch heilende Wirkung hat, kann uns den Weg zeigen.

Die Art und Weise der heilenden Tätigkeit des Analytikers ist zum Teil als Symbolisches zu verstehen. Er konstelliert Heilung—zum Teil —in Mythos und Ritual.

Nur im jungianischen Sinne ist es deshalb nicht zynisch, folgendes festzustellen: Zwei Jahre lang zwei Stunden pro Woche den Analytiker aufzusuchen ist zum Teil ein *Ritual,* das sich mit der leidenden Seele befasst und sie wichtig nimmt. Nur im jungianischen Sinne wirkt es nicht zynisch zu sagen: Auch unsere Ausbildung hat rituellen Charakter; sie ist ein gelebtes Symbol der Wichtigkeit der Seele. Die oft erwähnte Parallele zwischen Beichte und analytischer Psychologie liegt vielleicht in der Wichtigkeit des Rituellen bei beiden. Wir könnten von dem Rituellen der Beichte etwas lernen.

Auch nicht zynisch ist es zu vermuten, dass sogar die Art und Weise unserer Interpretation des seelischen Geschehens beim Patienten zum Teil rituellen Charakter hat und zum Teil eine poetische Mythologisierung des Schicksals des Kranken ist und nicht eine naturwissenschaftliche Erklärung. Eine freudianische Analyse ist z.B. eine grossartige rituelle Durchspielung des Oedipus-Komplexes.

Ist aber Erstarrung und Stagnation unserer Theorien und Methoden wirklich nötig, um den priesterlich-heilenden Faktor, das Ritual und den Mythos in unserer Arbeit zu bewahren?

Nur dann wird vielleicht Mythos zu Dogma und Ritual zu methodischer Starrheit, wenn wir die symbolische Natur unseres Handelns und Wissens entweder als naturwissenschaftliche Erkenntnis oder gar religiöse göttliche Offenbarung, ja sogar als Magie missverstehen. Unsere Erkenntnisse und Methoden sind weder naturwissenschaftlich, noch beruhen sie auf göttlicher Offenbarung. Wir sind keine Physiker, keine Chemiker; ein beachtlicher Teil unserer psychologischen Erkenntnisse sind eine symbolische Schau eines kaum fassbaren Geschehens, eine Mythologisierung und Ritualisierung, und in diesem Sinne schillernd. Wir sind auch keine religiösen Propheten, denen die Tiefen der Welt und Gottes offenbar wurden, auch dann nicht, wenn unsere Heilungen zum Teil auf Mythologisierung und Ritualen beruhen. Unsere Kenntnisse der psychologischen Seite des religiösen Phänomens dürfen nicht verwechselt werden mit religiösen Einsichten. Diese haben wir Analytiker weder mehr noch weniger als andere Menschen, als z.B. unsere Patienten.

Aber die illusionistische Ansicht, entweder Naturwissenschaftler oder Prophet oder beides zu sein, macht uns unsicher, ängstlich, allem Neuem abhold.

Unsere vielen hundert Stunden Ausbildungsanalyse sind nicht nur dazu da, um sich im naturwissenschaftlich psychologischen Sinne selber zu durchschauen und zu kennen, und die therapeutischen Fähigkeiten der eigenen Psyche richtig einsetzen zu können, sie sind auch ein gelebtes Symbol, ein Ritual des Wichtignehmens des Psychischen allgemein und der Psyche des Analytikers als heilender Faktor im speziellen. Selbstverständlich gibt es aber ganz verschiedene Symbole des Wichtignehmens der Psyche. Haben wir einmal das Symbolisch-Rituelle unseres Tuns ernst genommen, so können wir in jeder Hinsicht wiederum beweglich werden. Alle Hilfsmittel medikamentöser oder anderer Art sind willkommen und keine Bedrohung mehr, und wir können in diesem neuen Geist unsere Symbole kreativer, revolutionärer konzipieren.

Symbole sind etwas Lebendiges und ändern sich, verlieren ihre Wirksamkeit und werden immer wieder vom Unbewussten neu geschaffen und sollen von uns neu geschaut werden, die individuelle und kollektive Psyche ist dauernd in Bewegung. Symbole, die noch vor 40 Jahren Geltung hatten, wirksam waren, können zum Teil heute wirkungslos sein, nicht der psychischen Realität mehr entsprechend. Sowohl die grandiose Mythologisierung des Verhältnisses "Männlich-Weiblich" von Freud als auch die subtile Symbolik Jungs entsprechen nur noch beschränkt dem heutigen Weiblichen und Männlichen. Weiblich symbolisiert durch Eros, Mond, Männlich symbolisiert durch Logos, Sonne, oder vereinfacht freudianisch durch Sadismus-Masochismus, entspricht mehr dem Ende des 19. als dem des 20. Jahrhunderts. Ein starres Festhalten an Symbolen, die zur Zeit Jungs der psychischen Realität entsprachen, nicht aber der heutigen, schneidet uns den Zugang zu unserer Zeit völlig ab. Dieser unglückliche Konservativismus zeigt sich z.B. sehr oft in Abhandlungen konservativer Analytiker über das Weibliche.

Noch etwas zum Ritual: Dieses drückt ein psychisches Ereignis aus, in einer symbolischen Handlung, so dass das Symbol auf einen Kreis von Teilnehmenden wirkt. Eine gewisse Kontinuität gehört zum Ritual, wie zur Sprache, die nicht alle Tage geändert werden kann, da sie sonst unverständlich würde. Vielleicht verstehen wir Analytiker erstens zu wenig die rituelle Seite unseres Handelns und haben zweitens auch zu wenig Rituale. Diesen Mangel versuchen wir durch Erstarrung wettzumachen, wir lassen unsere Methoden und Theorien ritualistisch erstarren. Haben wir die Wichtigkeit der rituellen Seite unseres Handelns begriffen, so wird die Bahn wieder frei für mutiges Experimentieren und grundsätzliches In-Frage-Stellen. Dogmatische Erstarrung aber bedeutet für den heutigen Analytiker Verrat an sich selber und der Psychologie. Unsere Erstarrung, ganz gleichgültig ob sie sich auf Anima und Animus, auf das Selbst und die Individuation, auf die dogmatisch-konkretistisch statt mythologisch verstandenen Auseinandersetzungen des Kindes mit der Mutterbrust oder auf unsere Methoden bezieht, versuchte ich als psychologisch verständlich und in gewisser Hinsicht sogar als notwendig darzustellen. Dies ändert aber nichts daran, dass wir alles tun müssen, um aus unserer dogmatisch konservativen Haltung herauszukommen. Tun wir das nicht, so werden wir Analytiker mit der Zeit eine Sekte, deren Sektierertum nicht vor allem auf einem mutigen Widerstand gegen die kollektive Vermassung beruht sondern auf einer Unfähigkeit, die Hintergründe der Erstarrung zu durchschauen, und die entsprechenden Korrekturen an unserer Einstellung und unserer Arbeit vorzunehmen.

*

Lévi-Strauss (1967) hat in der Biographie eines Kwakiutl Schamanen unübertrefflich die Lage des modernen Analytikers beschrieben. Quesalid will Schamane werden, —Schamanen hatten in seinem Stamm vor allem heilende Funktionen—um deren Schwindel zu entlarven. Er erlernt unter anderem einen symbolisch zu verstehenden Taschenspielertrick, der darin besteht, dass er eine Feder in den Mund nimmt und diese im Mund mit Blut durchtränken kann. Wird ein Kranker behandelt, so wird diese blutgetränkte Feder aus dem Mund gespieen, und er behauptet, dies sei nun die Krankheit, die er in den Griff bekommen habe. Er wird dann einmal zu einem Kranken gerufen, der von einem andern Schamanen nicht geheilt werden konnte. Er mit seinem Trick kann helfen und ist sehr erstaunt über seine Wirkung. Er akzeptiert mit der Zeit seine eigenen Tricks und erlebt sie nicht mehr als Schwindel.

Er hat aber doch immer noch Zweifel an seinem Schamanentum und ist auf der Suche nach einem echten Schamanen. In seiner Biographie heisst es, er glaube, er sei vielleicht einmal einem echten Schamanen begegnet. Dieser nahm nie Geld für seine Heilungen und lachte nie. Diese Biographie beschreibt unsere widerspruchsvolle Situation, aus welcher heraus unsere therapeutische Stagnation etwas zu verstehen ist.

Wir müssen zum Teil den Heilungsprozess mit symbolisch-rituellen Handlungen konstellieren und das psychische Geschehen mythologisieren; aber wir sind keine Priester. Wir müssen alle Einsichten der Naturwissenschaftler für die Heilung einsetzen, aber wir sind keine Naturwissenschaftler.

Unsere Rituale und Zeremonien müssen wir ernst nehmen, gläubig durch sie heilen—aber wir müssen uns auch hüten, dieser Gläubigkeit starr zu verfallen, und nichts Neues zu versuchen.

Wir sind immer echt und unecht; gläubig und ungläubig, wie der oben beschriebene Schamane. Wir verlieren unsere heilende Wirkung, wenn wir unsere Rituale zu unserem Vorteil gebrauchen oder darüber lachen, spotten.

"Die edelste aller Künste ist die Heilkunst" soll Pythagoras gesagt haben. Die Widersprüche unserer Arbeit werden befruchtend in unserem Wissen, Diener dieser edelsten Kunst zu sein.

LITERATURE

LEVI-STRAUSS, CLAUDE (1967). "The sorcerer and his magic," in *Magic, witchcraft and curing,* ed. John Middleton. Garden City, New York, The Natural History Press.

Has Analysis Failed as
a Therapeutic Instrument?
Analytical Rigidity and Ritual

Besides all the esoteric intentions, the main aim of psychotherapy and analysis is to heal mental illness. We psychotherapists have to acknowledge with mixed feelings that the great advances in the treatment of psychosis in the last decades have come from the pharmaceutical industry. More humane forms of hospitalization too have increased the chances of curing psychotic people; only a small percentage of persons, however, who fall ill to a psychosis are unambiguously healed or improved through analytical treatment.

As analysts our main working areas are not psychotic illnesses but neurosis and psychosomatic ailments. But even here there is no reason for contentment. The percentage of neurosis and psychosomatic illnesses which are unambiguously cured or improved or whose course is shortened through analysis is too small. We certainly do not help decisively more than 10–40% of the people whom we see. In two ways we analysts cannot be happy with the results of our therapeutic endeavors: first, we do not heal enough of our treated cases; second, even if our treatment might now and again be successful it is always very expensive and time-consuming.

One must also admit that the Jungian school seems to have neither greater nor less therapeutic success than other schools of psychological thought.

At the turn of the century Freud, Jung, and other great physicians and psychologists began to treat by means of analysis the neuroses and psychosomatic disorders. Little or nothing indicates that the success of our contemporary therapeutic efforts is one whit greater than it was fifty years ago. We stand today at the same place, from a practical point of view, as did our predecessors, except that the treatment has become still more expensive.

If we observe the results of analysis against the background of general medical advances, there remains for us no alternative but to admit that analytical therapy, which at first promised much success, has stagnated and proven a therapeutic disappointment to the medically oriented.

What does a medical doctor ordinarily do in such an unsatisfactory situation? He looks for new methods, techniques, medicines, and general insights, in order to increase the rate of cure and improvement and to reduce the cost of therapy. What do analysts do in the same situation? We refine the established methods and techniques and "improve" our training, in the sense of increasing its length and its cost. We seek also to gain new realizations in detail, but we leave the fundamentals of theory and practice unchanged. Not only have we failed to make any decisive advances; we also have developed, and educated ourselves to, the position that we accept the insufficiency of our psychological techniques, methods, and insights. Rather than seeing our inadequacies for what they are, we devise defenses for their justification.

Although we find ourselves in a situation that should drive us to do everything possible to advance further, we seldom pose decisive, fundamental questions. For example: the effectiveness of analytical psychology as a therapeutic instrument probably lies not only in our psychological knowledge, our understanding of the psyche and our techniques, but also in ourselves, the practising analysts. Appropriately, therefore, not only the theoretical and scientific education of the analyst receives great attention, but we occupy ourselves also with the selection and the personal development of the analyst. Many hundred hours of training analysis are required as the precondition of our work. We refine and complicate our definitions of training and make them always more expensive and longer, hoping thereby to further an optimal unfolding of therapeutic ability. But has it ever been proved that nearly four hundred hours of analysis really do increase therapeutic ability? Has it ever been convincingly demonstrated that our system of training, which builds on academic qualifications and personal analysis that extends over many years, if possible with a man and with a woman, in the first place actually attracts therapeutically gifted people, and secondly increases the therapeutic capability of the candidate? Or, do we perhaps scare off the therapeutically gifted and diminish, through our training, the therapeutic gift? Are there better methods of selection and education?

In the training of nonmedical psychologists and even more in their practice, I notice a strange shying away from real mental disturbance. We should question this tendency. One tries to give nonmedical psychologists so-called easy cases and one warns them of the danger of patients with latent psychosis whose cases, so one says, should as soon as possible be given over to a psychiatrist. The same applies to suicidal cases. Might it be possible that by shielding our trainees from dealing with dangerous, suicidal, murderous, and psychotic cases, we attract the wrong people to train, people who might be more drawn to talking about interesting psychological phenomena than in dealing and battling with real psychic illness? It might not be a coincidence that so much of the insight even into the psychology of the healthy person has come from psychopathology. Thus the question could be raised whether it might not be better to have even nonmedical trainees plunge straight into the deepest psychopathology.

One often hears that the question of cure and improvement in analytical work is too subtle to define precisely. What exactly does the word "cure" mean in the case of neurotics and sufferers from psychosomatic ailments? It is therefore assumed that we need not worry in our field about results that seem unsatisfactory from the general perspective of the healing arts. Certainly, in our field it is more difficult to define cure and improvement than in the other areas of medicine. Statistical measurements are not easy, since the measured phenomenon resists definition. But we cannot hide ourselves behind this difficulty, for the relief from neurotic and psychosomatic symptoms, and the sense of personal well-being and the unfolding of social potential, can be determined. Genuine success could even be proven to a certain extent. However one judges the results of our healing efforts, whatever criteria may be used, whether we proceed from the experience of individual analysts or from a general over-view, we cannot avoid the conclusion that our degree of success is unsatisfactory.

It often seems to me as if we modern psychologists behave in a fashion similar to the old-time clergy. We refine our theories and methods, but seldom pose fundamental questions. We complicate and intensify rituals, but ask too infrequently whether they are basically effective. We resemble medieval theologians, not modern ones, for the latter place all their presuppositions in question. They wrestle with questions like: Is there a God? Is salvation a meaningful concept? Did Christ really come to us as the Son of God? But do we analysts pose questions like: Is there really such a thing as the unconscious? Is interpretation, amplification, or even dreaming itself, therapeutically effective? Is it therapeutically useful to see the patient regularly, and for an hour? Is analysis, as we practice it today, really the best possible instrument for reaching the goals we wish to achieve?

I am confining myself to the clinical aspects of analysis, but similar questions are justified in a broader framework. We may just as well ask them in relation to individuation, even if the meaning and aim of analysis and of individuation is seen differently by different analysts.

*

I believe I have answered the question whether analytical psychology has, at least in part, failed as a therapeutic instrument, and I could end my exposition here. Certainly it is worthwhile presenting a problematic situation even without showing a resolution of it. I cannot, however, conclude in this pessimistic spirit, for analytical therapy is of vital interest to me. Therefore I shall continue this exploration of the problem.

Perhaps one can find a way out of our unsatisfactory therapeutic situation in the motto, "Open the gate, open the door." Let us indiscriminately investigate and experiment! Our theoretical insights, our therapeutic experience, our training—everything must be experimented with and thought through in a new way. Every form of therapy should be tried; whether it fits our concepts or not makes no difference, if only we are enabled to heal and help.

One can of course discover among analytical psychologists and also among the members of other schools of psychology a few venturesome analysts who courageously continue to try new methods—family therapy, group therapy, marathon sessions, LSD, more relationship and less transference, etc. Yet, the impression remains that these courageous poly-experimentalists seem to have made but few pioneering theoretical breakthroughs; moreover, they have failed to realize even the therapeutic success of the classical analysts. The solution, "Open the gate, open the door," clearly does not bring us further.

Moreover on the purely personal, intuitive level I see a curious paradox. The conservatives among the analysts, who take their analytical perceptions either as unassailable proven facts or have the impression that their rituals have come, so to speak, directly from an inner voice of God and therefore never can be changed, mistaking their symbols as the only possible symbols, make a more serious and stirring impression than the poly-experimentalists. Furthermore, it often seems to me that these dogmatists and ritualists, who do not experiment but who follow the writings of the masters without doubt and little modification in practice, have a greater interest in the psyche and their therapeutic influence is pronounced.

Once again I have maneuvered myself into a blind alley. On the one hand I question the stagnation, the dogmatism and ritualism; on the other, I show no great admiration for the poly-experimentalists who, after all, might show a way out of our predicament. I must therefore let my thoughts play out once more.

In analytical work it seems to be somewhat clear that healing and improvement, in so far as they result from analytical therapy, rest in part on the relationship between analyst and patient, on the transference, on some sort of phenomenon that goes on between patient and analyst and on whose operation therapy is heavily dependent. Now, dogma and ritual belong partly to the priestly function; that healing powers are perhaps connected with the priestly function, in a psychological sense, is not a new proposition. Has then our dogmatic, ritualistic behavior perhaps some sort of existential justification? Does our priestly conduct perhaps further healing?

The patient is confused, suffering, and lives in psychic chaos. He seeks a healer who, he believes, knows the labyrinths of the soul and of illness. The legitimation for healing is for the patient most convincing if the healer shows at least the following qualifications: first, he has, behind him, certain initiation rites, such as an academic degree, authorized training analysis, etc.; secondly, he knows a set of techniques—or should we call them rituals?—such as seeing a patient three times a week, having him write down his dreams, etc.

Having gone himself through all the rituals and being able to perform them in a ceremonial way helps him to mobilize the healing power in the depth of the soul. Even if our therapeutic effectiveness is not very great, is it perhaps made possible at all by our being a modern variety of priest with his dogmas, rituals, and even magical practices?

*

Must we be either cynics or sectarian illusionists, as the opponents of every analysis assert? No, we must only make Jung's view more our own. His way of understanding the psyche can help both ourselves and other schools of psychology. His grasp of the symbolic, of the living symbol, which expresses something that cannot be formulated intellectually but has healing effectiveness, can show us the way.

The ways and means of the healing activity of the analyst must in part be understood symbolically. He constellates healing—in part— through myth and ritual. Only in the Jungian sense is it therefore not cynical to assert the following: to go to an analyst for two years, twice a week, is in part a *ritual* that concerns itself with the suffering soul and takes it seriously. Only in the Jungian sense is it not cynical to say also that our training has a ritualistic character; it is a lived symbol of the importance of the soul. The often referred to parallel between confession and analytical psychology rests perhaps on the importance for both of ritual. We can learn something from the ritual of confession.

Further, it is not cynical to suppose also that our interpretation of the psychic events of the patient has in part a ritualistic character and is in part a poetical mythologization of the sick person's fate, and is not a scientific explanation. Is not a Freudian analysis, for example, a grand ritualistic playing through of the Oedipus complex?

But is rigidity and stagnation in our theories and methods really necessary in order to protect the priestly healing factor, the ritual and myth, in our work? Perhaps myth will turn to dogma, ritual to methodological rigidity, only if we misinterpret the symbolic nature of our practice and knowledge, i.e., either as scientific knowledge or as religious revelation, even as magic. We are not physicists, not chemists; a considerable part of our psychological perceptions is a symbolic view of a highly elusive event and therefore opalescent. Furthermore, we are not religious prophets to whom the depths of the world and of God have been revealed, not even if our cures rest in part on mythologization and ritual. Our perceptions of the psychological side of religious phenomena must not be confused with religious insight. We analysts possess religion and religious insights no more or less than do other people, including our patients.

The prospect of being neither scientists nor prophets nor both, yet using some of the methods and insights of each, makes us uncertain, anxious, averse to everything new.

The discipline of many hundred hours of training analysis may be regarded not only in a natural-scientific way, i.e., that they are to enable one to activate properly the therapeutic capabilities of one's own psyche. This long course of hours is also a lived symbol, a ritual of taking seriously the psyche in general and the psyche of the analyst as a healing factor in particular. If we have once taken the symbolical-ritualistic aspect of our acts seriously, we can again become flexible in every respect. All means of helping, pharmacological or other, are welcome; there is no threat. In this spirit we can conceive our symbols in a more creative, a more revolutionary way.

Symbols live and change themselves, losing their effectiveness and coming into being ever anew out of the unconscious, and so we should look upon them in this way. The individual and the collective psyche are continuously in motion. Symbols that still had validity forty years ago and were vivid then can today be ineffective, no longer suiting psychic reality. Thus, Freud's grandiose mythologization of the relation "masculine-feminine," as also the more subtle symbolic presentation of this relation by Jung, conforms in only a limited sense to today's "feminine" and "masculine." Feminine as symbolized by eros, moon, and masculine by logos, sun, or as simplified by the Freudians to sado-masochism, accords more with the end of the nineteenth than with the end of the twentieth century. Every new generation has to re-examine the expressions and symbolizations of the feminine and the masculine. It is dangerous to standardize the fantasies, dreams, and behavior of our patients according to a view of what is feminine and masculine; this standardization, however, becomes even more grotesque when we use the view of a bygone epoch concerning what is feminine and masculine. By rigidly clinging to symbols that suited psychic reality in Jung's time but fail to do so today, we block entirely our entry into our own time.

A further word about ritual: Perhaps, first, we analysts understand too little the ritualistic side of our treatment, and, second, we have too few rituals. We try to make up for this lack through rigidification; we allow—perhaps even encourage—our methods and theories to ossify. If we grasp the importance of the ritualistic side of our practice, the way will again be made clear for courageous experimentation and for posing fundamental questions. Dogmatic rigidification, however, means for the analyst of today betrayal of himself and of psychology. Our rigidity—be it related to anima and animus, to the self and individuation, to the concrete rather than mythological understanding of the child's need to separate from the maternal breast, or to our methods, techniques, interpretations—I have tried to present as psychologically understandable and even in a certain respect as necessary. This alters not in the least the imperative that we do everything to abandon our dogmatic, conservative position. If we do not, we analysts will become in time a sect, whose sectarianism rests not on courageous opposition to collective mass consciousness but on the inability to examine the background of our rigidification and to undertake the relevant correctives in our attitude and work.

*

Lévi-Strauss (1967), in his life of a Kwakiutl shaman, has given an incomparable description of the modern analyst's situation. Quesalid wants to become a shaman—in his tribe the shaman has above all a healing function—in order to unmask their swindle. Among other things he learns a conjuring trick: it consists in taking a feather into his mouth and saturating it, while in his mouth, with blood. If a sick person be treated, this blood-saturated feather gets spit out of the mouth; it is believed that this is the disease and that he has managed to capture it. Once Quesalid is called to a sick person who could not be healed by another shaman. To his amazement his trick works! He actually can help with a trick. He is most surprised at its effectiveness. In time he accepts his trick and experiences it no longer as a swindle. But he continues to have doubts in his shamanism and is ever searching for a *real* shaman. Once, he believes, he did, perhaps, encounter a real shaman. This one never took money for his cures and never laughed.

This biography describes our contradictory situation. We must in part constellate the healing process with a symbolic-ritualistic treatment and mythologize psychic events, but we are not real priests. We must employ for the cure all the insights of natural science, but we are not real natural scientists.

We must take seriously our rituals and ceremonies, credulously using them to heal. But we must also guard ourselves against letting this credulity degenerate into rigidity and against resisting everything new.

We are always real and unreal, believing and skeptical, just as the shaman described above. We lose our healing effectiveness if we use our ritual for our own advantage, or laugh about it and make fun of it.

"The most excellent of all arts is the art of healing," Pythagoras is supposed to have said. The contradictions within our work can fructify our knowledge and become servants of this most excellent art.

Translated from German by Murray Stein
The English version is somewhat abridged

REFERENCES

Lévi-Strauss, Claude (1967). "The sorcerer and his magic," in *Magic, witchcraft and curing,* ed. John Middleton. Garden City, New York, The Natural History Press.

3

Three Ways of Failure
and Analysis

JAMES HILLMAN, *Zurich*

1. FAILURE IN ANALYSIS

We are each familiar with the failure of certain kinds of cases in analysis. Particularly difficult and unresponsive to successful therapy are people with styles of life in which homosexuality, alcoholism, or chronic depression are the major presenting "problems." To these can be added those with paranoid obsessions, the severe so-called character neuroses, and people who have been diagnosed as sociopaths and psychopaths. That so many and so varied kinds of cases for which analysis may have been considered the preferred method of treatment turn out to be failures gives cause for considering analysis afresh and in the light of these failures.

We are also familiar with another sort of failed cases, those in which a morbid cancer develops during the analysis, or which end in suicide, or where the countertransference reactions constellate such exorbitant fantasy and massive affect, or psychopathological lacunae, in the analyst that the case must be transferred or the analysis abandoned. Smaller failures perhaps go unrecognized—analyses that have as by-products estrangements within families, loss of extraverted adaptation, splintered friendships.

Through *clinical reflection* upon these various sorts of failures we may examine the kinds of cases which fail, or for which analysis fails, and we may bring our own failures as analysts to other analysts for scrutiny—all of which reflection attempts to correct present failures and minimize future ones. This manner of clinically reflecting is a function of the dominant empirical and moral theme of our culture: learning through mistakes, trial and error, getting better through working at it, if at first you don't succeed try, try again, in which the model is one of improvement away from mistakes, error, and failure, towards competence.

Failure in this metaphor is linked in a polarity with success, and we tend to measure failures normatively, that is as a privation of success. Failure is the obverse of successful treatment; success equals the minimum of failure. A successful analysis would then mean success with those areas of failure in the case—the dominating presenting complaints of homosexuality, alcoholism, delusions—and a failure would mean their continuation despite the personality development and insight gained through the analysis.

This model of failure, simple though it might seem, has nonetheless encouraged some sophisticated discussions of analysis. Existential analysis would do away with normative criteria of success and failure altogether. On the other hand, behavior therapy would consider failure wholly in terms of the normative criteria of positive functioning, making suspect the belief in analysis as a method of personality growth and increase of consciousness unless there is positive evidence of symptom elimination and relief of distress.

That by which we define analysis will also define its success and failure: an analysis that aims for increase of consciousness or individuation cannot be judged a failure if it does not cure symptoms, and vice versa an analysis that aims at removing a crippling phobia cannot be called a failure if it never goes into the patient's dreams or integrates the phobia into meaningfulness.

Of course this simple, normative model of success (as optimum health, psychic order, or wholeness) neglects the fact that success and failure may be conceived not as opposites or poles of a continuum, but as an identity, so that *every analysis is both a failure and a success at the same time,* and every part of every analysis is both right and wrong, leading and misleading, constructively growing and destructively killing, implying that for analysis to succeed at all it must always fail.

2. FAILURE OF ANALYSIS

The inevitability of the first kind of failure opens a larger perspective, and we may move the question from specific failures in analysis to the general failure of analysis. Since analysis always shows certain sorts of failures, is there not something general about analysis which brings about failure, so that analysis itself may be considered a failure?

The literature shows that as there are discussions about the failure *in* analysis in certain kinds of cases, there are also discussion on the failure of analysis as a whole. Freud's late reflections on "Analysis terminable or interminable" is the *locus classicus* for this kind of pessimistic consideration.

Does analysis ever reach its end, in time or fulfilment; is transference ever resolved, individuation ever achieved? Even if analysis does not satisfy the goal of cure, does it indeed yield enlargement of consciousness, depth of personality, finer love, better adaptation, significant life? If we look at the analysts, ourselves, as the paradigms for the process in which we sit for many years, what effect has analysis had upon our adaptation, our consciousness, our loving?

From another perspective, where are the validating statistics in regard to kinds of cases and kinds of improvement within such classes, and how may we ever formulate such statistics since nosological classifications into which we might class our cases are today all in doubt? Is "paranoic" a valid term with an actual referent? Where are the "manics" and "hysterics" of yesteryear? How can we assess success and failure of a treatment without agreed criteria for what we are treating, i.e., what is psychic illness and psychic health which gives meaning in general to an idea of "treatment"?

The view that analysis in general has failed comes from critics from many sides. Experimentalists ask for public evidence of achievement; clinicians ask for evidence of improvement through analytical treatment; societal critics see analysis as the establishment's tool for maintaining our notions of sickness, of exclusive individuality, and of professionalism, perpetuating a system of bourgeois capitalism. Theologians and philosophers consider its failure more profoundly, regarding analysis to have an inadequate ideational critique and a suspect method that is more like brainwashing or initiation into a religious sect than either a therapeutic treatment or an empirical science of personality exploration which it claims to be. It fails because its subliminal premises differ from its overt intentions. Finally historians (of ideas, social movements, and medicine) see analysis within its setting of the twentieth century, as a response to a specific failure within that civilization, and that what was right for early twentieth century men is insufficient for us today.

Through just such *historical reflection* upon the failure of analysis we may recall that analysis did arise out of failure, in that it was a specific method for dealing with those peculiar kinds of cases that had failed to be understood, or even find a hearing by the prevailing system, e.g., the hysterics of Freud and Breuer and the schizophrenics of Jung and Bleuler. These were the medically and socially failed, and psychotherapy was invented as a specific response to these specific failures. If analysis arises from the maladapted, the peculiar neurotic discontents of our civilization who hitherto could find no meaningful place, the failed so to speak, then a third perspective opens in regard to the relationship between analysis and failure.

3. FAILURE AS ANALYSIS

Despite the critique of the first kind—that analysis fails in many specific instances—and the critiques of the second kind—that analysis as such is a failure—for me, and I shall assume for us preponderantly, the merits of classical analysis are so obvious that one need not dwell upon them. A panegyric here, or even an apology, is hardly in place, so let us turn instead to the defects of the merits. Let us take the clinical and historical reflection upon the failure of classical analysis one step further into an *archetypal reflection*.

By classical analysis I mean a course of treatment in an atmosphere of sympathy and confidence of one person by another person for a fee, which treatment may be conceived as educative (in various senses) or therapeutic (in various senses) and which proceeds principally through the joint interpretative exploration of habitual behavior and of classes of mental events that have been traditionally called fantasies, feelings, memories, dreams, and ideas, and where the exploration follows a coherent set of methods, concepts, and beliefs stemming mainly from Freud and from Jung, where focus is preferably upon the unanticipated and affectively charged, and whose goal is the improvement (subjectively and/or objectively determined) of the analysand and the termination of the treatment. This description leaves room for many versions of improvement—from alleviation of symptoms to individuation and mystical revelation. This description also leaves room for various aspects of Freud's and Jung's methods, concepts, and beliefs as they receive differing emphasis according to place, time, and practitioner.

An archetypal reflection upon failure in and of analysis would leave untouched its definition, that is, we would not attempt to improve analysis in specific instances, nor redefine (update) it in general so that it becomes a more adequate response to contemporary psychic ills. Rather I would suggest—and this shall be my final point—that analysis may continue as before even where it conceives itself not only as having failed historically and clinically, but as *being failure archetypally;* as being concerned with failure in the dictionary senses of failure: weakness, defectiveness, absence of victory, bankruptcy, deception, lack, and incompletion.

Failure would be regarded as one fundamental psychic factor in terms of which every man lives his life. Existentialism calls this category "scheitern," or the consciousness that arises from shipwreck. Alchemy has considered it under the rubrics of *dissolutio, mortificatio, putrefactio.* Buddhism speaks of inherent decay; D. H. Lawrence of the "ship of death."

Were analysis to be imagined in terms of its inherent failure (which merely parallels the inherent failure of every life) emphasis would no longer be placed too onesidedly upon the integrative, increasing, enlarging, and upward-striving metaphor, the eros aspect of ever more unions, a metaphor which may be condensed into the key-word "growth" (which already has taken on overtones of escalation, proliferation, and cancer). Instead we would return to that tradition of the analysis of the soul which recognizes "two opposite propensities in the human frame; one constantly and uniformly tending to corruption and decay, the other to life and health"—a sentence from Ernst Stahl, the eighteenth-century German physician-philosopher who placed the soul at the center of his concerns. But the sentence might as well have come from Freud's contrast of Eros and Thanatos. Thanatos provides the archetypal reflection to our theme of failure.

When analysis follows the models of thought of nineteenth-century medical philosophy, its heroic and Great-Mother Nature determined consciousness, then it will tend, as with Bichat, to define life as "the sum of forces which oppose death," and then it will consider the unconscious—as did Schopenhauer, von Hartmann, Carus, and even Bergson—as an organic life force that develops and has, as Freud said, no negation. I believe we still tend to view the unconscious in this nine-tenth-century model, as the creative will of life slumbering in the soul, which unfurls into time and which if read rightly can keep us from failing.

Were analysis to take its historical origins (as a response to failure) also as its archetypal base, then its perspective might derive more from Thanatos and the statement of Bichat could be reversed. Analysis explores failure in terms of death, and it is called into existence as the psyche's preferred instrument to explore failure in terms of all the forces which oppose life, i.e., to look for Thanatos and its related archetypal dominants wherever life is blocked, defeated, bankrupt, and failed.

This approach investigates (analyzes) failure less to remove it for new growth, than to lead each mistake, error, and weakness into failure (be "psychopompos" to it) by leading it to its final consequences, its psychic goal in death. Then every mistake of life, every weakness and error in and of analysis, instead of being set straight in repentance or wrung for its drop of consciousness or transformed and integrated, becomes rather the entrance to failure, an opening into the reversal of all values. Rather than as a block in Eros and the flow of life, we might consider failures as constellated, intended, even finally caused by the underworld which wants life to fail in order that other attitudes governed by other archetypal principles be recognized.

The gods then which we would consider to be the dominants of analysis would particularly be those who govern what the Romantics called the "nightside of the soul" (Fechner). Analysis would derive its attitudes from those archetypal dominants personified in the gods who have a special relationship with the invisible, underground night-time world of death, terror, and tragedy, such as Hermes, Hades, Saturn, Persephone, Dionysos (Lord of Souls and source of tragedy), and especially the Children of Night described by Hesiod (*Theogony*): doom, old age, death, murder, destiny, fate, deception, sleep, dreams, quarrels, grievances, misery, nemesis. These personifications of Hesiod are the main content of analysis and they are partly what we today call failures, since we have placed analysis among the healing, helping professions of positivism with its emphasis upon the gods and heroes of above, visible in Apollonian light, god and goddesses of city, field, life, and deed. Even love we tend to conceive in the concrete manner of Aphrodite, forgetting the subtle intimacy of Eros and Thanatos, even their identity in Renaissance Neoplatonism.

We may do more justice with the failures in analysis and the failure of analysis when we consider analysis as a process in failure, and even individuation as a movement in the realm of Hades, invisibly, where the literalisms of life are reflected in the metaphors of death. Then individuation, the uniqueness of individual personality, will be recognized as Unamuno characterized it in the tragic sense of life, which has its own joy, its own comedy.

When I am in despair, I do not want to be told of rebirth; when I am ageing and decaying and the civilization around me collapsing from its over-growth that is over-kill, I cannot tolerate that word "growth," and when I am falling to bits in my complexities, I cannot abide the defensive simplistics of mandalas, nor the sentimentalities of individuation as unity and wholeness. These are formulae presented through a fantasy of opposites—the disintegration shall be compensated by integration. But what of cure through likeness where like takes care of like? I want the right background to the failure of life; I want to hear with precision of those gods who are served by and thrive upon and can hence provide an archetypal background to and even an eros connection with defeat, decay, and dismemberment, because these dominants would reflect the *experienced* psyche, not in its Aristotelian conceptualization as belonging to life, but in the actuality of its own known goal, which is also both its way and its substance, death.

4

The Timing of Analysis

DAVID HOLT, *London*

In the half hour which is all the time I have now, I want to say something about success and failure in analysis in terms of time. And in case my time should run out before I can conclude, let me start by stating what that conclusion is. It is this: that the time of the psyche has the power and the shape of a promise, and that if we are to work with this promise we must subordinate the concept of success and failure to that of resistance. But I am going to use this word resistance, deliberately, in a sense other than that of classical psychoanalysis. For me, the analysis of the psyche works with, and through, and in, the resistance which holds between the keeping and breaking of a promise. The success or failure of analysis must be judged in terms of this resistance.

Such is my conclusion. My starting point is the need for a meeting ground between the practice of Jung's psychology and the wider scientific community of which we are all members. Throughout Jung's work there is a deeply felt concern for the problem of time, from the recognition in 1912 of what he then called "the etiological significance of the actual present" to his later writings on synchronicity. These concepts are at the center of my own personal engagement with Jung's work, and of the professional method I was taught in Zurich. But in applying them, and in arguing their relevance with various audiences, I have come to feel that Jung's psychology implies an experience of time which overflows the containment of any one science. So my thinking has turned for help to that discipline which makes the overflowing of time its special concern: history.

It seems to me that philosophers of history, in arguing about the time of history and about man's action within that time, have developed ideas which have an immediate relevance for practicing analysts. The implications of this new historical self-consciousness are changing the whole climate of the culture in which we live in ways of which we are still unconscious. This change centers on what we can describe, with some risk of over-simplification, as the hidden identity of interpretation and cause.

In our own work, we are familiar with such a hidden identity in our experience of projection and transference. Philosophers of history share our interest in how the dialogue of question and answer that is traditional to the natural sciences proves inadequate to an understanding of human action. Like us, they are familiar with the uncomfortable stretch in which this dialogue seems to insist on "triangulating" itself, so that the interpretation and the cause of action seem to be working together to actualize some third power latent in them both; and they argue that if we are to understand this "triangulation," we must put the questioning of time at the center of our method.

So I want to say something now about points of contact between one aspect of Jung's thought and one aspect of the philosophy of history. I shall do so with reference to memory and hope. I shall argue that if we are to do justice to the varieties of memory and hope the analyst of the psyche must be constantly questioning the nature of time. I shall suggest that this questioning is helped if we make a tentative distinction between two ways in which we experience time. One of these I call successional, the other intentional. Within successional time, our interest is held by change between a before and an after. Within intentional time, our interest is held by completion between a beginning and an end. Psychology and history share a common concern for the act which reconciles our interest in change with our interest in completion.

2

A 31-year-old man dreamed that he was being questioned by detectives who were trying to get him to admit to an unspecified crime of which he was convinced he was innocent. A terrifying sense of guilt was growing. The mood of deepening nightmare came to a climax when he suddenly cried out: "I have no memory!" With that cry he admitted to the crime and accepted as authentic the memory of the detectives. As a result of this confession he himself then remembered, still within the dream, being held as a desperately struggling baby in the huge hands of his father, and hating, hating, hating, where he should have loved.

Now such a dream is evidently typical of the material from which analysts of the psyche have developed their varying theories of resistance in the etiology of human behavior. The lectures of 1912 in which Jung used the phrase, "the etiological significance of the actual present" (as a heading in the English language version only) are given over to the question of how we should interpret such material. Since then, experiences like these, both in dreams and in waking states, have been widely discussed, inside and outside professional psychological circles.

My interest in the dream now is limited to the word "memory." Itself a memory, this dream uses the word "memory" strangely. I want to consider that use.

The dreamer remembered when he confessed that he had no memory. In the moment when he renounced his own private link with the past, he accepted the memory of the investigating detective as valid for himself. What are we to make of this surrender of memory which establishes memory? Is this the overcoming of childhood amnesia under the guidance of a more experienced inquirer who has himself learned to raise the curtain that separates us all from the determining events of our infancy? Or is this, as many enemies of psychoanalysis would argue, the education of an artificial memory: education of a kind familiar in those cultures where the publicly shared remembrance of times past is directed by a specially trained caste of priests and commissars?

The thesis I am presenting is that questions as to true and false memory, or as to spontaneous and artificial memory, open up into questions which distinguish memory from history. In history, the present has knowledge of the past of a kind not accessible to memory. We can call this knowledge artificial if we like, but then we must recognize that the interpretation of action in successional time is grounded in the resistance of another kind of time altogether, a time that does not "follow on."

3

In the eighteenth century it was still reasonable to treat history as the organization of recorded memories. But this is no longer the case. During the last two hundred years historians have been discovering within their own discipline a truth long familiar in the theory and practice of law: that someone not present at the time of an action can nevertheless know that action in ways not open to those who were present.

The action with which the historian is concerned has to be reconstructed to be known. It can only be reconstructed by entering into the thinking of those who carried the action, by thinking their thoughts again. At the level of first hand historical research the question "What really happened?" resolves itself into a more complex questioning of the relation between thought and action. What did they think they were doing? How did their thinking compare with their doing? And how does the difference between the two enable us to know now what was done then? This three level questioning stretches our whole understanding of action. Action is never a fact, never a thing done and completed. It is inherently and indefinitely open. In the court of history, as in a court of law, the need to get at the facts is secondary to a more radical impulse: the need to persuade persons that action is always "to be answered for."

Such answering for action requires time for its unfolding, yet also relies on its ability to arrest time in order that the answer given can reconstitute the original action. The historian's method is a rhythm of questions and answer. But the beat of this rhythm exploits a hiatus between past and present. It exploits the fact that although past and present are continuous, they must also be in some sense discontinuous if there is to be time for the present to know the past.

This is a critical point in my attempt to relate history to the analysis of the psyche. History, like the psyche, only arises as a question that provokes reflection because the otherness of a "then" and a "now" insists on being taken more seriously than their continuity. When we read history books, as when we read some analytic case histories, we read of a succession of events. But the historian reconstructs that succession by a method that exploits a hiatus or flaw in his experience of succession, so that he can have immediate knowledge of a past "now" without that knowledge being mediated to him by the times in between. In this immediacy of a past present with a present present the historian's method introduces us to an experience of time which is absolutely different from that presupposed by, for instance, theories of biological evolution.

This historical time is reflexive. Past and present are related in both directions. It is not only a question of a present initiative recalling the past event. The evidence of the past evokes the questioning of the present, and the dialogue between the two develops out of a power common to both. As one philosopher of history has put it, historical knowledge "is that special case of memory where the object of present thought is past thought, the gap between present and past being bridged not only by the power of present thought to think of the past, but also by the power of past thought to reawaken itself in the present."

It is this two-way movement that constitutes history. It is a reflexive act which, in allowing time to pass between two presents, establishes agency outside the passing of time. It is this experience of agency outside succession to which I want to draw attention in contrasting history and memory to an audience of practicing psychologists.

However, since Hegel first wrestled with these problems it has become evident that it is not going to be easy to define the precise relationship between action within successional time and the reflexive answering for action which constitutes history. There is no agreement among historians or philosophers of history as to how we can describe this conjunction. But for the psychologist working with the casualties of autobiographical succession there is, I believe, one very valuable lesson to be learned from the arguments deployed by historians over the last two hundred years. It is this: that when we try to "answer for action" the resistance which constitutes the threshold between our unconsciousness and our consciousness is determined by something other than memory or its repression. It is determined by our ability to experience time not only as a medium in which reality is enacted, but also as an agent which itself acts on reality.

4

And it is this observation that brings me right to the heart of what I have to say this morning. It seems to me that this distinction between time as medium and time as agent is essential to an understanding of Jung's psychology. It is this distinction which justifies, and controls, the interpretation of biography in terms of myth. Between the time of biography and the time of myth we share the time of history. In history we are conscious of time not only as flowing between a before and after, but also as the constant presence of a power that reflects that flow. If we interpret this power as a resistance to be overcome so that time may flow more easily, we collapse a tension that is inherent in being. For we have our being both in the flowing of time and in the power which reflects that flow, and it is this double standing toward time which opens us to the hidden identity of interpretation and cause in which the psyche acts.

But if we can distinguish these two modes of time by analyzing the relationship between present and past, we are left with the more pressing problem of whether we can establish and confirm this insight in our living between present and future. Here is seems to me that the analysis of memory has to be complemented by the analysis of hope.

It is not easy to develop a science in terms of something as elusive and unreliable as hope, which is perhaps one reason why this perennial inspiration of human action is allowed, under its own name, no central place in psychoanalytical theory. But in our practice hope is a factor with which we are working every day. There can be no presenting situation without hope, and what we make of hope determines everything we do. There is need to integrate our theory and practice with regard to hope, and here I believe the study of history can help, by showing how what we call resistance can be understood as the interdependence of hope and time.

In the philosophy of history we know ourselves as heirs to two kinds of belief in time. We can call one Greek, the other Jewish and Christian. The Greek view of time is close to that of myth. Here time is natural, it recurs as in the seasons of the year, and it has no beginning and no end. The Jewish and Christian tradition on the other hand has broken self-consciously with the time of myth. History is experienced as closer to autobiography than to myth. Time is not natural, it is made, and being made it has an absolute beginning and an absolute end.

On an intellectual plane this distinction is widely recognized. But what is not so widely realized is that with the secularization of mythical and religious belief during the last three hundred years the psychic reality of this distinction can easily remain unconscious. It is this reality which we must be able to analyze if we are to do justice to the nature of hope. Otherwise our experience of hope will be determined by a choice which we are not conscious of having made. For if we remain within what I have called the Greek tradition, we will treat hope as derived from what happens to us in time. But if we respond to the Jewish and Christian tradition, then our hope is in a power that *makes* both beginning and end. In that case, the time which completes our lives between birth and death does not teach us hope. On the contrary: it is itself sustained by hope.

This distinction between a hope that is derived from experience, and can therefore always be disproved by what comes afterwards, and a hope that sustains the very framework of experience and is therefore itself the proof of what is to come, seems to be crucial for the analysis of the psyche. For it enables us to recognize an interdependence between hope and time at the heart of our method. What we make of time determines what we make of hope, and what we make of hope determines what we make of time. It is because of this interdependence between time and hope that hope appears to be so untrustworthy. But it is precisely in this interdependence that the psyche discovers itself as able to convert succession into intention, and intention into succession. When hope in the passing of time fails we must ask whether this failure may not discover hope of a different kind altogether: hope that is quite literally *in* a joining of end and beginning which transcends what passes in between. And when for some reason we are afraid to remember what is past, we must ask to what extent this fear has been learned and to what extent it discovers a fear that negates all learning: the fear that there may be no ground for hope outside succession.

It is in this context that I can understand what Jung has written about the rival claims of etiology and teleology to explain what is present. Both exhaust themselves, and serve only to empty out the fullness of what is, if we understand time as given to us irrespective of any activity of our own. But both are justified if we choose to believe that we can have personal access, through hope and its negation, to the energy which may or may not sustain time. Our search for causes is then taken up into the realization of hope, and the psyche presents itself as a question that can be lived but never answered: by what power do we reconcile succession with an end and a beginning of our making? Or, more simply: by what power do we reconcile change with completion?

5

We meet this power, so I believe, in resistance, but it will be clear to you by now that I am using this word resistance with a very different meaning from that of classical psychoanalysis. In psychology as in history we interpret plots in which we are also the actors. Our interpretation moves between a now and a then, but the convention by which we think of that "then" as a before and after obscures our interest in another kind of then, a then that is always both beginning and end. This interest derives from, and also condemns us to, an intention of which we are necessarily unconscious within passing time, so that in trying to interpret our plots from within the acting of them we meet a resistance that is always reconstituting itself as the present making of the plot.

It is in trying to analyze the constant presence of this resistance that I have come to give such weight to the idea of promise. For it seems to me that in our everyday experience of promise we come closest to understanding how the same power that resists the interpretation of a plot also sustains the action of the plot. It is a power with two characteristics. It moves, but its movement is always contained between an unmoved beginning and end of its own making: just as a promise overcomes the passing of time yet needs that passing for its own realization. And it exists only by virtue of its own negation: just as a promise can only be kept if it can also be broken.

In our lives this power proves itself when memory and hope which are personal fail in the presence of memory and hope which are transpersonal. Jung has taught us to analyze the psyche in terms of the interaction of personal biography and transpersonal myth. He has taught us to question whether our amnesia of times we have known may conceal an anamnesis of times we have not known. But history teaches us that when we thus invoke times we have not known to interpret times we do know, the distinction between amnesia and anamnesis opens up into a distinction of another kind altogether: the distinction between a hope that is learned from experience and a hope without which there can be no experience. Jung has shown us how to analyze the tension between these two kinds of hope, and between their two very different kinds of negation, in his work on the archetypes and on the relation between the personal and the collective unconscious. This tension, this psychic energy, becomes actual for us when we recognize that life has an obligation towards time that is active as well as passive; that life is bound by a promise to convert the spending and the saving of time one into the other.

This promise to convert the spending and the saving of time one into the other is, so I believe, the presence of the psyche. Any professional method that claims to analyze the psyche finds itself bound by this promise, so that the resistance which holds between the keeping and breaking of this promise determines the timing of our work. It is in analyzing this resistance that we can help secure the foundations of psychology.

5

Ending Phase as an Indicator of the Success or Failure of Psychotherapy

MICHAEL FORDHAM, *London*

It is often hard to decide how much of a success or failure a case of psychotherapy has been. This is because criteria by which to judge the result are vague. To be sure anybody who has developed a reliable theory may use it to assess his work, and since he is familiar with it and knows how it can be applied, his conclusions will be valuable. There are, however, many theories not easy to compare with one another; so it may be useful to focus on the ending of psychotherapy as a specific situation having definable characteristics, with the qualification that however skilfully it is conducted or however long the therapy goes on, ending has a way of taking place without the therapist's aim being achieved.

No doubt appreciating the difficulties, Jung had little to say about endings: he described one in *Two Essays* and made a list of eight reasons for stopping in *Psychology and Alchemy* and that is about all. He headed his list with those patients who only need a piece of good advice and concluded it with those for whom the individuation process makes therapy interminable. It is the last class of people which has most bedevilled our ideas about the value of even considering whether success and failure are useful concepts at all. Indeed, medical, philosophic, social, or religious models all tend to break down in face of them.

Because of the short time which the conference committee has wisely given each speaker, I shall not enter into the problems these reflections raise and instead will start from some axioms about analytical psychotherapy. They are:

1) For a radical therapy to take place two people must meet regularly over a prolonged period.

2) There arrives a time when they separate.

3) At the start the relationship is asymmetrical, the therapist being more experienced, knowledgeable, etc., than the patient.

4) As the process proceeds the asymmetry diminishes—though it never disappears—and the patient achieves greater insight and control over his affects.

How ending occurs depends most on the last axiom, and numerous factors enter into it that may be grouped under headings: finance and the demands of every day life on the one hand, the transference and countertransference set-up on the other. There are however so many significant details that it is tempting to fall back on a rule of thumb so as to cut through them all: to rely on a fantasy sequence, or indications from dreams or practical realities or the overt state of the transference. Though all these come into the picture, it is most important not to base ending on any one and to take as much as possible into account.

Let us assume a patient who has been in therapy long enough to have worked through and understood the main conflicts for which he or she arrived for treatment. During that time, a reasonably good alliance between therapist and patient will have been made, so that a transference will have formed and been worked on both in its positive (loving) and negative (hating) aspects. In the course of this work, associations, many dreams, and fantasies including active imagination will have been understood and if necessary analyzed in relation to the past and present, personal and collective.

At last a time comes when the material begins to thin out; the associations have little in them; dreams diminish in number and become superficial in character; fantasies lose their compelling power; every day personal and social difficulties become manageable and there are no transference crises. So it is not surprising if therapist and patient begin to think their work is drawing to a close; they may even mention it almost at the same time or one may do so and the other may reveal that he had been thinking about it also. The ending phase has begun. Once the idea has been expressed, it is not difficult to agree that separation will take place, and a date may thereupon be agreed to. It seems sad that such a long partnership should end just as the patient becomes truly viable, but both therapist and patient recognize that to go on with therapy may be less fruitful than ending it. Will it be forever? That is still an open question. At this time the therapy as a whole may come under review and also the history of earlier separations from birth onwards. Recorded information and hearsay about earlier situations is relevant, but they need to be linked up with previous situations in which separation has taken place during the therapy: how has the patient reacted to holiday breaks? How much distress have they caused? And also, if the patient has been coming five times a week, what have the weekend breaks meant to him? It is also relevant to look at patterns in the way a patient ends his interviews and to analyze them. Thinking about all this introduces quite a number of problems about ending. Amongst them is one which needs special care: how to end so as not to reproduce unresolvable traumatic situations from the past.

It is likely that if patient and therapist start to work on ending together, the separations during therapy have already become tolerable to the patient; but they have all been occasions when meeting will again take place in a relatively short time. This time, the separation will be the end of meetings.

It is very likely that when an ending is contemplated, or even mutually decided upon, the patient may start by reviewing all the faults of his analyst with which he has not dared to confront him before; alternatively or concurrently, gratitude may become easier to express. One patient, having decided that ending was desirable, felt it to be an invasion, in which himself was holding out with remaining bits of the self that were left intact: the integration of this situation led to driving home that his ego still needed to relinquish its omnipotent fantasies. Again, dependent feelings may reassert themselves in that the patient's whole life seems once again to depend upon fantasies of blissful union with his therapist. These examples must serve to show something of the variety of reactions to thinking about ending; they could be greatly multiplied.

Working on his first reactions, the patient may hope, before ending, to be reconciled to the analyst's failings or to gain a more and more realistic assessment of his gifts or internally of his (the patient's) own limitations and merits. Very often the ending response focuses the first problem that he came for, and sometimes there results a sort of miniature re-analysis of his essential conflicts. But however different the ending period may be, there is one group of feelings that may be looked for: sadness that what was hoped for has not been achieved, corresponding to sadness at parting—the loss of the therapist—combined with gratitude for all that has been achieved.

It would be a travesty of the truth if the therapist thought that the ending work was one-sided, for he also is going to lose a patient with whom he has been more or less deeply involved, so that he also will hope to feel sadness at a worthwhile parting. However, to say that he needs to do as much work on arriving at this position would be false; gratitude will, it may be hoped, figure less and satisfaction with work well done will figure more.

To illustrate a satisfactory ending I now wish to describe one which demonstrates some of the characteristics so far enumerated and especially how the therapist may feel about it.

The patient, a middle-aged woman, had been in therapy with numerous analysts. Her first analysis began when she was in her late adolescence, and there had never been a break of more than a few years up to the time I saw her. A characteristic of each ending was this: it had either been deliberately induced by her analyst or else it had been dictated by circumstances: it had never been decided upon by herself.

When she began to approach the subject of parting from me, she tried rather directly to arrange that I should decide how and when it should take place. It was easy, in view of her history, to show her what she was doing and to point out that if I did as she wished the way would be opened for her to repeat the earlier traumatic parting from the only good parent figure she remembered—an uncle. It was after this interpretation that she made up her own mind and fixed a date. Though I was in agreement with her decision, I found that I was without any feeling of sadness or regret at the impending event, neither did I experience any satisfaction at having made it possible for her to arrive at her decision.

Upon reflection, it was not clear to me why reviving her memory had been so decisive; but next time it was easier to understand. She had never been able to share her despair at her uncle's loss; she had been told secretly of it and secret her feelings had to remain. As we went over this situation her feelings emerged and were communicated, for the first time; she became alive, pleasant, and attractive, and so my feelings of loss at the impending end could combine with satisfaction at what the decision had produced. When she left, she expressed her gratitude in balanced and convincing language. From personal knowledge I am as certain that the ending was a true one; she has not been in analysis again and shows every sign of not doing so. That is over ten years ago.

But is it justifiable to think of a separation as the end of therapy? We know that it is not and that any good analysis means that self-analysis will continue. (I want to interpolate here that self-analysis is not primarily a conscious process but rather a continuation in the unconscious of what has taken place in the therapy.) It may be that the ex-patient will return to his therapist not so long after separation has taken place to finish off a bit of analysis which had been left out. When this happens it is very striking how he takes up where he has left off and that what is necessary to be done can often be accomplished in one or a few interviews. So another analysis does not start, though the return interview may be repeated in my experience over a year or even more.

It is this observation that gives rise to the idea of there being a post-therapy phase in which the patient's identification with the analyst continues to need reinforcement before the patient can establish himself in the new avenues for living that have been opened up to him by his therapy.

This completes the outline picture of successful endings. The cases I have referred to all went through long periods of therapy. Many of them had been coming four or five times a week over many years. The one I described never came so often, and I have rather deliberately chosen her to refute the idea that the features of ending I have enumerated only apply to frequent or everyday analytic therapy. It can be worked out in more detail with more frequent sessions, but in principle it is the same with others.

I now wish to consider an example of how ending shows up analytic failure. It is of a patient whom I had seen over a very long time, so long that I cannot remember exactly, but it was about twenty years. The treatment was divided into two parts and the first part ended because she, as I thought, needed more frequent and regular interviews.

The second part showed up a delusional transference which led to a state of bewildering identity rather like the one Jung described in his paper "The Realities of Practical Psychotherapy." After a very long time I succeeded in defining my own position sufficiently to make sure that I no longer contributed significantly to the form of her transference. I worked for about six months from this position and became convinced that her transference could not be resolved by analytic means.

When, therefore, her delusional pattern emerged once again I said, firmly, that we had been in this situation too often, and as no solution to it could be found, we must regard it as a failure of the analysis. I stated that though I did not intend to stop immediately I would set a date for ending at the Christmas break—about three months ahead. She went away to consider it. After a session or two she started on a familiar maneuver: she appeared to accept what I said, but proceeded as if nothing had happened. This raised suspicions in my mind, so I told her what I thought she was doing and said that I did not want there to be any misapprehension as to my intention. It was then that she gave indirect and distorted indications of acceptance. She told her husband that *she* (believe it or not) was ending her analysis. He replied, "Don't go back on it."

The most striking event that took place in the ending period was as follows. She sat in a chair (previously she had been on the couch out of preference) and delivered herself of a detailed statement on why I had made a mistake in a paper I wrote which contained a reference to her. After several interviews she expressed her dissatisfaction at what was going on and returned to the couch. For my part, I thought her argument lacked conviction; I received the impression that she might have a dawning idea as to the nature of her argument, but that her predominant thought was probably that it was futile to continue with it because I was, in her view, as defensive as ever (projective identification).

The end came. It was an open declaration of love. She held out both hands and I got the impression that I was intended to take them and go on to take her in my arms. Somewhat regretfully I took her hands and uttered a platitude which I cannot bring myself to repeat.

This case illustrates very well how ending crystallizes a failure in a particular area just as the other ones helped me to know what was a success.

The features of the failure are the following:

1) The decision to end was one-sided; it was resisted by the patient to the end, as the declaration of love showed, and only gave semblance of agreement by developing a reversed view of it: she asserted that it was *she* who had decided to end and so, by implication, *not* me.

2) The central anxiety for which she came was not resolved and so neither was her transference.

3) There was no expression of sadness or gratitude on her part, nor

did I derive any corresponding feelings of satisfaction from all the work that had been done.

The case could be considered nonetheless as therapeutically successful. My patient's personal life had become enriched; she was, in a somewhat unusual way, very successful and creative in her work. She had always possessed a rich inner life, but now it was more valued, more understood, and better related to reality than before. I record this because I believe that the subject of success or failure needs more penetrating understanding than overt therapeutic success.

To conclude: Jung wrote that he learned much more from his failures than his successes. I think we can all understand what he meant: a failure, which may not be so understood by the patient at all, presents the therapist with a problem to be solved. Therefore failures are more interesting, and I hope that this paper will go some way towards providing a criterion for detecting them. Only so doing can we define areas in which we, personally or collectively, need to undertake research that involves further individuation.

REFERENCES

JUNG, C. G. (1935). "The relations between the ego and the unconscious," in *C.W.* 7.

—— (1937). "The realities of practical psychotherapy," in *C.W.* 16 (2nd edition, revised.)

—— (1952). *Psychology and Alchemy. C.W.* 12.

6

Die Konstellierung der Gegenübertragung beim Auftauchen archetypischer Träume
Untersuchungsmethoden und -ergebnisse

H. Dieckmann, *Berlin*

1929 sagte C. G. Jung: (1958b, S. 76) "Denn, wie man es auch drehen und wenden mag, die Beziehung zwischen Arzt und Patient ist eine persönliche Beziehung innerhalb des unpersönlichen Rahmens der ärztlichen Behandlung. Es ist mit keinem Kunstgriff zu vermeiden, daß die Behandlung das Produkt einer gegenseitigen Beeinflussung ist, an welcher das ganze Wesen des Patienten sowohl wie das des Arztes teilhat. In der Behandlung findet die Begegnung zweier irrationaler Gegebenheiten, nämlich zweier Menschen statt, die nicht abgegrenzte, bestimmbare Größen sind, sondern neben ihrem vielleicht bestimmten Bewußtsein eine unbestimmbar ausgedehnte Sphäre von Unbewußtheit mitbringen."

Mit dieser zweifelsohne richtigen und sehr wichtigen Feststellung Jungs ist in der Psychotherapie nur sehr langsam, sehr unzureichend und zögernd Ernst gemacht worden. Befangen in dem cartesianischen

Denken der alten Naturwissenschaften strebte man bewußt oder unbewußt danach, den therapeutischen Prozeß beim Patienten weitgehend
zu objektivieren. So war und ist zu einem großen Teil noch heute—
abgesehen van neueren Entwicklungen, die die Empathie mit einbeziehen—für die Psychoanalyse die Gegenübertragung ein pathologi-
scher und störender Prozeß, der durch eigene Bewußtmachung und
Analyse des Analytikers nach Möglichkeit weitgehend ausgeschaltet
werden sollte. 1946 veröffentlichte Jung in seiner "Psychologie der
Übertragung" (1958a) eine differenzierte Darstellung des therapeutischen Feldes zwischen Arzt und Patient im Schema der Cross-Cousin-
Marriage und eine Beschreibung jener "Vermischung zweier chemi-
scher Körper" (1958b, S. 77), wie er an anderer Stelle früher meta-
phorisch gesagt hatte. Er relativierte aber leider in einem Vorwort diesen Prozeß auf jene weiche . . . "höheren Formen der Psychotherapie,
. . . den ganzen Menschen in die Schranken fordern" (1958a, S. 190). Er
spricht gleichzeitig von der Fällen, wo die Übertragung milde verläuft
oder sich praktisch nicht bemerkbar macht, eine Feststellung, von der
wir heute wissen, daß sie falsch ist und Abwehr beschreibt.

1957 differenzierte Fordham (1957, S. 91ff) die Gegenübertragungs-
reaktion und unterschied eine illusionäre, d. h. projektive, von den
Komplexen des Analytikers ausgehende Gegenübertragung von einer
syntonen, bei der der Patient den Analytiker emotional in die Rolle
einer Beziehungsperson spielt. Auch G. Adler (1967, S. 344 ff.) faßt
die Gegenübertragung als fundamentalen Punkt in Theorie und Praxis
der Analytischen Psychologie auf und unterscheidet die Gegenübertragung von der Gegenprojektion (1968, S. 172). Er hebt insbesondere den
positiven Wert der Gegenübertragung hervor, die einen Indikator für
die konstruktive subjektive Reaktion des Analytikers darstellt, die aus
dessen eigenem Unbewußten kommt und die analytische Beziehung
aktiviert.

Das Problem in der Gegenübertragungsforschung liegt nun darin,
daß alle Aussagen, die wir bisher in der Literatur darüber finden konnten, unkontrolliert und gewissermaßen naiv sind. Der Analytiker
macht eine Aussage über etwas, was ihm als eigene innere Reaktion an
einer bestimmten Stelle der Therapie auffällt, die auch wieder unkontrolliert von ihm selbst gewählt wurde. Der Analytiker spricht
zudem über sein eigenes Unbewußtes und deutet es selbst. Mit Recht
sprechen wir uns sicher die Fähigkeit zu, gelernt zu haben, mit dem
eigenen Unbewußten umzugehen; aber mit dem gleichen Recht und
der entsprechenden Bescheidenheit müssen wir auch

zugeben, daß wir überall und immer noch in diesem Prozeß über blinde Flecken verfügen. Niemand von uns wird auf die Idee kommen, von sich zu behaupten, er sei ein fertig individuierter Mensch. Wir sind vielmehr alle Anfänger in diesem großen Prozeß der Individuation und haben auch unsere eigenen Probleme mit Persona, Schatten und Anima, und mitunter glückt es uns, einen kleinen Einblick in das Erlebnis des Selbst zu erhaschen.

Wir haben nun in den letzten Jahren in Berlin den Versuch unternommen, wenigstens in einer gewissen kontrollierten Situation die Gegenübertragungsreaktionen zu erfassen. Wir bildeten eine Gruppe von vier Analytikern, die bereits über langjährige praktische Erfahrung verfügten, und der außer dem Referenten Herr R. Blomeyer, Herr E. Jung und Herr H. J. Wilke angehören. In diese Gruppe wurde jeweils von einem der Analytiker die Darstellung einer einzelnen Analysenstunde mit einem archetypischen Traum gebracht, in der außer den Assoziationen des Patienten auch die Einfälle des Analytikers synchron aufgezeichnet waren. Hierbei wurde auch der Inhalt der vorhergehenden Stunde und die nachfolgende Entwicklung berücksichtigt. Dieses wurde in der Gruppensituation eingehend analysiert.

Ehe ich nun einen Bericht über die vorläufigen Ergebnisse dieser Untersuchung gebe, muß ich noch einiges zur Methodik sagen. Entsprechend dem bereits vorher historisch Gesagten ist unsere therapeutische Haltung mehr oder weniger weitgehend auf den Patienten konzentriert. Das extreme Beispiel hierfür ist die alte Spiegelhaltung Freuds, aber auch die Haltung freischwebender Aufmerksamkeit oder das Sich-leer-Machen, um die Inhalte des Patienten aufzunehmen, sowie ähnliche therapeutische Haltungen beruhen auf einer bewußten Konzentration auf das Unbewußte und das Bewußtsein des Patienten. Als anderes Extrem steht diesem das Beispiel des Regenmachers gegenüber, das Jung oft benutzte (Vgl. 1970, S. 419, n. 211). Hier liegt die Richtung der Konzentration ausschließlich auf dem eigenen Unbewußten, das von der Umweltstörung in Disharmonie gerät. Die Wiederherstellung der eigenen inneren Harmonie bedingt dann auch die Behebung der äußeren Störung.

Auch wir sind von einem ähnlichen Vorstellungsmodell wie dem letzteren—d. h. dem Regenmacher—ausgegangen, wobei wir uns allerdings bemüht haben, einen mittleren Weg zu finden. Mir schwebt hier das Metapher von einem Instrument vor, das die Psyche des Analytikers bildet, und auf dem der Patient spielt. Lauscht man den Tönen und der Melodie, die dieses Instrument hervorbringt, ist man in der Lage, viel Zusätzliches neben dem auszusagen, was man am Patienten beobachtet. Das Metapher hinkt insofern, als die analytische Veränderung ja nicht nur den Patienten, sondern auch den Arzt betrifft. Es ist nun, wie wir erfahren haben, gar nicht so einfach, neben den Assoziationen des Patienten auch noch den eigenen, unbewußten Prozeß zu beobachten, und ihn zeitgerecht parallel einzuordnen, d. h. mit dem einen Auge nach außen und mit dem anderen nach innen zu sehen. Es erfordert vielmehr einen langwierigen Lernprozeß, der sich u. a. darin dokumentiert, daß in dem ersten Arbeitsjahr zu einer Therapiestunde des Patienten durchschnittlich etwa 8 Assoziationen des Analytikers mitgeteilt wurden, während diese Zahl im zweiten Arbeitsjahr bereits auf 17 anstieg. Selbstverständlich sind wir uns darüber klar, daß es infolge solcher technischer Probleme, wozu u. a. auch die Schwierigkeit der Protokollführung gehört, unmöglich ist, ein vollständiges Bild der beiderseitigen assoziativen, beziehungsweise amplifikatorischen Prozesse darzustellen. Wir sind uns auch darüber klar gewesen, daß in dieser Methode eine gewisse narzistische Gefahr des Mehr-sich-selbst-Bespiegelns als auf den Patienten zu achten liegt, und wir sind anfangs und auch heute noch sehr vorsichtig damit umgegangen. Eine solche Entgleisung ist aber nicht eingetreten, sondern wir haben im Gegenteil in unseren Kontrollen auch sehr gute therapeutische Erfahrungen feststellen können.

Wir haben ein bestimmtes Auswahlkriterium angewandt für die Stunden, die wir in die Untersuchung einbeziehen wollten. Es sollte sich, wie bereits gesagt, um Stunden handeln, in denen von dem Pat. ein archetypischer Traum berichtet wurde, wobei wir mehr Wert auf die Stärke der im Traum enthaltenen Emotionen als auf die Klassik der Mythologeme legten. Wir sind hierbei von der Vorstellung ausgegangen, daß wir zunächst einmal die Stunden beobachten wollten, in denen eine hohe emotionale Aktivität des Pat. unbewußt auf den Analytiker einwirkte. Wir erwarteten, daß identifikatorische, projektive und partizipatorische Reaktionen an diesen Stellen besonders deutlich auftreten mußten.

Insgesamt wurden bisher 25 derartige Fälle eingehend in der Gruppe (bei ca. dreistündigen Sitzungen) analysiert. Das Hintergrundmaterial, über das wir verfügen, ist natürlich erheblich größer, da jeder von uns wesentlich mehr Fälle nach dieser Methode aufzeichnete bzw. beobachtete, als er in die Gruppe bringen konnte. Auch diese Erfahrungen sind hier mitberücksichtigt. Ich möchte nicht daran vorbeigehen zu erwähnen, daß durch dieses Verfahren selbstverständlich auch ein gruppendynamischer Prozeß ausgelöst wurde, der ebenfalls eine Reihe recht interessanter Phänomene aufwies, den ich aber hier zunächst ausklammern muß, und über den wir später an anderer Stelle berichten werden. Auch das auftretende Typenproblem ist hier noch nicht einbezogen, da es noch von Herrn Wilke bearbeitet wird.

Ich möchte nun zunächst versuchen, eine gewisse Einteilung der Einfälle zu geben, die von Seiten der Analytiker bei uns berichtet wurden. Als Einfälle haben wir selbstverständlich keine bewußten Überlegungen, sondern nur spontan aus dem Unbewußten auftauchende Assoziationen gerechnet. Die größte Gruppe bildete, wie es zu erwarten war, Assoziationen, die sich auf das Thema der Stunde, ihrer Symbolik und auf die Lebensgeschichte des Pat. bezogen. Es gab hier Einfälle zur archetypischen Amplifikation, zur Genese und zur aktuellen Lebenssituation des Patienten.

Eine zweite Gruppe bezog sich auf Assoziationen, die die Lebensgeschichte und die Probleme des Analytikers betrafen, d. h. Einfälle aus der Genese und der aktuellen Situation des Arztes.

Drittens traten rein emotionale Reaktionen auf, und es ist vielleicht sehr interessant, daß gerade diese Gruppe im zweiten Arbeitsjahr den zahlenmäßig höchsten Anstieg zeigte (von ca. einer Reaktion pro Pat. und Stunde im ersten Jahr zu 4 Reaktionen pro Pat. und Stunde im zweiten Jahr) und daß diese Reaktionen zunehmend differenzierter wurden. Es scheint, daß das kollektive Tabu, daß ein Wissenschaftler seine Gefühle beobachtet und in seine Arbeit miteinbringt, trotz besserem rationalen Wissen auch für uns noch recht weitgehend zutraf. Die Differenzierung, Kultivierung und Erziehung der Fühlfunktion, sowie ihr bewußter Einsatz, scheint mir überhaupt eines der großen Probleme unserer Zeit zu sein, dessen Vernachlässigung sich immer wieder rächt.

Als letzteres wären noch die somatischen Reaktionen des Analytikers zu erwähnen sowohl im vegetativen als auch im motorischen Bereich wie Herzklopfen, Druckgefühle, Spannungen, Müdigkeit und Gähnen, Kratzen etc. Ausnahmslos konnte hinter diesen in der Gruppenanalyse ein gemeinsames Stück Unbewußtheit zwischen Arzt und Patient aufgedeckt werden.

Das von uns vielleicht als am erstaunlichsten erlebte Ergebnis war das des psychologischen Zusammenhanges der Assoziationsreihe des Analytikers mit der des Patienten. Es ist für den Psychotherapeuten zwar eine selbstverständliche Erfahrung, daß die Reihe der freien Einfälle einen psychologisch sinnvollen Zusammenhang hat. So war es auch zu erwarten, daß dieser Zusammenhang nicht nur in der Assoziationskette des Pat., sondern auch in der des Analytikers bestand; daß aber beide Ketten unter sich wieder sinnentsprechend verknüpft waren, und zwar in vollem Umfang, hatten wir nicht in dieser Form erwartet. Der spontane Ausspruch eines unserer Mitglieder: "Die Patienten sagen ja dauernd das, was ich im Augenblick denke und fühle!" charakterisiert vielleicht am besten diese Situation. Natürlich ist dieser Ausspruch nicht wörtlich zu nehmen, denn erstens handelt es sich um Sinnentsprechungen, obwohl auch die formalen und inhaltlichen Vorstellungsinhalte bei beiden Personen oft verblüffend ähnlich waren, und zweitens dachte und fühlte auch der Analytiker oft, was der Patient sagte, d. h. die Assoziationen des Analytikers wurden durch die Worte und Emotionen des Pat. bestimmt. Einen ausführlichen derartigen Stundenbericht wird Herr Blomeyer in dem folgenden Vortrag vorlegen können (vgl. diesen Band). Wichtig erscheint mir, daß auch die archetypischen Amplifikationen, die dem Analytiker einfielen, von seinem persönlichen Hintergrund her bestimmt waren, und dieser rastete wieder in das Problem des Patienten ein. Ich möchte hierfür ein kurzes Beispiel geben:

Eine 37jährige Patientin, ein borderline case, mit einer psychotischen Mutter, träumte vor der 496. Stunde: "Ich hatte ein Gewand an wie ein Teufel, ein Gott oder ein König, es kann auch vom Tod getragen werden. Ich wollte das Böse abtun und meinte den Mantel. Dann kam mein Freund. In meiner Angst wollte ich mich an ihn klammern, aber als ich nun sagte: "Weiche von mir Satan," konnte man denken, dieser Ausspruch bezieht sich auf ihn. Ich hatte furchtbare Angst, wollte ihn umarmen, und er wollte mich fast gleichzeitig umarmen. In der Dunkelheit hatte ich Zweifel und Angst, ob er es auch ist und von dieser Angst bin ich aufgewacht."

Dem Analytiker fällt zunächst ohne besondere Emotion Mephistopheles und eine Szene aus dem Beginn des Faustdramas ein, wo Faust glaubt, den Teufel gefangen zu haben, dieser aber entweicht.

Nun berichtet die Patientin wie sie nie ohne furchtbare Angst mit der Mutter in einem Raum schlafen konnte, weil sie fürchtete, von dieser mit der Axt erschlagen zu werden. Dem Analytiker fallen nun mit Emotionen frühe eigene Kinderängste von Tod, Sterben und Abschluß des Lebens ein, was ja auch eine Beziehung zu der Figur des alten Faust und seinem Schritt in ein anderes Leben hat.

Die Patientin berichtet dann weiter von ihrer völligen Entwurzelung bei der Evakuierung in einer Kleinstadt, während dem Therapeuten eine mittelalterliche Stadt vorschwebt mit der Geborgenheit in ihren Mauern und einer glücklichen Zeit in einer solchen Stadt auf seiner Hochzeitsreise. (Zur Zeit d. Analysenstunde hatte er dagegen Eheprobleme. Gefühlsmäßig war er in der Lage, diese zu ertragen, da er diesen alten Rückhalt einer glücklichen und harmonischen Beziehung auf der anderen Seite im Hintergrund besaß.) Der Therapeut findet gewissermaßen innerlich ein emotionalers pièce de resistance, von dem aus ein

Konflikt zu bewältigen ist. Genau in diesem Augenblick berichtet die Patientin, daß sie während der Evakuierungszeit einen festen, sicheren Punkt auf der Tenne einer Scheune gefunden hatte, wohin, sie sich immer mit ihrem Bruder zurückzog und Karten spielte, wenn die Mutter lieblos war. Es tritt hier also eines der von uns sehr häufig beobachteten Synchronizitätsphänomene auf, indem Analytiker und Patient innerlich gleichzeitig einen Temenos finden, aus dem heraus man dem dämonischen und überwältigenden Mutteranimus begegnen kann. Von hier aus ist der erste Ansatzpunkt zur Verarbeitung des Problems, das heißt der zwischen Arzt und Patientin in der Übertragungssituation stehenden Angst, gegeben, und die Analyse verläuft zunächst fruchtbar weiter. Ich bin mir natürlich darüber klar, daß man die Situation auch als gemeinsame Flucht vor dem Mutterdämon deuten kann, was aber hier nicht zutrifft.

Differenzieren wir noch einmal das Geschehen: Beim Analytiker treten zunächst archetypische Amplifikationen auf, die sich um die nicht gelungene Bannung des Teufels drehen. Diese werden vom persönlichen Unbewußten mit den entsprechenden Emotionen aus der Kindheitsgenese belebt, nun geht die Reihe in die aktuelle Situation über, und der Archetyp (mittelalterliche Stadt—Fauststube-Hochzeit) mit den aktuellen Emotionen zusammen vermittelt eine innere Bewältigungsmöglichkeit der Situation.

Die Patientin verbleibt im Bereich ihrer eigenen Genese und begibt sich in ihre schweren noch existenten Kindheitsängste, findet aber gleichzeitig mit dem Analytiker einen rettenden Punkt in diesem Chaos, und im weiteren Verlauf dieser und der nächsten Stunden können Ängste fruchtbar verarbeitet werden. Dieser ganze Vorgang, dieser geschilderte erste Teil einer Stunde, ist ohne jede Deutung von Seiten des Analytikers verlaufen, trotzdem tritt eine gefühlsmäßige Steuerung der Situation auch für die Patientin ein. Natürlich gibt es auch das umgekehrte Phänomen, daß die Einfälle des Analytikers zuerst persönlich emotional sind, und daraus eine archetypische Amplifikation entsteht, die geäußert wird, je nachdem wie es die Situation erfordert.

In diesem kurzen Beispiel ist bereits die Gruppenverarbeitung enthalten. Während des Stundenverlaufes und auch nachher bei der Ausarbeitung waren dem Analytiker diese inneren Zusammenhänge noch nicht bewußt, wozu noch wichtige Hintergrundaspekte in der Problematik des Analytikers in der Gruppe verarbeitet werden konnten. So war auch zum Beispiel nur die Assoziation Hochzeitsreise in der Stunde vorhanden, die Beziehung dieser Reise zum Aktualkonflikt und die von daher stammende Bedeutung dagegen wurde ihm erst in der Gruppe voll bewußt. Es ist für uns alle immer wieder eine beeindruckende Erfahrung gewesen, in welchem Umfang durch diese Analyse des Analytikers wesentliche, neue Gesichtspunkte und eine viel umfangreichere Bewußtwerdung des analytischen Prozesses erfolgten. Wir haben einfach nicht damit gerechnet, daß man mit dieser Methode erfahrenen Analytikern soviel Aha-Erlebnisse über den therapeutischen Prozeß vermitteln könnte, der zwischen ihnen und den Patienten in einer derartigen Stunde ablief. Wenn wir nicht schon vorher von der Aussage Jungs überzeugt gewesen wären: "Die unvermeidliche psychische Induktion bringt es mit sich, daß beide von der Wandlung des Dritten ergriffen und gewandelt werden, wobei allein das Wissen des Arztes wie ein flackerndes Lämpchen die tiefe Dunkelheit des Geschehens spärlich erhellt", (1958a, S. 211) so hätten wir nach diesen Erfahrungen nicht umhin gekonnt, es zu sein. Innerhalb der Analyse gibt es also auch auf Seiten des Analytikers die beiden Formen der Individuation: die autonome unbewußte Teilnahme der Psyche des Arztes am Wandlungsprozeß des Patienten und die bewußt erlebte, analytisch geförderte und verarbeitete Individuation. Letztere kann genau wie die bewußte Individuation des Patienten eine größere Entfaltung, stärkere Bereicherung und Bewußtheit des therapeutischen Prozesses hervorrufen. Man kann zwar auch allein mit den eigenen Einfällen viel anfangen. Wesentliche neue Gesichtspunkte ergeben sich aber zusätzlich in der Gruppe. Der Analytiker hat eben blinde Flecke, und die Aussagen über Gegenübertragung werden erheblich schlüssiger, wenn sie in der Gruppe oder durch einen anderen Analytiker kontrolliert werden.

Obwohl in dem oben berichteten Fall bereits die kompensatorische Funktion des kollektiven Unbewußten deutlich wird, sind doch die korrespondierenden Elemente überwiegend. Ich möchte daher ein zweites Beispiel schildern von einer schweren Neurose mit starken schizoiden Elementen, in dem die kompensatorische Funktion überwiegt. Die Patientin träumte vor der 147. Stunde: "Ich bin in ein Haus umgezogen. Da war noch eine andere Frau drin. Dann kam plötzlich ein Mann und wollte uns vergewaltigen. Da er bei der anderen anfing, bin ich weggelaufen, um Hilfe zu holen, aber als ich auß Sichtweite war, habe ich mich auf einen Baumstumpf gesetzt und abgewartet. Als ich nach einer Weile zum Haus zurückkam, waren sie beide weg. Ich habe dann die Betten frisch bezogen. Ich hatte furchtbare Angst in dem Traum und wachte ganz erschöpft auf."

Da die Patientin bisher vor jeder Konfrontation mit dem Unbewußten fortgelaufen war und die schweren Fluchttendenzen, die bis zu einer ganzen Serie von Suizidversuchen voranalytisch und zu Beginn der Analyse gegangen waren, hier immer noch anhielten, merkte der Analytiker ein leises Ärger- und Ungeduldsgefühl in sich aufklingen.

Dann tauchte der Einfall Hades-Persephone-Demeter auf, und es trat zunächst eine emotionale Identifikation mit der Hadesfigur ein: "So müßte man es doch endlich machen wie der Hades", dachte er, "greifen und festhalten". Als nächster Einfall kam dann aber ein eigener archetypischer Traum aus dem Beginn seiner Ausbildungszeit. In diesem Traum befand sich unter einer alten Burgruine eine Höhlenwelt, in der praktisch alle Schätze der Welt ausgestellt waren, unter anderem auch eine Abteilung, in der sämtliche möglichen sexuellen Beziehungsformen von lebenden Menschen dargestellt waren. Hierbei befanden sich die Vorstellenden hinter einer Gitterwand wie im Zoo. In diesem Augenblick berichtet die Patientin folgenden Erweiterungseinfall zu dem Traum: "Das Haus hatte jene Glaswand, und es war kein Vorhang zugezogen. Die meisten Dinge erlebe ich ja auch hinter einer Glaswand."

Der Hintergrund, der in der Gruppe herauskam, war folgender: Analytiker und Patientin waren in stark puritanischen Elternhäusern aufgewachsen, in denen Sexualität ausgeklammert und als ekelhaft erlebt wurde. Die Patientin hatte bis zu diesem Zeitpunkt nie über Sexualität gesprochen und auch bis auf wenige Durchbrüche unter Alkohol alle sexuellen Impulse verdrängt. Der Analytiker befand sich zur Zeit seines damaligen Traumes in erheblichen Schwierigkeiten, in die ihn seine sehr archaische und turbulente Sexualität gebracht hatte. Es war ihm damals doch sehr peinlich gewesen, diesen Traum seiner Lehranalytikerin zu erzählen, zumal er durch die dargestellten Sexualakte recht angeregt war. Er erinnerte sich deutlich an das befreiende und erlösende Gefühl, als seine Analytikerin diesen Traum nicht so ekelhaft fand wie seine Mutter, sondern ganz der Ansicht des Unbewußten war, es handele sich um höchste Werte, die sie verständnisvoll und eher freudig annahm. Diese Erinnerung veränderte nun merkbar die Haltung des Analytikers, und der weitere Verlauf der Analysenstunde mit seiner Patientin war von seiner Seite her durch die positive mütterliche Gefühlserfahrung von damals getönt. Die Libido aus dem kollektiven Unbewußten füllte also nicht die Figur des ungeduldigen und vergewaltigenden Hades auf, sondern mobilisierte den Demeter-Archetyp. Dadurch gelang es dem Analytiker, eine mütterliche Haltung anzunehmen und im weiteren Verlauf der Stunde die Angst der Patientin abzubauen. Am nächsten Tag rief diese den Analytiker an: "Ich kann es nur am Telefon sagen. Die Glasscheibe ist zerbrochen. Nach der letzten Stunde hatte ich eine Flut von sexuellen Phantasien, und erstmalig in meinen Phantasien hatten die Menschen überhaupt Gesichter und dann auch noch mir bekannte. Sie selbst waren übrigens auch dabei!"

Ich glaube, daß es an diesem Beispiel deutlich wird, wie hier das kollektive Unbewußte die bewußten, bzw. aus dem persönlichen Unbewußten aufsteigenden, Tendenzen und Impulse kompensiert und in eine analytisch fruchtbare Richtung bringt.

Dieser Fall leitet damit über zu einem weiteren Problem, dem des Widerstandes. Ich meine hier nun ausdrücklich den Widerstand des Analytikers gegen das Unbewußte des Patienten.

Wir haben in unseren Fällen eine doch recht aufschlußreiche Erfahrung gemacht. Der Widerstand des Analytikers ging eigentlich immer vom persönlichen Unbewußten aus, während das kollektive Unbewußte sich bemühte, die Analyse wieder in die Progression zu bekommen. Es war in einem Fall geradezu drastisch, mit welcher rührenden Verzweiflung das kollektive Unbewußte eine prospektive Amplifikation nach der anderen nach oben schickte, um den Analytiker zu korrigieren, der auf der Basis einer alten Kinderangst, also einer illusionären Gegenübertragung bzw. Gegenprojektion, mit seinen Deutungen immer genau daneben lag. Hierbei hatte die Patientin einen Traum gehabt, der das Motiv der Todeshochzeit enthielt mit einem prospektiven und gefühlsmäßig positiven Ausgang. Dieser Traum mobilisierte beim Analytiker aber eine alte Hingabeproblematik aus der Kindheit mit Ohnmachtssymptomatik und entsprechenden begleitenden Ängsten.

Er verwandte den Rest der Stunde in Überlegungen, wieso die Patientin dieses Motiv positiv erleben könnte, während aus seinem kollektiven Unbewußten laufend Amplifikationen auftauchten, die prospektiven Charakter hatten, wie z. B. Amor und Psyche.

Wir glauben im übrigen sagen zu dürfen, daß das Problem des Widerstandes, der vom Analytiker ausgeht und den Prozeß blockiert, von nicht zu unterschätzender Wichtigkeit ist. Hätte in dem zweiten Fallbeispiel der Analytiker nicht auf sein kollektives Unbewußtes gehört, wäre die Glasscheibe nicht zerbrochen, nnd die Patientin weiter geflüchtet. Ich sage damit in diesem Kreise sicher nichts Neues, wenn ich noch einmal auf die Realität der Metapher Jungs vom Regenmacher hinweise. Ich hoffe, daß Ihnen bereits an den beiden Beispielen klar geworden ist, wie die psychische Induktion, die aus der Emotion des Patienten auf die Psyche des Analytikers überspringt, bei diesem so etwas wie eine abgeschwächte Infektion mit der Neurose des Pat. hervorruft und die Neurotoide mobilisiert. Es entsteht so eine Unordnung in der Psyche des Analytikers, eine vielleicht oft disharmonische Hintergrundsmusik. Wenn der Analytiker diese in sich ordnet und bewältigt, was natürlich oft über viele Stunden bzw. die ganze Analyse geht, ordnet sich auch in der Psyche des Pat. etwas, und dieses sogar vielfach, ohne daß es ausgesprochen werden muß. Das klingt zwar mystisch, ist aber für uns im Laufe der zwei Jahre zu einer sehr handfesten Realität geworden.

Widerstand, d. h. eben der Widerstand von Seiten des Analytikers, tritt dann auf, wenn der Analytiker es versäumt, diesen Prozeß in sich selbst durchzuführen. Ich muß aus zeitlichen Gründen hier darauf verzichten, ein ausführliches Beispiel zu bringen.

Widerstand bzw. Fehldeutungen des analytischen Prozesses treten ebenfalls auf, wenn das Bewußtsein des Analytikers zu irrational anmutende Einfälle nicht akzeptiert. Ich möchte hierfür ein Beispiel aus der Analyse einer 42jährigen Patientin anführen:

Es handelte sich um die 259. Analysenstunde, in der die Patientin einen Traum berichtete, in dem mehrere Familienmitglieder starben bzw. umkamen. Im Mittelpunkt des Traumes stand die Figur eines ihrer Brüder, der recht grausam im Feuer ums Leben kam, und an dem sie sehr gehangen hatte. Der Analytiker faßte den Traum zunächst so auf, als ob hier noch einmal unerledigter Geschwisterkonflikt aufflammte, eine latente Aggression gagen den Bruder. Die ersten Einfälle der Patientin handelten mehr von den anderen Personen, was der Analytiker als Abwehr verstand. Zu diesem Zeitpunkt kam ihm der völlig irrationale Einfall: "Gartenzwerg". Dieser Einfall war ihm in der ernsten Situation nicht gerade angenehm und erschien ihm als zu kitschig. Als guter Jungianer ersetzte er daraufhin den Gartenzwerg schleunigst in Gedanken durch einen richtigen Zwerg, um wieder bei seinen geliebten Archetypen zu sein. Nun fiel ihm aber nichts mehr ein. Die Patientin assoziierte weiter, aber die Situation wurde dem Analytiker immer unverständlicher, mit dem Zwerg ließ sich nichts anfangen. Es war auch wie verhext, es fiel ihm nicht mehr ein konkreter, vernünftiger Zwerg ein. Schließlich kapitulierte er und kehrte reumütig zu seinem Gartenzwerg zurück. Dabei merkte er, daß ihm kurz vor dem Gartenzwerg ganz subliminar noch etwas viel Schlimmeres eingefallen war, nämlich solch ein Gummizwerg für Babys, der quietscht, wenn man raufdrückt. Er akzeptiert jetzt auch diesen Einfall und erinnerte sich, daß sich vor 10 Jahren seine kleine Tochter einen solchen Zwerk glühend gewünscht hatte, und er von Pontius zu Pilatus gelaufen war, um ihn ihr zu besorgen. Inzwischen war die Tochter in die Pubertät gekommen, und er hatte kurze Zeit zuvor mit ihr ein Gespräch über Suicid-Ideen geführt, die ihr im Rahmen des Ablösungsprozesses von den Eltern kamen. Er hatte versucht, sie in ihrer Selbständigkeit bzw. -werdung zu unterstützen, und sie in ihrer Ablösung bestätigt. Nun fiel es ihm wie Schuppen von den Augen, daß alle Einfälle der Patientin auf einen derartigen Ablösungs- und Einschmelzungsprozeß hingingen, und er deutete den Traum in dieser Richtung.

Die Deutung traf, und die Patientin verstand jetzt, was der ihr vorher unverständliche Traum sagen wollte. Unmittelbar nach der Deutung berichtete sie zusätzlich, daß ihre früheren Suicid-Ideen, die sie eigentlich völlig überwunden geglaubt hatte, wieder aufgetaucht seien, aber mit einer für sie merkwürdigen, eher symbolischen und angstfreien emotionalen Besetzung, d. h. im Sinne einer Wandlungssymbolik. Wieder war hier in beiden Unbewußten eine Participation eingegangen worden, und der scheinbar ganz abseits liegende Einfall erwies sich als der Treffer ins Schwarze bzw. als das Symbol, über dessen Brücke das Bewußtsein des Analytikers das unbewußte Problem der Patientin erfassen konnte, wofür er vorher blind gewesen war.

Ich möchte nun aus dem bisher vorgelegtem Material mit aller Vorsicht folgende Schlüsse ziehen:

1. Beim Auftreten von archetypischen Träumen innerhalb einer Analyse, d. h. in emotional hochgespannten Situationen, kommt es zu einer engen Participation zwischen dem Unbewußten des Analytikers und dem des Patienten, so daß die Assoziationsketten, bzw. die Amplifikationen, ohne Ausnahme um einen gemeinsamen Zentralpunkt kreisen, oder, anders ausgedrückt: Der archetypische Traum des Patienten konstelliert spezielle archetypische und individuelle Inhalte im Unbewußten des Therapeuten. Diese können korrespondierend oder kompensierend sein.

Wir können hier in größerem Umfang und mit einer andern Methode das von Furrer vorgelegte Material in seinem Buch: *Objektivierung des Unbewußten* (1969) bestätigen. Furrer hat diese Participation bei gleichzeitigen Krakelzeichnungen von Arzt und Patient in Schweigestunden gefunden.

2. Große Teile des Widerstandes in der Analyse beruhen auf einem Widerstand des Analytikers gegen dis psychische Induktion durch das Unbewußte des Patienten. Bei unseren Analytikern verhielt sich das kollektive Unbewußte in solchen Situationen prospektiv und progressiv, während das persönliche Unbewußte und der Ich-Komplex mit Abwehrvorgängen reagierte. Vermutlich wird dieser Tatbestand die Voraussetzung erfordern, daß der Analytiker innerhalb der eigenen Lehranalyse gelernt hat, eine Beziehung zu den Inhalten seines kollektiven Unbewußten zu finden und mit ihnen zu arbeiten.

3. Wir haben bisher keine vergleichenden Untersuchungen über Analysestunden ohne Auftreten von Archetypik. Stichproben haben uns aber zu der Auffassung geführt, daß auch hier mehr an Participation vorhanden ist, als wir bisher wissen.

Für die theoretisch-rationale Erfassung dieses Prozesses hat sich mir nach längerem Suchen die Piaget'sche Theorie der Wahrnehmung als recht fruchtbar erwiesen. Unter dem Aspekt dieser Theorie kommt es über die Wahrnehmung subliminarer Signale zu einer unbewußten Assimilation auf der symbolischen Ebene mit dem Erleben des Patienten. Zweitens tritt eine Akkomodation ein, die im kollektiven Unbewußten die archetypischen Prozesse beim Analytiker konstelliert, die versuchen, den Prozeß zu steuern. Von beiden Vorgängen, der Assimilation und der Akkommodation, wird insbesondere die Akkommodation ins Bewusstsein gebracht. Die Akkomodation der Sinnesorgane an den Gegenstand, und die Akkomodation der Bewegungen dieser Organe an die Bewegungen der Dinge, stellt bei Piaget keine primäre Gegebenheit dar, sondern bleibt immer abhängig von der Assimilation des Objektes an die Aktivität des Subjektes (1969). Eine ähnliche Konzeption vertritt auch des Gestaltkreis Victor v. Weizsäckers (1947).

Unter diesem theoretischen Ansatz läßt sich zur Not sogar solch ein Synchronizitätsphänomen wie im zweiten Fallbeispiel verstehen, nämlich daß dem Analytiker ein eigener Traum mit Sexualität hinter Gittern einfällt, und unmittelbar danach bzw. gleichzeitig die Patientin die Assoziation Sexualität hinter einer Glasscheibe hat. Glasscheibe und Gitter stammen ja aus dem gleichen Symbolkreis. Trotzdem erscheint mir schon hier, wenn man die Gleichzeitigkeit bzw. die unmittelbare Aufeinanderfolge in zeitlicher Hinsicht miteinbezieht, die Theorie der Wahrscheinlichkeit etwas überstrapaziert. Ich möchte zu diesem Problem eine weiteres Beispiel anführen:

Es handelte sich um eine Patientin Anfang 30, die sich in einer aktuellen Spannungssituation mit ihrem Freund befand. Sie träumte vor der 170. Stunde:

"Ich ging mit meinem Hund in Kanada (wo sie längere Zeit gelebt hatte) im Wald spazieren. Es waren dort Männer mit Baumstämmen beschäftigt. Es wurden Bäume gefällt und Flöße in einem Fluß zusammengestellt. Plötzlich rissen sich die Stämme im Fluß los, es wurde sehr gefährlich, und es bestand die Gefahr, erschlagen zu werden."

Der Analytiker bezog den Traum natürlich innerlich zunächst auf die aktuelle Situation mit dem Freund und erwartete mit einer gewissen Spannung, daß die Patientin über die weitere Entwicklung ihrer Beziehung zu diesem Freund, die zwischen dieser und der vorigen Stunde stattgefunden hatte, berichten würde. Dies geschah aber nicht, sondern die Einfälle der Patientin bewegten sich um Gerüche, darum, daß Hunde eine Nase für gewisse Dinge hätten, und daß ihr selbst ein solches Ahnungsvermögen völlig abginge. Sie könnte mit der Intuition eigentlich nichts anfangen und verstünde auch nicht so recht, was sie überhaupt bedeutete. Der Analytiker entschied sich an dieser Stelle aus bestimmten Gründen, etwas Erklärendes über Intuition zu sagen, wozu er ein von ihm sehr häufig benutztes Beispiel von einem Förster nahm, der eine Nase für den Wildwechsel von Rehen zu einer bestimmten Zeit hat. Merkwürdigerweise drängte sich ihm dabei von Anfang an, schon als er seine Erklärung überlegte, das Beispiel nicht wie üblich mit den Rehen, sondern mit Wildschweinen auf, zu denen er sonst gar keine weitere Beziehung hatte. Er sprach trotzdem von Rehen, äußerte aber am Ende der Erklärung beiläufig den Satz. "Komisch, ich hatte dauernd den Impuls, anstatt von Rehen von Wildschweinen zu sprechen". Die Patientin sah sehr erstaunt auf und antwortete: "Kurz bevor ich das von der Intuition sagte, hatte ich eine ganz flüchtige Vorstellung von einem Spaziergang zur Saubucht (die einzige Stelle in Berlin, wo es Wildschweine gibt), den ich gestern gemacht habe. Sie war aber so flüchtig, daß ich sie gar nicht recht beachtet habe und mitteilen konnte. Auf diesem Spaziergang habe ich sehr intensiv über mein Problem mit meinem Freund nachgedacht. Er hatte mir kurz zuvor einen Traum von sich erzählt, der mich irgendwie sehr berührt hatte, und in dessen Mittelpunkt ein Wesen stand, das halb Fuchs, halb Wildschwein war."

Das führte dann in der Stunde dazu, daß aus dem mehr theoretischen Beginn eine lebendige Auseinandersetzung um das Kernproblem der Patientin wurde.

Ich muß nun noch etwas differenizerter werden. Die Wildschwein-Assoziation war zunächst auch beim Analytiker sehr subliminar und lag zeitlich identisch mit der flüchtigen Vorstellung der Patientin. Innerhalb der Gruppe war bei uns einige Zeit vorher das Problem der Wichtigkeit solcher subliminarer irrationaler Einfälle beim Analytiker durchgesprochen worden. Wir hatten angefangen, diesen Einfällen erhöhte Aufmerksamkeit zu schenken. Normalerweise wäre die flüchtige Assoziation "Wildschwein" beim Analytiker, wenn sie überhaupt bewußt geworden wäre, mit Leichtigkeit wieder verdrängt worden. Jetzt hatte sie eine erhöhte Libidobesetzung erhalten und persistierte bzw. drängte sich so stark auf, daß der Analytiker sich zu einer vorsichtigen Mitteilung an die Patientin entschloß. Ich teile diesen Vorgang deswegen so genau mit, weil wir die Erfahrung gemacht haben, daß gerade diese subliminaren Einfälle wesentliche und analytisch wichtige Dinge berühren, und außerdem in ihnen häufiger Phänomene zu beobachten waren, die sich kaum anders als durch eine *extra-sensory perception* erklären lassen.

Das in unserer Gruppe durchgearbeitete Material zeigte nun in den ersten zehn Fällen acht solcher Phänomene, während diese Zahl bei den zweiten zehn Fällen auf elf stieg und in der nächsten Gruppe von zehn, die noch nicht ganz vollständig ist, auch weiterhin ansteigt. Wir waren bei der Auswahl dessen, was wir als ESP gelten lassen wollten, auch eher kritisch als großzügig, schon weil wir einen grundsätzlichen Skeptiker in unserer Gruppe hatten. Trotzdem scheinen uns die Zahlen relativ hoch zu sein, und enthalten außerdem einen Trend, der den bisherigen Beobachtungen über die ESP zu widersprechen scheint. Mit der Literatur (Jung 1967a, b; Rhine 1962; Bender 1966) stimmen unsere Beobachtungen insoweit überein, als zum Auftreten der ESP ein höherer emotionaler Spannungszustand gehört und eine nicht-abwehrende, interessierte Zuwendung. Übereinstimmend wird aber auch berichtet, daß in Wiederholungssituationen, und das trifft ja auch für Jungs astrologisches Experiment zu, die ESP nachläßt, absinkt oder ganz verschwindet. Bei uns trat nun genau das Umgekehrte ein, nämlich eine Steigerung. Ich möchte hier noch hinzufügen, daß von meiner Erfahrung ganz allgemein in allen meinen Analysen die Beobachtung von derartigen Phänomenen erheblich häufiger geworden ist als in früheren Jahren, seit wir uns mit diesen Gegenübertragungsproblemen beschäftigen und die Methode einer gleichzeitigen Beobachtung beider Unbewußter anwenden. Das wirft eine Reihe von außerordentlich spannenden und interessanten Fragen auf. Zunächst bestünde eine Erklärung wohl darin, daß im Gegensatz zu Karten- oder Würfelexperimenten die emotionale Situation in einer Analyse bei der Evozierung eines Archetyps ja jedesmal neu aufgeladen wird, und man dadurch eigentlich nie ein Wiederholungsexperiment macht. Es kam vielleicht von daher allmählich zu einer steigenden Apperzeption der ESP-Phänomene, nicht nur bei mir, sondern auch bei anderen Gruppenmitgliedern, allerdings nur durch den sehr allmählichen langjährigen Übungsvorgang, das eigene Unbewußte in emotionalen Situationen differenziert zu beobachten.

Nach der Konzeption von Jung und der späteren von Spitz (1960) beruhen die sogenannten parapsychologischen Wahrnehmungen beim Menschen auf der Tätigkeit eines phylogenetisch älteren Wahrnehmungssystems aus dem Reich des Sympathicus und Parasympathicus, das Spitz als das co-inaesthetische Wahrnehmungssystem bezeichnet hat. Im Laufe der Ich-Bildung wird dieses System ersetzt bzw. überlagert durch das übliche diakritische Wahrnehmungssystem und praktisch ausgeschaltet. Hierfür sprechen auch die von M. L. v. Franz (1964) angeführten Beobachtungen, daß bei Sensitiven mit parapsychologischen Fähigkeiten im Verlaufe einer analytischen Ich-Stabilisierung diese Fähigkeiten verlorengehen. Für uns wirft sich hier aber die Frage auf, ob dieser Vorgang irreversibel ist. Gelingt es unter bestimmten Umständen oder bei Anwendung bestimmter Methoden vielleicht eben doch auch bei einem stabilen Ich, diese Schicht zu mobilisieren, was durch die Emotionen geschieht, und die Ich-Grenzen für die Apperceptionen aus diesem Bereich transparent zu machen?

Ich habe mit voller Absicht gerade das obige Beispiel gewählt. Hätte in diesem Fall der Analytiker die Patientin nicht auf seine eigene Assoziation hin angesprochen, was ja an sich in der Analyse nicht unbedingt üblich ist, wäre die ESP gar nicht bewußt geworden, da es sich beiderseits um etwas Subliminares handelte, was üblicherweise nicht einmal in der Analyse, geschweige denn in sonstigen kommunikativen Prozessen hochkommt. Es ist zu erwarten, und ich bin durch andere Erfahrungen ähnlicher Art davon überzeugt, daß die Kommunikation zweier Menschen auf dieser Ebene sehr viel häufiger und dichter ist, als wir gemeinhin anzunehmen pflegen. Das noch geringe Material (25 in der Gruppe kontrollierter Fälle und über 200 allein aus meiner Praxis auf diese Art sorgfältig geführter Protokolle), und die auch mit 2 Jahren noch nicht sehr lange Zeit reichen nicht aus, um hierauf eine endgültige Antwort zu geben. Es ist durchaus möglich, daß auch der von uns eingeschlagene Weg an dieser Stelle nicht weiterführen wird. Es bleiben Fragen, die mir aber doch einer Diskussion wert erscheinen oder einer Anregung an andere, ähnliche Versuche. Am Schluß meiner Ausführungen möchte ich sagen, daß wir nichts getan und untersucht haben, was nicht schon von Jung selbst oder anderen gesagt oder beobachtet worden ist. Wir haben lediglich ehrlich versucht, das Problem der Gegenübertragung als eines produktiven therapeutischen Instrumentes sehr Ernst zu nehmen, und es möglichst kontrolliert auf uns selbst anzuwenden, oder, um es in einem Bild auszudrücken: wir haben wenigstens mit einem Auge versucht, das Metapher vom Regenmacher praktisch auszuprobieren und zu untersuchen, und dabei festgestellt, daß es weitaus besser funktioniert, als wir es zu denken wagten. Das, was uns bei diesen ganzen Untersuchungen am meisten beeindruckt hat, ist, daß das übliche kausale Modell von Übertragung und Gegenübertragung, d. h. Aktion und Reaktion, bzw. Beeinflussung und Gegenbeeinflussung, zur Erfassung der Phänomene nicht ausreichte. Der analytischen Situation liegt in einer tieferen Schicht ein vom Selbst ausgehender synchronistischer Prozeß zugrunde, für dessen Differenzierung uns heute noch die Begriffswelt fehlt, und für den wir den Mut und die Offenheit aufbringen müssen, einen Schritt in das Unbekannte und Unübliche zu wagen.

Literatur

Adler, G. (1967). "Methods of treatment in analytical psychology," in *Psychoanalytic techniques,* ed. B. B. Wolman. New York, Basic Books.

——— (1968). *Das lebendige Symbol*. München/Berlin/Wien, Urban & Schwarzenberg.

BENDER, H. (1966). *Parapsychologie. Entwicklung, Ergebnisse, Probleme*. Darmstadt, Wissenschaftliche Buchgesellschaft.

FORDHAM, M. (1957). *New developments in analytical psychology*. London, Routledge.

FRANZ, M.-L. VON (1964). "Religiöse oder magische Einstellung zum Unbewussten," in *Psychotherapeutische Probleme*. Zurich, Rascher.

FURRER, W. (1969). *Objektivierung des Unbewussten*. Bern/Stuttgart/Wien, Huber.

JUNG, C. G. (1958a). "Die Psychologie der Uebertragung," in *Ges.W.* 16.

——— (1958b). "Die Probleme der modernen Psychotherapie," in *Ges.W.* 16.

——— (1967a). "Synchronizität als Prinzip akausaler Zusammenhänge," in *Ges. W.* 8.

——— (1967b). "Ueber Synchronizität," in *Ges.W.* 8.

——— (1970). *Mysterium coniunctionis*. *C.W.* 14, 2nd ed.

PIAGET, J. (1969). *Nachahmung, Spiel und Traum*. Stuttgart, Klett.

RHINE, J. B. and PRATT, J. G. (1962). *Parapsychologie, Grenzwissenschaft der Psyche*. Bern und München, Francke.

SPITZ, R. A. (1960). *Die Entstehung der ersten Objektbeziehungen*. Stuttgart, Klett.

WEIZSÄCKER, V. VON (1947). *Der Gestaltkreis*. Stuttgart, Thieme.

The Constellation of the Countertransference in Relation to the Presentation of Archetypal Dreams
Research Methods and Results

In 1929, C.G. Jung wrote: "For, twist and turn the matter as we may, the relation between doctor and patient remains a personal one within the impersonal framework of professional treatment. By no device can the treatment be anything but the product of mutual influence, in which the whole being of the doctor as well as that of his patient plays its part. In the treatment there is an encounter between two irrational factors, that is to say, between two persons who are not fixed and determinable quantities but who bring with them, besides their more or less clearly defined fields of consciousness, an indefinitely extended sphere of non-consciousness" (1966b, par. 163).

Although psychotherapists have gradually come to take this very important statement of Jung's with the seriousness it deserves, they have been slow to assimilate its full implications. Caught in the Cartesian thinking of the old classical sciences they have striven—consciously or unconsciously—to make the patient the central object of the therapeutic process. Thus for psychoanalysis in the past, and still to a large extent today—aside from more recent developments that involve empathy—the countertransference was and is a pathological and disturbing process which should be eliminated as far as possible by the analyst's increasing consciousness and analysis of himself. In 1946 Jung published in "The Psychology of the Transference" (1966a) a differentiated account of the therapeutic field between patient and doctor, using the schema of the cross-cousin marriage, and a description of that "mixing [of] two different chemical substances," as he called it metaphorically in his earlier paper (1966b, par. 163). Unfortunately he later relativized this process and confined it to "the higher [forms of] psychotherapy . . . that set tasks which challenge the whole man" (1966a, par. 367). He also speaks of cases "when there is only a mild transference or when it is practically unnoticeable" (1966a, par. 359), a statement which we know today is incorrect and indicative of a defence.

In 1957 Fordham (1957, pp. 91ff.) differentiated the countertransference reaction and distinguished an illusory, i.e., projective countertransference originating in the analyst's own complexes from a syntonic one in which the patient makes the analyst play the emotional role of a partner in the relationship. Adler too (1967, pp. 344ff.) regards the countertransference as the focal point in the theory and practice of analytical psychology and distinguishes between countertransference and counterprojection (1961, p. 217). He lays particular stress on the positive value of the countertransference as an indicator of the constructive subjective reaction of the analyst which springs from his own unconscious and activates the analytical relationship.

Now the problem of investigating the countertransference lies in the fact that all statements we have so far been able to find in the literature on the subject have not been scientifically controlled and are somewhat naïve. The analyst makes a statement about something that strikes him as being his own inner reaction at a particular point in the therapeutic process, a reaction which again was not subject to control and was chosen by him. Moreover the analyst is speaking about his own unconscious and interpreting it himself. We can rightly credit ourselves with the faculty of having learnt how to deal with our own unconscious; but with equal right, and with commensurate modesty and honesty, we must also admit that everywhere in this process we still have our blind spots. None of us would ever dream of asserting that he was a fully individuated person. Rather, we are all beginners in this great process of individuation and have our own problems with the persona, shadow, animus and anima, and now and then we are fortunate enough to catch a glimpse of the experience of the self.

During the last few years, we have been making an attempt in Berlin at least to investigate countertransference reactions in a situation with proper scientific controls. We formed a group of four analysts with many years of practical experience behind them; its members consist of R. Blomeyer, E. Jung, H.-J. Wilke, and myself. At each meeting, one of the analysts presented a report of a single analytical session together with a patient's archetypal dream; the patient's associations as well as the analyst's were noted down synchronously. Account was also taken of the content of the previous session and its subsequent development. All this was thoroughly analyzed in the group situation.

Before reporting on the provisional results of this investigation, I must say a few words about our method. As I stated at the beginning, historically considered the therapist's attitude has been concentrated more or less exclusively on the patient. The extreme example of this is Freud's old technique of "holding up a mirror" to him; but the attitude of free-floating attention or of "emptying oneself" in order to take in the psychic contents of the patient, and similar therapeutic attitudes, are all based on conscious concentration on the patient's unconscious and what is going on in his conscious mind. At the other extreme we have the example of the rainmaker, cited by Jung (1970, par. 604, n. 211). Here concentration is directed exclusively to one's own unconscious, which has been thrown into disharmony by a disturbance in the outer world. The restoration of inner harmony in oneself also brings about the removal of the outer disturbance.

We too started off with a conceptual model similar to that of the rainmaker, though we certainly endeavoured to find a middle way. The metaphor I have in mind is of the analyst's psyche as a musical instrument upon which the patient plays. If we listen to the sounds and the melody this instrument gives out, we are in a position to make many statements that supplement our observations of the patient.

The metaphor limps inasmuch as the change of analytical procedure affects not only the patient but the analyst as well. We found that it is not so simple to observe, side by side, the patient's associations and our own unconscious processes and coordinate them in their proper temporal sequence; that is, to look outwards with one eye and inwards with the other. On the contrary, a wearisome learning process was needed, as is shown by the fact that during the first year of work the analysts reported an average of 8 of their own associations per therapeutic session, a figure which rose to 17 during the second year. Naturally it was clear to us that as a result of such technical problems, including among others the difficulty of keeping the records, it was impossible to give a complete picture of the associations on both sides and of the amplificatory processes. It was also clear that there was inherent in this method a narcissistic danger that the analyst would tend to gaze more admiringly at himself than to pay due attention to the patient, and from the beginning we set about it very circumspectly and still do today. However, lapses of this kind did not occur and our therapeutic experiences have on the contrary been very favorable thanks to strict scientific controls.

A definite criterion of selection was employed for the sessions which we wished to include in our investigation. As I have already said, the sessions were to be confined to those in which an archetypal dream had been reported by the patient, we ourselves setting more value on the intensity of the emotions contained in the dream than on "classic" mythological motifs. The idea we started off with was that we would observe first of all those sessions where the strong emotional activity of the patient unconsciously affected the analyst. We expected that identificatory, projective, and participatory reactions would be especially noticeable at these points.

Altogether, 25 such cases have been thoroughly analyzed in the group so far, each session lasting 3 hours. The background material at our disposal is of course much larger, since the method allowed each of us to write up or observe considerably more cases than he was able to present to the group. These experiences, too, are taken into account here. I must not omit to mention, either, that as a result of this procedure a group-dynamic process was also constellated which likewise showed a number of extremely interesting phenomena. I shall not go into it here as we intend to report on it in another place. Nor can I include the manifestations of the type problem which is still being worked out by H.-J. Wilke.

I shall try first of all to classify the associations which were reported to us by the analysts themselves. It goes without saying that we did not count as associations any conscious reflections but only ideas that arose spontaneously out of the unconscious. The largest group, as might be expected, consisted of associations relating to the theme of the session, its symbolic content and the patient's life history. Among them were associations evoked by archetypal amplification or referring to the genesis of the patient's illness and his actual situation.

A second group related to associations concerning the life history and problems of the analyst, i.e., ideas evoked by his past and present situation.

Thirdly, there were purely emotional reactions, and it is perhaps interesting to note that it was just this group that showed the highest rate of increase during the second year of work (from about 1 reaction per session in the first year to 4 reactions per session in the second), and that these reactions became increasingly more differentiated. This unexpected result seems to show that despite our better rational knowledge we were still affected to a very large extent by the taboo against a scientist observing his feelings and importing them into his work. The differentiation, cultivation, and education of the feeling function as well as its conscious application seem to me one of the greatest problems of our time, and its neglect has to be paid for again and again.

Finally, I should mention the somatic reactions of the analyst in the vegetative as well as the motor sphere, such as pounding of the heart, feeling of strain, tension, fatigue, yawning, scratching, etc. Without exception an area of unconsciousness common to both analyst and patient could be found behind these symptoms during the group analysis.

Perhaps the most astonishing result for us was the psychological connection between the analysts's chains of association and the patient's. For the psychotherapist it is, of course, self-evident that the chain of free associations should be connected together in a psychologically meaningful way. So it was to be expected that this connection would be found not only in the patient's chain of association but in the analyst's as well; what we had not expected was that the two chains would again be connected with each other so that they again corresponded meaningfully all along the line. Perhaps the situation may best be characterized by the spontaneous exclamation of one of our members: "The patients continually say what I am thinking and feeling at the moment!" Naturally this exclamation is not to be taken literally, because firstly it concerned only the correspondences in meaning, although in both persons the formal and material content of the associations often showed the most amazing similarities, and secondly the analyst himself was often thinking and feeling what the patient was saying—that is, the analyst's associations were determined by the patient's words and emotions. R. Blomeyer will give a detailed report of one of these sessions (cf. this volume, below). It seems significant to me that the archetypal amplifications which occurred to the analyst were also determined by his personal background, which in turn fitted in with the patient's problem. I would like to give a brief example of this:

A 37-year-old woman patient, a borderline case with a psychotic mother, brought this dream to the 496th session: "*I had on a robe like a devil's, a god's, or a king's, it might also have been worn by death. I wanted to cast aside the evil, which for me was represented by the robe. Then my friend came. In my fear I wanted to cling to him, but when I said 'Get thee behind me, Satan,' he might have thought this saying referred to him. I felt terribly afraid, wanted to embrace him, and he wanted to embrace me at the same time. In the darkness I was beset by doubt and fear whether it was really he, and this fear woke me up."*

Without any particular emotion the analyst associated this with Mephistopheles and a scene from the beginning of the drama, where Faust thinks he has caught the devil, but the devil escapes.

The patient then told him that she could never sleep without terrible fear in the same room with her mother because she was afraid her mother would kill her with an axe. Full of emotion, the analyst recalled his own early childhood fears of death, dying and extinction, all of which was connected with the figure of the old Faust and his entry into another life.

Then, as the patient went on to speak of her complete uprooting when she was evacuated to a small town, the analyst saw in his mind's eye a medieval city nestling behind the security of its walls, and remembered the happy time he had spent in such a city on his honeymoon. (At the time of the analytical session the analyst had marital problems. Emotionally he was able to bear them, because he had this old support of a happy and harmonious relationship in the background.) He had found within himself a kind of emotional stronghold from which to overcome the conflict. At this very moment the patient said that during the period of evacuation she had found a safe place of refuge on the threshing floor of a barn, where she always withdrew with her brother to play cards when their mother was unkind. So here we have one of those synchronistic phenomena which we frequently observed: analyst and patient simultaneously find within themselves a temenos from which they can face the daemonic and overwhelming maternal animus. This gave us the first *point d'appui* for working out the problem of fear between analyst and patient in the transference situation, and from then on the analysis took a fruitful turn. I am naturally aware that the situation could also be interpreted as mutual flight from the maternal daemon, but this interpretation does not hold good.

Let us recapitulate what has happened: archetypal amplifications occur to the analyst which gravitate round the unsuccessful banishment of the devil. These become activated by the personal unconscious with corresponding emotions from his childhood history, the chain of associations now passes over into the actual situation, and the archetype (mediaeval city—Faust's study—marriage) together with the actual emotions affords an inner possibility of mastering the situation.

The patient remains within the sphere of her own history and exposes herself to her severe and still existing childhood fears, but simultaneously finds with the analyst a place of refuge in this chaos, so that in the course of this and the following sessions the fears could be fruitfully worked through. This whole process took place without any interpretation on the part of the analyst, despite which the situation appeared to be emotionally guided for the patient as well. Naturally the contrary phenomenon also exists, where the analyst's associations begin by being personal and emotional, and then give rise to an archetypal amplification which is expressed as the situation demands.

In this brief example the work done by the group has been included. During the session and also in working through the material afterwards the analyst was not yet conscious of these inner connections, there were also other important background aspects of the analyst's problem that could be worked out in the group. For instance, only the honeymoon association occurred during the session, but only in the group did he become fully conscious of its relation to the actual conflict and of its resulting significance. Again and again it has been an impressive experience for all of us to see to what extent the analysis of the analyst resulted in essentially new points of view and in a much more comprehensive consciousness of the analytical process. We had simply not reckoned with the fact that this method could convey to seasoned analysts so many "Aha experiences" concerning the therapeutic process going on between them and their patients in this kind of session. Had we not already been convinced of the truth of Jung's statement, "Psychological induction inevitably causes the two parties to get involved in the transformation of the third and to be themselves transformed in the process, and all the time the doctor's knowledge, like a flickering lamp, is the one dim light in the darkness" (1966a, par. 399), we could not have failed to be so after these experiences. Thus, analysis allows for both forms of individuation on the part of the analyst too: the autonomous, unconscious participation of his psyche in the transformation process of the patient, and an individuation consciously experienced, promoted and worked through by self-analysis. The second kind, just like the conscious individuation of the patient, can engender a greater development, a stronger enrichment and fuller awareness of the therapeutic process. Of course one can do a great deal by oneself with one's own associations. Essentially new viewpoints, however, emerge supplementarily only in the group. The analyst, as I have said, has his blind spots, and the statements made about the countertransference become considerably more conclusive when they are controlled in the group or by another analyst.

Although the compensatory function of the collective unconscious is clear enough in the case reported above, the parallelistic elements are still predominant. I should therefore like to give a second example of a severe neurosis with marked schizoid tendencies, where the compensatory function predominates. A woman patient brought this dream to the 147th session: *"I have moved into a house. There was another woman in it. Suddenly a man came along and tried to rape us. As he had started on the other woman, I ran off to get help, but as soon as I was out of sight I sat down on a tree stump and waited. When I went back to the house after a while, they had both gone. I put clean sheets on the bed. I was terribly frightened in the dream and woke up quite exhausted."*

Since the patient had until then run away from any confrontation with the unconscious, and the pronounced flight tendencies which had led to a whole series of suicide attempts before and at the beginning of the analysis still persisted, the analyst noticed in himself faint stirrings of annoyance and impatience. Then the idea of Hades-Persephone-Demeter dropped into his head, and he felt an emotional identification with the figure of Hades: "In the end one should do it like Hades did," he thought, "seize and hold fast." The next association was an archetypal dream of his own from the beginning of his training period. In this dream, *beneath the ruins of an old castle, there was a world of caves where practically all the treasures of the earth were on display, among other things a department in which all the possible forms of sexual intercourse were enacted by living people. The performers were kept behind a wire grille as in a zoo.* At that moment the patient reported the following additional association to the dream: *"The house had a glass wall, and none of the curtains was drawn. I myself experience most things behind a glass wall."*

The background that came out in the group was as follows: analyst and patient had both been brought up in strictly puritanical homes where sex was taboo and considered disgusting. Up till this point the patient had never spoken of sex, and except for an occasional breakthrough under alcohol had repressed all her sexual impulses. At the time of his dream the analyst had been thrown into considerable difficulties by his very archaic and turbulent sexuality. It had been most embarrassing for him to tell this dream to his training analyst—a woman—especially as he was thoroughly aroused by the sexual acts he had witnessed. He clearly remembered the feeling of liberation and redemption when she did not find the dream as disgusting as his mother would have done, but sided entirely with the unconscious in thinking that it represented supreme values which she accepted understandingly and even joyfully. This memory now effected a noticeable change in the analyst's attitude, and the rest of the session with the patient was colored on his side by the positive maternal feeling he had experienced at that time. The libido from the collective unconscious was no longer soaked up by the figure of the impatient ravisher Hades, but mobilized the Demeter archetype. In this way the analyst succeeded in adopting a maternal attitude and in breaking down his patient's fear. The next day she rang him up: "I can only say it over the telephone. The glass pane has been shattered. After the last session I had a flood of sexual fantasies, and for the first time in my fantasies the people had faces, some of them known to me. Yours was among them too!"

I think it is clear from this example how the collective unconscious compensates the conscious tendencies and impulses as well as those arising out of the personal unconscious and turns them in an analytically fruitful direction.

This case leads on to a further problem, that of resistance. Here I am thinking specifically of the analyst's resistance to the unconscious of the patient.

Our cases have afforded us one very instructive experience. The analyst's resistance always proceeded from the personal unconscious, whereas the collective unconscious was endeavoring to get the analysis moving forward again. In one drastic instance it was positively touching to see how desperately the collective unconscious sent up one prospective amplification after another in order to correct the analyst, whose interpretations invariably missed the mark because of an old childhood fear, that is, because of an illusory countertransference or counterprojection. The patient had had a dream that contained the motif of the death-marriage with a prospective and emotionally positive outcome. But this dream mobilized in the analyst an old problem of self-surrender from his childhood with symptoms of fainting and all the accompanying fears.

He spent the rest of the session reflecting how the patient was able to experience this motif positively, while from his collective unconscious there emerged a series of amplifications which had a prospective character, e.g., Amor and Psyche.

In any case we think we can say that the problem of resistance which originates with the analyst and blocks the process is very important and should not be underestimated. If in the second example the analyst had not listened to his collective unconscious the glass pane would not have been shattered and the patient would have taken to flight again. In the present company I am certainly saying nothing new when I point once more to the reality of Jung's metaphor of the rainmaker.

I hope it has already become clear to you from both these examples how the psychic induction which springs across from the patient's emotion to the psyche of the analyst results in something like a diluted infection with the patient's neurosis and mobilizes his neurotic tendencies. In this way a disorder arises in the psyche of the analyst, a background music that is often disharmonious. If he can put these tendencies in order in himself and subdue them—which naturally often extends over many sessions or even over the whole analysis—something also put itself in order in the psyche of the patient, sometimes without anything having to be said. I know this sounds mystical, but during our two years of work it has become for us a very palpable reality.

Resistance on the part of the analyst always appears when he fails to carry out this process in himself. For lack of time I must refrain from giving a detailed example of this.

Resistances in the form of erroneous interpretations of the analytical process likewise appear when the conscious mind of the analyst cannot accept associations that strike him as too irrational. I would like to give an example from the analysis of a 42-year-old woman patient:

During the 259th session the patient reported a dream in which *several members of her family had died or lost their lives.* The central figure of the dream was one of her brothers, of whom she had been very fond, who suffered a cruel death in a fire. The analyst began by interpreting the dream as though an unresolved brother-sister conflict had flared up again, indicating a latent aggression against the brother. The patient's first associations referred more to other people, which the analyst took as a defense reaction. At this moment a completely irrational association came to him: "Garden dwarf." Considering the gravity of the situation, this association was not exactly pleasant and seemed to him too sentimental. As a good Jungian he swiftly replaced the garden dwarf in his thoughts by a proper dwarf in order to get back to his beloved archetypes. After that he had no more associations. The patient went on associating, but the situation became more and more incomprehensible to the analyst, and nothing could be done with the dwarf. Everything seemed bewitched, and the analyst could no longer produce associations with a concrete, rational dwarf. Finally he capitulated and turned back ruefully to his garden dwarf. He then noticed that shortly before the appearance of the garden dwarf, something far worse had occurred to him quite subliminally: one of these rubber dwarfs for babies, which squeaks when you squeeze it. He now accepted this association too and remembered that ten years previously his little daughter had ardently wished for such a dwarf, and how he had searched high and low in order to get one for her. In the meantime his daughter had reached the age of puberty, and a short while before he had had a talk with her about the suicide ideas that had come into her head in connection with the process of separating from her parents. He had tried to support her becoming independent and confirmed her need for separation. Now the scales fell from his eyes: he saw that all the patient's associations pointed to just such a process of separation and transformation, and he interpreted the dream in this sense. The interpretation struck home, and the patient now understood what the previously incomprehensible dream was trying to tell her. Immediately after the interpretataion she reported additionally that her former suicide ideas, which she thought she had overcome completely, had reappeared, but with a remarkable emotional charge that was free of anxiety and more symbolic of a process of transformation. Here again her unconscious and the analyst's had entered into participation, and the apparently far-fetched association had proved to be a direct hit, a symbol that served as a bridge and enabled the conscious mind of the analyst to grasp the patient's problem for which he had no eyes before.

I would now like to draw the following conclusions with all due caution from the material that has been presented so far:

1. When archetypal dreams appear in an analysis, that is, in highly charged emotional situations, there is a close participation between the analyst's unconscious and the patient's, so that without exception the chains of association and the amplifications gravitate round a central point common to both. To put it in another way: the archetypal dream of the patient constellates specifically archetypal and individual contents in the unconscious of the therapist. These contents may be either parallelistic or compensatory.

Here we can largely confirm with the help of a different method the material put forward by Furrer in his book *Objectivierung des Unbewussten* (1969). Furrer discovered the same participation when analyst and patient simultaneously engaged in silent doodling sessions.

2. Much of the resistance in analysis is due to the analyst's resistance to the psychic induction caused by the patient's unconscious. In the case of our analysts, the behavior of the collective unconscious in such situations was prospective and progressive, whereas the personal unconscious and the ego complex reacted with defensive measures. Presumably this fact will require as a precondition that the analyst has learnt in his own training analysis to relate to the contents of his collective unconscious and to work with them.

3. So far we have no comparative studies of analytical sessions in

which no archetypal symbolism appeared. But samplings have led us to believe that here too more participation is present than we would expect.

For the theoretical and rational understanding of this process I have found after a long search that Piaget's theory of perception has been extremely fruitful. According to this theory, the perception of sub-liminal signals results in an unconscious assimilation of the patient's experience on the symbolic level. Secondly, an accommodation occurs whereby archetypal factors are constellated in the collective uncon-scious of the analyst which seek to guide the process. Both the assimila-tion and the accommodation conditions, are brought into consciousness, in particular the process of accommodation. The accommodation of the sense organs to the object and the accommodation of the movements of these organs to the movements of things are, for Piaget, not a prime datum but always remain dependent on the assimilation of the object to the activity of the subject (1951). A similar conception has been advanced by Victor von Weizsäcker in his book *Der Gestaltkreis* (1947).

From this theoretical starting-point we can even understand such a synchronistic phenomenon as was reported in the second case, where the analyst recalls a dream of his own about sexual scenes behind a wire grille, and immediately afterwards, or even simultaneously, the patient has the association of sexuality behind a glass pane. Glass pane and grille belong to the same class of symbols. Nevertheless it seems to me that if we include simultaneity or immediate succession in time, the theory of probability is being somewhat overstrained. I would like to give a further example of this problem:

It concerned a woman patient in her early 30's who was in an actual situation of conflict with her friend. She brought this dream to the 170th session:

"I was walking with my dog in a wood in Canada (where she had lived for a long time). *Some men were busy with tree trunks. They were cutting down trees and making rafts in a river. Suddenly the logs broke loose, it became very dangerous, and I was in danger of being killed."*

At first the analyst inwardly related the dream to the actual situation with the friend, and was eagerly expecting the patient to tell him about the latest developments in their relationship which had taken place between this and the previous session. But she didn't. Instead, the patient's associations revolved round the subject of smells: she said dogs had a nose for certain things and that she herself entirely lacked any such flair. She could do nothing with intuition and did not really understand what it was all about. At this juncture the analyst decided for certain reasons to say something explanatory about intuition, choosing, as he had often done before, the example of a forester who had a nose for the route followed by deer at a particular season. Remarkably enough, even before he had started his explanation, the image that thrust itself upon him was not the usual one of the deer, but of wild boars, with which normally he had no connection to at all. He nevertheless talked about the deer, but at the end of his explanation he remarked in passing: "Funny, all the time I had the impulse to speak not of deer but of wild boars." The patient looked very astonished and answered: "Just before I said that about intuition, I had a fleeting vision of a walk I took yesterday to Saubucht [the only place in Berlin where there are wild boars]. But it was so fleeting that I did not really notice it and could not tell it to you. On this walk I was thinking very hard about the problem with my friend. Shortly before he had told me a dream of his that somehow moved me very much, and the central figure in it was a creature that was half fox and half wild boar."

The result was that during the rest of the session this somewhat theoretical starting-point led to a lively discussion concerning the core of the patient's problem.

I must now become still more specific. The wild-boar association was to begin with a very subliminal one for the analyst too and coincided in time with the fleeting vision of the patient. Not long before this we had been discussing in the group the problem of the importance of these subliminal, irrational associations on the part of the analyst. We had begun to pay increasing attention to them. Normally the analyst's fleeting association "wild boar"—if it had reached consciousness at all—might easily have been repressed again. Now it had acquired an intensified libido charge and persisted or obtruded itself so strongly that the analyst decided to communicate it cautiously to the patient. I have described this procedure so precisely because experience has taught us that it is just these subliminal associations that stir up essential and analytically important details, and also because phenomena could frequently be observed in them which can hardly be explained except in terms of extrasensory perception.

The material we worked through in the group showed eight such phenomena in the first ten cases, a figure which rose to eleven in the second ten cases and is still rising in the next group of ten, where the results are not yet quite complete. In selecting what we would count as ESP we were more critical than broad-minded, if only because we had some thoroughgoing skeptics among us. Even so, the figures seem to us to be relatively high and also to contain a trend that appears to contradict the previous observations concerning ESP. Our observations agree with those reported in the literature (Jung, 1969a, b; Rhine, 1957; Bender, 1966) in so far as a heightened state of emotional tension and a non-defensive attitude of attentive interest are needed for ESP phenomena to manifest themselves. Equally it is reported that in repetitive situations—and this is true also of Jung's astrological experiment—ESP slackens, decreases, or disappears altogether. Now exactly the opposite happened with us: there was an increase. Here I would like to add that so far as my own experience goes the observation of such phenomena in all my analyses has become much more frequent than in earlier years, ever since we began to concern ourselves with these countertransference problems and to apply the method of simultaneously observing the unconscious of both analyst and patient. This raises a number of exciting and extraordinarily interesting questions. A provisional explanation might be that, unlike the experiments with cards or dice, the emotional situation in an analysis is recharged each time by the evocation of an archetype, so that actually a repetitive experiment is never made. This may have gradually led to an increasing apperception of ESP phenomena, not only in my case but also among the other members of the group, and only, of course, as a result of training oneself for many years to observe with great exactitude one's own unconscious in emotional situations.

According to Jung and the later views of Spitz (1954), the so-called parapsychological perceptions in man are based on the activity of a phylogenetically older perceptual system located in the region of the sympathetic and parasympathetic systems, which Spitz designates as the coenaesthetic perceptual system. In the course of ego-formation this system is replaced or overlaid by the usual diacritical perceptual system and practically eliminated. This view is supported by the observations adduced by M.-L. von Franz (1964), that sensitive persons with parapsychological faculties lose these faculties during the process of stabilizing the ego in analysis. For us the question that arises is whether this process is reversible. Would it be possible, under special conditions or with the use of special methods, to mobilize the coenaesthetic perceptual system by the arousal of emotion even in the case of a stable ego, and to make the ego-boundaries transparent for apperceptions coming from this sphere?

The case I described above was chosen for a definite purpose. Had the analyst not talked to the patient about his own association—which in itself is not exactly customary in analysis—the ESP phenomenon would not have reached consciousness inasmuch as it was something subliminal for both of them, and normally this does not come to the surface even in analysis, let alone in other processes of communication. It is to be expected—and other experiences of a similar nature have convinced me of this—that communication between two people on this level is much more frequent and much closer than we are generally inclined to assume. The small amount of material available at present (25 group-controlled cases and over 200 careful reports I myself have made on the basis of the procedure here described) and the relatively short two-year period of work are not sufficient for a final answer to be given. It is quite possible that the path we have struck out on will not lead us any further. Nevertheless, questions remain which seem to me worth discussing, or worth stimulating others to make similar experiments.

In conclusion I would like to say that we have not done or investigated anything that has not already been written about or observed by Jung himself and others. We have merely made an honest attempt to take the problem of countertransference very seriously as a productive therapeutic agent and to apply it to ourselves under strictly controlled conditions. Or, to express it in an image: we have tried at least with one eye to put the metaphor of the rainmaker to a practical test, and in so doing have found that it functions far better than we ever dared to think. What has impressed us most throughout our investigations is that the usual causal model of transference and countertransference, i.e., of action and reaction or influence and counterinfluence, has not sufficed as a means of grasping the phenomena in question. In a deeper layer underlying the analytical situation there is a synchronistic process regulated by the self, a process that cannot yet be differentiated further for lack of the requisite conceptual tools, and for the investigation of which we must summon up the courage and open-mindedness to venture into unknown realms far removed from the conventional disciplines.

Translated from the German by R. F. C. Hull

REFERENCES

ADLER, G. (1961). *The living symbol.* London, Routledge; New York, Bollingen/Pantheon.
—— (1967). "Methods of treatment in analytical psychology," in *Psychoanalytic techniques,* ed. B. B. Wolman. New York, Basic Books.
BENDER, H. (1966). *Parapsychologie. Entwicklung, Ergebnisse, Probleme.* Darmstadt, Wissenschaftliche Buchgesellschaft.
FORDHAM, M. (1957). *New developments in analytical psychology.* London, Routledge.

FRANZ, M.-L. VON (1964). "Religiöse oder magische Einstellung zum Unbewussten," in *Psychotherapeutische Probleme*. Zurich, Rascher.

FURRER, W. (1969). *Objektivierung des Unbewussten*. Bern et al., Huber.

JUNG, C. G. (1966a). "The psychology of the transference," in *C.W.* 16, 2nd edn.

—— (1966b). "Problems of modern psychotherapy," in *C.W.* 16, 2nd edn.

—— (1969a). "Synchronicity: an acausal connecting principle," in *C.W.* 8, 2nd edn.

—— (1969b). "On synchronicity," in *C.W.* 8, 2nd edn.

—— (1970). *Mysterium coniunctionis. C.W.* 14, 2nd edn.

PIAGET, J. (1951). *Play, dreams, and imitation in childhood.* London, Routledge; New York, Norton.

RHINE, J. B. and PRATT, J. G. (1957). *Parapsychology: frontier science of the mind.* Springfield, Ill., Thomas; Oxford, Blackwell.

SPITZ, R. A. (1954). "Genèse des premières relations objectales; observations directes sur le nourrisson pendant sa première année," *Revue française de psychanalyse,* 18 (1954), 479–575.

WEIZSÄCKER, V. VON. (1947). *Der Gestaltkreis.* Stuttgart, Thieme.

7

Die Konstellierung der Gegenübertragung beim Auftauchen archetypischer Träume
Kasuistik

Rudolf Blomeyer, *Berlin*

Die 30. Behandlungsstunde einer 23jährigen Patientin

Die praktische Darstellung der Gegenübertragung stößt, wenn man wirklich informieren will (und kein "Alter Weiser" sein will), auf Schwierigkeiten: Einerseits ist es korrekt, wenn der Analytiker möglichst offen über seine Patienten berichtet. Er muß dabei nur—und das wird auch hier geschehen—durch leichte Veränderungen deren Identität schützen. Anderseits aber wirkt es indezent, wenn er viel über sich selber spricht, was man jedoch in Kauf nehmen muss.

Im November 1969 suchte mich eine 23jährige Patientin auf, die von Kind an an einer Phobie litt. Sie wog um 80 kg und wirkte ein bißchen wie ein Kumpel, ein bißchen wie ein Trampel. Sie erschien dabei resolut und selbständig, aber dem traute ich nicht. Man weiß ja, wenn es sich um eine Phobie handelt, daß man es nachher mit einem hilflosen kleinen Mädchen zu tun hat, das erst propulsiv vorprellt und dann furchtbare Angst bekommt und schreiend bei Mutter Schutz sucht. Ich erfuhr:

—Sie hatte ihren Vater nie gekannt. Er war schon vor ihrer Geburt auf Nimmerwiedersehen verschwunden.

—Die Mutter wechselte in der Kindheit alle 4-5 Jahre ihre männlichen Beziehungspersonen und hatte schlecht und recht für die Patientin gesorgt. Sie übte jetzt hinsichtlich der Phobie eine Schutzfunktion aus.

—Die Patientin war frühreif gewesen, hatte verschiedene Männerbeziehungen gehabt, war aber frigide.

—Sie hatte mit 18 Jahren geheiratet und einen Sohn bekommen. Dieser Entwicklungsansatz war zusammengebrochen: Die Ehe war wegen eines anderen Mannes geschieden worden, und der Sohn war kurz darauf an einer Infektion gestorben.

—Seither hatte die Patientin noch viel mehr Angst als früher. Sie fürchtete, an einem Herzschlag sterben zu müssen oder verrückt zu werden.

Sie erschien sehr infantil, in ihren Einstellungen ambivalent, kaum zu einer klaren Entscheidung fähig. Sie war sehr in Not und suchte ganz dringend und sofort einen Behandlungsplatz.

Sie sagte zu ihrer Angst noch etwas Wichtiges, was auf ein gewisses Verständnis schließen ließ: "Es ist, als ob da etwas Gefährliches in mir wäre, und ich weiß nicht, wie ich damit fertig werden soll".

Nun brauchen sehr viele Patienten "ganz dringend" einen Behandlungsplatz, und ich hatte gar keinen frei. Ich gab ihr, wenn auch mit dem Bemerken, es werde sich zunächst um eine lockere Betreuung handeln müssen, trotzdem einen. Das heißt aber: ich hatte mich überfahren lassen. Mein Unbewußtes mußte auf sie angesprochen und das Bewußte überredet haben, ihr außer der Reihe einen Platz zu geben. Wenn ich damals gefragt worden wäre, worauf ich angesprochen hätte, hätte ich vermutlich auf ihre Krankheitseinsicht oder ihre Hilfsbedürftigkeit hingewiesen, aber das Wesentliche nicht recht formulieren können. Vielleicht hätte ich immerhin gesagt, etwas Spontanes in ihr hätte mich angesprochen. Vielleicht hätte ich sogar hinzugefügt, ich meinte mit dem Spontanen genauer etwas Animalisches. Aber das hätte ich wahrscheinlich gleich wieder bagatellisiert, und ein erfahrener Beobachter hätte zu Recht vermutet, da müsse der Kern des

Problems liegen. Es dauerte lange, bis ich ihn erfaßt hatte; und es wird etwas Geduld brauchen, mir auf dem Weg dahin zu folgen.

Die Behandlung lief zögernd und unregelmäßig an. Die Patientin agiertestark außerhalb der Behandlung. Sie tat dabei anfangs etwas positiv Erscheinendes: Sie trennte sich endgültig von ihrem geschiedenen Mann, mit dem sie—typisch für ihre Ambivalenz und Entscheidungsunfähigkeit—immer noch zusammengelebt hatte. Aber dann verlobte sie sich Hals über Kopf mit einem 18jährigen, löste die Verlobung wieder und lernte gleich anschließend einen anderen, diesmal etwas älteren Mann kennen, den sie sofort heiraten wollte. Sie war mur dadurch davon zurückzuhalten, daß *e r* nicht wollte. Damit ging sie in die Sommerferien. In der ersten Stunde nach den Ferien, Mitte September, teilte sie mit, er wolle nun doch heiraten. Für Ende Oktober sei die Hochzeit angesetzt.

Gegen Ende der darauffolgenden 29. Behandlungsstunde wurde sie nachdenklich und äußerte, sie habe ein schlechtes Gewissen dem Mann gegenüber. Er wisse doch gar nicht, *w i e* neurotisch sie sei. Sie fragte sich außerdem, ob sie eigentlich Kinder haben wolle oder nicht. Er wolle sicher keine Kinder. Aber es stehe doch in der Bibel (aber natürlich glaube sie nicht an Gott, aber sie wisse es doch nicht): "Seid fruchtbar und mehret euch!" Ob ich ihr denn nicht sagen könne, was sie tun solle? Ich sagte, nein, sie müsse in sich selbst eine Antwort suchen.

Zur 30. Stunde berichtete sie, sie habe einen Traum gehabt. Er habe sie, obwohl sie ihn nicht verstanden habe, sehr beeindruckt, und sie habe ihn deshalb sogar aufgeschrieben (sie hatte sonst nie Träume aufgeschrieben). Leider hätte sie bei all dem Trubel aber den Zettel vergessen. Natürlich sprach sie dann erst einmal nicht von dem Traum, sondern von dem Trubel. Ich saß in einer Mischung aus analytischer Geduld und menschlicher Ungeduld abwartend dabei.

Sie kam schließlich von sich aus auf den Traum zurück. Er hatte mehrere Teile, die die Patientin in mehreren Ansätzen mit Wiederholungen und Ergänzungen schilderte. Es kamen dann noch Einfälle von ihr dazu. Alles ging ziemlich durcheinander, gehört aber rückblickend in einen psychologisch klaren Zusammenhang. Ich stelle die Inhalte hier vereinfachend nach Themen geordnet dar. Ich lasse einige Einzelheiten, so wichtig sie sein mögen, aus. Ich verfahre ebenso mit meinen eigenen Einfällen, die in der Stunde dem Gedankengang der Patientin folgten.

Die Patientin hatte im Traum in einer Zeitschrift ein Bild gesehen, dazu eine Überschrift, die lautete: "Der Tanz der kleinen Nurnen". Das Wort "Nurnen" war ihr so wenig wie mir im Bewußten geläufig.

Ihr Unbewußtes hatte es gebildet. Die Nurnen waren, wie sie sagte, Göttinnen, so daß die Überschrift übersetzt lauten würde: Der Tanz der kleinen Göttinnen.

Das Traumbild zeigte eine auffallende Symmetrie. Es bestand aus 7 von oben nach unten verlaufenden Reihen. In der ersten und der siebenten Reihe, also den beiden äußeren Reihen, sah man die Nurnen, dann kam zur Mitte hin (in der 2. und 5. Reihe) jeweils eine Reihe "Stacheltiere oder Tausendfüßer" ("die hießen eben so") und dann neben der vertikalen Mittelachse je eine freie, leere Reihe, ein "Niemandsland". Das Ganze war also spiegelbildlich angeordnet. Die Nurnen tanzten von außen nach innen zur Mitte hin, glitten aber immer wieder an den Stacheltieren oder Tausendfüßern ab und tanzten aufs Neue zu ihnen hin, (ein Bild, etwa wie Wogen, die auf flache Steine auflaufen, zurücklaufen, wieder auflaufen usw.). Das war das Traumbild. Man "wußte" noch etwas dazu: In der Mitte mußte der Vater sein. Zu dem wollten die Nurnen hintanzen. Und während sie tanzten, war Mutter gestorben.

1	2	3	4	5	6	7
N	S	.	V	.	S	N
U	T	.	A	.	T	U
R	A	.	T	.	A	R
N	C	.	E	.	C	N
E	H	.	R	.	H	E
N	E	.		.	E	N
	L	.		.	L	
	T	.		.	T	
	I	.		.	I	
	E	.		.	E	
	R	.		.	R	
	E	.		.	E	

Dieses archetypisch-kollektive Bild mit dem Suchen nach einer Mitte und dem Wiederabgleiten wurde in 2 weiteren Traumteilen auf einer persönlichen Ebene wiederholt:

Im ersten schmuste die Patientin mit dem Analytiker auf einer Camping-Liege. Er sagte dann, wie sonst am Stundenende: "Nun ist es gut" und war damit verschwunden.

Im zweiten Traumteil schmuste sie mit einer Freundin, Gaby, die als "jung, flatterhaft, nichtssagend" geschildert wurde, also wohl für einen Schattenanteil stand, in dem eine Entwicklungspotenz liegen konnte. Gaby saß breitbeinig auf der Patientin und sagte: "Lass sein, ich habe einen Tampon drin, ich habe meine Tage". Das Thema

Suchen und Abgewiesen- oder Enttäuschtwerden tauchte in der Stunde noch mehrmals direkt auf:

a) Die Patientin erzählte, nach der letzten Stunde habe sie beim Weggehen gedacht, sie müsse umkehren, zurück zum Analytiker, anstatt zu Mutter, die sie zur Behandlung begleitet hatte und draussen wartete.

b) Sie berichtete von einer Phantasie, die sie kürzlich hatte: Ihr Sohn lebe noch. In Wirklichkeit hatte aber eine Bekannte einen Sohn bekommen, nicht sie.

c) Sie klagte über Schwierigkeiten mit ihrer Frauenärztin (ein eingewachsenes Pessar sollte entfernt werden) und fragte, ob sie nicht meine Frau, die eine gynäkologische Praxis hat, aufsuchen könnte. Sie mußte erfahren, dass das nicht ginge.

d) Sie äußerte danach: "Ich muß gerade denken, so was wie Sie möchte ich heiraten". Daß das nicht ginge, wußte sie selbst.

Sie machte also, wie die Nurnen, Ansatz um Ansatz auf eine Beziehung hin und glitt jedesmal wieder ab. In der Mitte stand der "Vater", aber sie wechselte, wenn sie abgewiesen wurde, auf die gleichgeschlechtliche Ebene zu ihrer Freundin oder zur Frau des Analytikers.

Das Wichtigste und allem gemeinsame ist vielleicht der "Sohn", ein Entwicklungsansatz, der gesucht und verfehlt wird. Sie muß offenbar aus einer matriarchalen Gebundenheit heraus zu "Vater", aber der Weg ist versperrt. Die Progression wird nur über eine Regression zu den Stacheltieren oder Tausendfüßern möglich sein. Das sind ganz undifferenzierte, uroborische Tiere mit Elementarcharakter. Die Tausendfüßer mögen auch die Ambivalenz der Patientin charakterisieren. Die Stacheltiere scheinen für ein eingekrustetes Mütterlich-Weibliches zu stehen, das die "Frauenärztin" aus ihnen herauslösen müßte. Auf der archetypischen Ebene hat das Bild mit den Nurnen und Stacheltieren einen transpersonalen Charakter. Gegenüber der vordergründigen Sexualität in der Übertragungsbeziehung hat es mit den "Göttinnen" einen religiösen Aspekt. Die Symmetrie des Bildes verweist auf eine Tendenz nach Ordnung und Zentrierung. Die Stunde hatte ein reichliches Material gebracht, das man auf seinen verschiedenen Bezugsebenen noch weit differenzierter ausdeuten könnte. Der Analytiker müßte glücklich gewesen sein. Mir war aber nicht glücklich zumute. Im Gegenteil, ich fühlte mich trotz der scheinbar klaren Zusammenhänge irgendwie ratlos und irritiert. Ich sagte der Patientin am Stundenende so etwa, es sei da ein Problem, aber wir wüßten noch nicht einmal genau, wie es aussehe, geschweige denn, wie es zu lösen sei.

Dabei hatte die Stunde, nachdem die Patientin erst einmal auf ihren Traum zurückgekommen war, gut angefangen. Ich freute mich, daß sie an ihr Problem heranging. Ich fand interessant, was sie brachte, und es erschien mir auch analytisch einleuchtend. Aber rückblickend würde ich sagen, daß ich die Stunde über irgendwie gespalten, "wie schizophren" war. Ein Teil von mir saß ruhig da, registrierte und dachte. Ein zweiter nahm intensiv an einem unterschwelligen Prozeß teil und geriet dabei zunehmend in Erregung und Angst, was der erste zwar auch registrierte, aber, und das war das Eigenartige, so, als ob es ihn eigentlich nichts anginge.

Zu den Nurnen fielen mir gleich anfangs Nornen ein, später Urnen: Schicksal und Tod. Dazu noch, zu den tanzenden kleinen Göttinnen: tanzende Nymphen in hauchdünnen Kleidchen, die ich wie lebendig vor mir sah: Eros, Schicksal und Tod. Das Ganze in symmetrischer Ordnung: "wie ein Mandala" dachte ich.

Diesem positiven, lebendigen Aspekt stand von Anfang an ein negativer, starrer oder destruktiver gegenüber. Bevor ich die Nurnen als Nymphen sah, —ich komme später auf die Nymphen zurück—, und bevor die Patientin die Stacheltiere überhaupt erwähnt hatte, sah ich die "kleinen Göttinnen" als eine Reihe von kalten, unlebendigen Schönheitsköniginnen, wie sie auf Miß-Wahlen paradieren. Die antiken Göttinnen waren bei mir zu modernen "Göttinnen" erstarrt und pervertiert. Darin lag einerseits eine projektive Gegenübertragung, auf deren Hintergrund ich hier nicht eingehen will, andererseits eine syntone, einfühlende: Mein Unbewußtes hatte mit den kalten Schönheitsköniginnen die "Stacheltiere" und die "Gaby" vorweggenommen. Die Patientin brachte von sich aus (ich hatte von den "Schönheitsköniginnen" nichts gesagt) mehrere Bestätigungen dazu:

a) Ihr fielen zu den "Nurnen" Nutten ein,

b) die Nurnen hatten Faschingskleider getragen und

c) zuletzt, wie ich gesagt hatte, wir wüßten noch nicht einmal genau, wie das Problem aussehe, fiel ihr dazu ein früherer Traum ein, in dem sich zwei große, kalte Schönheiten bitterböse gegenüberstehen.

Der Schattenaspekt dieser gefühlskalten, phallisch-narzißtischen, die weibliche Rolle ablehnenden und *pervertierten* Frauen ist, verbunden mit dem Infantilen und Leeren, in der jungen, flatterhaften, nichtssagenden Gaby mit personifiziert. Gaby hemmt vorerst die Entwicklung, weist das Traum-Ich der Patientin ab. Das Bild hat sich mir in der Stunde sogar noch schärfer, destruktiver dargestellt: Während die Patientin nur schilderte, daß Gaby sagte: "Laß sein", tauchte vor mir flüchtig ein Bild auf, in dem Gaby auf der Patientin saß und ihr mit einem Messer zwischen die Brüste stach. Der Schatten will das Traum-Ich umbringen. Ich habe dieses Bild in der Stunde relativ unbeteiligt registriert. Es wird später wichtig werden.

Emotional betonter, etwas beunruhigender, war eine flüchtige Wort- und Klangvorstellung, die zu den Tausendfüßern und als Nachassoziation zu den Nornen auftauchte: "Yggdrasil, Ratatösk". Meine Denkseite nahm das ganze harmlos auf: Zu den Nornen gehört die Weltenesche Yggdrasil; und Ratatösk ist das Eichhörnchen, das an der Esche auf und ab läuft und zugleich zu den Tausendfüßern paßt.

Für einen Augenblick wirklich beunruhigt war ich, als mir dann eine Witzzeichnung einfiel, die ich vor etwa 15 Jahren gesehen haben muß: Ein Mann erschreckt seinen Angreifer, eine Schlange, dadurch, daß er sein Hemd aufreißt und seine Brust zeigt, auf der eine Schlange tätowiert ist. Das war recht irritierend. Ich konnte nichts damit anfangen und mir auch nicht erklären, warum ich gleich anschließend an Siegfried im Kampf mit dem Drachen dachte.

Bald nach der Stunde arbeitete ich mein Protokoll aus, weil ich den Fall in die Gruppe bringen wollte. Irgendetwas stimmte nicht, aber ich wußte nicht, was. Am Morgen vor der Gruppensitzung ging mir nach dem Aufwachen der Fall noch einmal durch den Kopf. Ich war sehr erschrocken, als ich dabei plötzlich einen primitivheftigen Affekt gegen die Patientin spürte: "Das dicke, dumme Schwein!" dachte ich. Gleich darauf fiel mir auf, daß ich bei der Ausarbeitung des Protokolls etwas weggeschoben hatte: Ich mußte bei dem Bild von Gaby, die die Patientin zwischen die Brüste stach, in der Stunde eine vage sadistische Lust gespürt haben. Und dann hatte das Bild bei der Ausarbeitung der Protokolls plötzlich gewechselt. Nicht Gaby, sondern ich saß auf der Patientin und stach auf sie ein.

Es wird jetzt verständlicher, weshalb ich mich in der Stunde so irritiert-ratlos und gespalten gefühlt hatte, und was die eigenartige Witzzeichnung von dem Mann, der die Schlange mit der Schlange abwehrt, und das Bild von Siegfried im Kampf mit dem Drachen bedeuteten: Ich war zutiefst einbezogen und hatte Angst. "Schlange" stand gegen "Schlange", und "Siegfried" hatte sich des "Drachens" zu erwehren.

Wir wissen zwar, daß der Analytiker den ganzen Kosmos des Unbewußten mit allen Entwicklungsschichten bis hinunter zu den archaichsten in sich trägt, und daß von Fall zu Fall bald diese, bald jene Schicht ein Problem des Patienten aufnimmt und mitschwingt; aber es macht trotzdem Angst, wenn es, so wie hier, geschieht.

Wir haben in der Gruppe versucht, die Hintergründe zu klären. Es hat sich nach und nach Folgendes ergeben: Das gemeinsame Problem zwischen Patient und Analytiker ist eine erhebliche Ambivalenz im Versuch der Herstellung einer Beziehung und der gegenläufigen Abwehr dieser Beziehung. Die Beziehung wird ebenso gesucht wie gefürchtet. Dem Bild von den Nurnen, die zum "Vater" tanzen wollen und an den "Tausendfüssern" abgleiten, entspricht beim Analytiker das Bild vom Eichhörnchen Ratatösk, das an der Weltenesche Yggdrasil emsig auf und ab läuft und Botschaften zwischen dem Adler im Wipfel (dem Vater-Geist) und dem (uroborisch mütterlichen) Drachen Nidhögg an der Wurzel hin- und herträgt. Dort, beim Drachen sind an der Weltenesche übrigens Zwerge angesiedelt die die Wurzelfasern der Esche zernagen. Einer von ihnen, Davalin, ist der Vater der Nornen, des Schicksals. (Ich will hier nachtragen, daß die Nornen-Assoziation, die ja von mir stammte, der Patientin in der Stunde schließlich angeboten wurde. Sie verstand die Assoziation sofort und antwortete spontan: "Ja, die Nornen, das Schicksal! Das (Traum-)Bild ist doch eigentlich ganz logisch: Ich tanze von außen in ein Niemandsland zu Vater, den ich nie finde, und habe zugleich Angst, Mutter stirbt." Wir dürfen die Assoziation also als "richtig" im Sinne einer kompensatorischen Reaktion aus dem kollektiven Unbewussten einsetzen.)

Das Wesentliche am Ratatösk ist nun etwas, was in der Gruppe noch nicht recht klar wurde und erst hinterher nachgelesen werden mußte: Ich hatte 1½ Jahr zuvor die Ratatösk-Arbeit von Frau Veszy-Wagner (*Psyche* XXIII/3, März 1969) gelesen und deren Inhalt partiell verdrängt. Die Arbeit heißt: "Ratatösk—Die Rolle des *pervertierten* Intellekts". (Das Ratatösk als *pervertiertes* Männliches korrespondiert hier mit der *Nutte* als *pervertiertem* Weiblichen.) Nach der Arbeit von Frau Wagner überbringt das Ratatösk "entstellte" Botschaften. Es sei ein "zerstörerischer" Intellekt, "bar jeglicher ethischen Wärme". "Die ambivalente Gestalt des Ratatösk" schreibt Frau Wagner, "scheint in einem beinahe psychotischen Seelenzustand eine noch nicht völlig abgespaltene Kraft darzustellen. . . . Das Ziel der Integration ist noch nicht ganz aufgegeben, aber alle Aktivität in dieser Richtung ist zum Scheitern verurteilt; es scheint ein schrecklicher Mangel an Koordination zwischen den Kräften zu herrschen".

Ohne Beachtung der Gegenübertragung und des Gesamtbildes würden wir sagen: Das Ratatösk ist eine Amplifikation zu den Nurnen und den Tausendfüßern. Der Analytiker hat damit ein Bild gefunden, das das beziehungsherstellende und doch in blinder Aktivität fast beziehungslose, unkoordinierte Denken der Patientin gut beschreibt. Mit Beachtung der Gegenübertragung müssen wir aber anders formulieren und sagen: Der Analytiker hat auch sich selbst, sein Gespaltensein in der Stunde, abgebildet. Unter dem Druck emotionaler Spannung und dem Andrängen archaischer Impulse oder in Konfrontation mit dem "Drachen" Nidhögg (einer deutlichen, aber dynamisch weit stärkeren Parallele zu den "Stacheltieren") ist auch das Denken des Analytikers entgleist und trägt "entstellte Botschaften" hin und her. Weniger bildhaft: Er regrediert ins Formale, hält noch eine Beziehung aufrecht, wird aber fast blind für den Hintergrund, den ihm das Unbewußte deutlich anbietet. Das Bewußte koordiniert nicht mehr, nimmt andererseits aber immerhin die Aufforderung, sich dem Drachenkampf zu stellen, wahr und stellt sich auch später.

Wir haben etwas über das Ratatösk und seine Bedeutung gesagt, meinen auch mit dem Bild vom Analytiker, der auf die Patientin einsticht, zu verstehen, daß sich hinter dem "Drachen" ein archaisch-regressives Inzestmotiv verbirgt, das für die Libido eine hohe Faszination, für das Ich aber etwas sehr Erschreckendes hat. Man kann zunächst an einen uroborischen Inzest etwa auf der Stufe des Einbruchs des patriarchalen Uroboros nach E. Neumann denken und hat damit sicher Richtiges erfaßt. Der Konflikt spielt hier aber spezifischer (in der Regression einen Schritt weiter) auf einer uroborisch-theriomorphen Ebene, die tiefer im matriarchal-uroborischen Raum zu liegen scheint. Nicht nur die Geschlechter sind in der Differenzierung unsicher, sondern auch Mensch und Tier sind noch miteinander vermengt. Ich habe erwähnt, daß ich anfangs "etwas Animalisches" in der Patientin gespürt und am Ende gedacht hatte: "Das dicke, dumme Schwein!". Letzteres war gewiß nicht wörtlich gemeint; aber wir haben gute Gründe zu sagen: Doch, das Unbewußte hat wirklich "Schwein" gemeint!

In der Gruppe wurde nämlich relativ früh zu den "Nymphen" PAN assoziiert, und wir glauben, damit auf das zentrale archetypische Leitbild gestoßen zu sein, das sich auch hinter dem "Vater" im Traum der Patientin verbirgt.— Pan, der bocksgestaltige Gott, von dem auch der Teufel abgeleitet ist, ist nach verschiedenen Versionen u.a. einmal der Sohn von Hermes und der Ziegennymphe Amaltheia, ein andermal von Zeus und der Nymphe Kallisto, die eine Gefährtin der Artemis ist. Kallisto heißt übersetzt: Die Schönste. Kallisto wollte jungfräulich bleiben (s. die "Schönheitsköniginnen" und die Frigidität der Patientin). Es wird gesagt, daß Zeus sich als Bär mit der Kallisto vereinigte, oder daß Kallisto als Bärin dem Zeus begegnete, oder daß Artemis, als sie die daraus resultierende Schwangerschaft entdeckte, Kallisto in eine Bärin verwandelte (sie steht jetzt als "großer Bär" am Himmel). In der Amaltheia- wie in der Kallisto-Version geht es, wie in der Gestalt des Pan, um eine Vermengung von Mensch und Tier, um das Motiv der Hochzeit mit dem Tier, die einerseits tiefe Regression bedeutet, in der andererseits in der Rückbeziehung auf das Tier eine enorm dynamische, rauschhafte Kraft liegen kann. Die kühle psychologische Formel "Rückbeziehung auf das Tier" ist zweifellos richtig, aber für den hier zugrundeliegenden Konflikt unvollständig. Sie muß

ergänzt heißen: Rückbeziehung auf das Tier unter zumindest poten-
tieller Aufgabe des Geistes oder des Menschlichen überhaupt. Erst
wenn man das einfügt, kann man etwas von der Faszination und der
Versuchung, die in dem Motiv liegen, spüren; aber man spürt zugleich
den Schrecken und die panische Angst, die entstehen, weil so viel
Natur die geistgerichtete Ichstruktur des Menschen unwiderbringlich
zu überwältigen und aufzuschlucken droht. Der Mensch wehrt verzweifelt ab (und die "Sodomie" gilt als eine der schimpflichsten und primi-
tivsten Perversionen).

Dass es sich wirklich um "Pan" handelte, der abgewehrt wurde, dass
also die Amplifikation in der Gruppe richtig und Ernst zu nehmen war,
lässt sich in unserem Fall (u.a. habe ich ihn deshalb ausgewaehlt)
zweifelsfrei belegen. Nicht nur, daß mir entsprechende sodomistische
Phantasien aus meiner Frühgeschichte wieder eingefallen wären (sie
waren schon früher in meiner eigenen Analyse aufgetaucht, aber ich
hatte lange nicht mehr daran gedacht), sondern auch, daß die Patientin
in die erste Behandlungsstunde nach der Gruppensitzung (sie hatte
also inzwischen keinen Kontakt mit mir gehabt) den folgenden, eindeutig bestätigenden Traum mitbrachte: "Zwei Hunde, ein Rüde und
eine Hündin, sind mit ihren Besitzern" (zwei Schatten sind mit ihren
Ichs) "über die Straße gerannt. Der Rüde wollte die Hündin besprin-
gen, aber sie hat ihn weggebissen. Da kam ein feister, dicker Mann;
er sah wild aus mit Schlapphut und Zigarre und weit offenem Mantel.
Der hat die Hündin besprungen".—Pan!—Die Patientin brachte
wieder eine Stunde später sehr widerstrebend die Erinnerung an sodomistische Kinderspiele mit einem Hund.

Auch bei mir sind dann noch weitere Erinnerungen, die ich bis
dahin nicht mit dem Fall in Zusammenhang gebracht hatte, aufgetaucht. Ich überlegte noch einmal, was die Patientin wohl anfangs bei
mir angesprochen hätte. Es müsse doch mit meiner Anima und/oder
mit meinem Schatten zusammengehangen haben, meinte ich. Aber zur
Anima schien sie mir zunächst so gar nicht zu passen. Mir fielen dann
zwei Mädchen aus der Studentenzeit ein, die der Patientin in gewis-
sem Sinne ähnlich waren, und die mich einigermaßen interessiert hatten. Dahinter tauchte das Bild einer polnischen Landarbeiterin, die
mir in der Pubertät begegnet war, auf und dahinter wieder, zu meinem
großen Erstaunen, das Bild meiner Mutter, und zwar in einer ganz
bestimmten Situation: Mutter mit dem Ganter. Das war ein ziemlich
bösartiger Ganter, der mit seinem spitzen Schnabel heftig auf Mensch
oder Tier einhacken konnte (s. das Bild vom Analytiker, der auf die
Patientin einsticht). Alle hatten vor ihm Angst, nur Mutter konnte
mit ihm umgehen, z.B. hingehen und ihm den Kopf streicheln. Das hat

mir damals sehr imponiert. Man kann das Bild zwanglos orthodox-analytisch deuten oder an eine Art "Leda mit dem Schwan auf dem Dorfe" denken. Aber ich glaube, es handelt sich um ein entwicklungs-geschichtlich tiefer liegendes Motiv, um das der "Großen Mutter als der Herrin der Tiere".

Hier schließt sich der Kreis. Ich kann die große, erregende, geheim-nisvolle und teils auch verbotene Welt der Tiere, die für mich hinter diesem Bild steht, und die mich als Kind tief beeindruckt hat, hier nicht schildern. Aber es ist wohl deutlich, daß das Bild dem Pan gegen-über, der in seiner naiven und furchtbaren Dynamik allein zwar eine Verlebendigung, aber keine Lösung bringt, ein Gegengewicht bildet und einen fruchtbaren Ansatz zu einer Bewältigung auf einer dem Pan adäquaten Bewußtseinsebene darstellt. Das Unbewußte hatte eine Antwort auf Pan gefunden. Diese Antwort war übrigens schon in der Stunde angeklungen: Im Traum der Patientin hieß es (s.o.), Mutter sei gestorben. Dazu war mir in der Stunde der Tod meiner eigenen Mutter eingefallen. Später, in der Gruppenbesprechung, tauchte eine Erinne-rung daran auf, daß ich vor dem Tod der Mutter in einem großen Wald (*"bei Pan"*) von einer großen, tiefen Traurigkeit ergriffen worden war. In dieser Erinnerung waren Pan und die Mutter schon einander zugeordnet.—Das Muttermotiv ist aber zusammen mit dem Animali-schen und dem Angstmotiv (Phobie, Pan, panische Angst) und einem Wandlungsmotiv, das Erlösung von der Angst und eine Erneuerung bringt, sehr verdichtet bereits im Bild der Esche Yggdrasil enthalten: Yggdrasil (s. C.G. Jung: *Symbole der Wandlung*) heißt übersetzt "Schreckroß"; und im Holz der Weltenesche ist beim Weltuntergang ein Menschenpaar begorgen, von dem dann die Geschlechter der erneuer-ten Welt abstammen. Im Moment des Weltuntergangs wird die Wel-tenesche zur bewahrenden Mutter. Sie ist zugleich Toten- und Lebens-baum. In der scheinbar entferntliegenden Assoziation "Yggdrasil" war die Gesamtthematik zusammen mit einem Lösungsentwurf verborgen. Ich habe geschildert, wie sich das Erleben der Patientin im Therapeu-ten abbildet. Ich will nun nach auf eine Umkehrung hinweisen, damit das Bild nicht zu einseitig bleibt. Es handelt sich ja um eine zweiseitige unbewußte Beziehung.

Ich wähle das Beispiel einer unbewußten Participation, in der die Patientin—außerhalb irgendwie als "neurotisch" zu beschreibender Phänomene—ein ihr mit Sicherheit im Bewußten unbekanntes Erleben des Analytikers im Traum als ihr eigenes wiedergibt:

Ich mußte mich für eine Reise einer Pockenimpfung unterziehen. Es kam zu einer allergischen Reaktion, die in der Folgezeit (im Sinne einer Kälteurticaria) durch Kälte und Nässe auslösbar war. An einem

Mittwoch bildeten sich, nachdem ich in zu kaltem Wasser geschwommen hatte, am ganzen Körper erst kleine, dann große, juckende Quaddeln, und es kam zu einem recht üblen Kreislaufkollaps. Die Patientin wußte von all dem nichts. Am darauffolgendem Montag berichtete sie, sie habe am Mittwoch im Traum einen Bikini anprobiert. Dabei habe sie kleine Pickel am Körper bekommen. Daraus seien große, flatschige Blasen geworden, und sie habe Angst gehabt, ersticken zu müssen. Die Angst zu ersticken habe sich am Freitag im Traum wiederholt mit dem Zusatz: "Weil sie die Blattern (Pocken) hätte". Sie sprach dann die ganze Stunde über vom Schwimmen.

Zum Abschluß noch eine Kleinigkeit über Namen welche zwar nicht immer ein Omen sein müssen, aber doch häufig Träger von Bedeutungen sind oder Bedeutsames konstellieren: Die Patientin hat zwei Namen, einen, mit dem sie gerufen wird und sich gern rufen läßt, und einen "richtigen", den Taufnamen. Sie wird "Petruschka" gerufen, und dazu ist ihr "Peter Pan" eingefallen. Ihr richtiger Name ist aber ein Tiername, etwa entsprechend dem Namen Ursula (die Bärin, s. Kallisto). Auch ich habe zwei Namen: Gerufen wurde ich lange Zeit Peter. Aber ich heiße "richtig" (nach dem Bruder meiner Mutter— s.o.—) Rudolf. Das ist aus dem althochdeutschen "Hrodulf" entstanden und heißt "wölfisch" oder "der Wolf Wotans" (s.o.).—Patientin und Analytiker waren also von Anfang an durch den "Peter" und den Tiernamen miteinander verbunden.

Zusammenfassung

Die Konstellierung der Gegenübertragung und ihre Handhabung werden an einem Behandlungsfall gezeigt: Innerhalb des analytischen Prozesses wurde eine gemeinsame Regression von Patient und Analytiker auf eine Schicht, in der sich "Pan" und "die große Mutter als Herrin der Tiere" gegenüberstehen, deutlich und mit Hilfe der Gruppe durchgearbeitet.

The Constellation of the Countertransference in Relation to the Presentation of Archetypal Dreams
Clinical Aspects

Case History: 30th session with a 23-year-old female patient

The practical description of the countertransference presents difficulties if you really want it to be informative without wishing to assume the role of a "Wise Old Man." It is correct on the one hand for the analyst to be as frank as possible in his reports of patients. Only he must—and this will be the case here too—protect their identity by means of slight alterations. On the other hand it is indecent if he talks too much about himself, but I'm afraid this cannot be avoided.

In November 1969 I was visited by a 23-year-old female patient who had suffered from a phobia since childhood. She weighed about 80 kilos and gave the impression partly of chumminess and partly of clumsiness. At the same time she seemed determined and independent, but I had my suspicions. For we know that when it is a phobia we find ourselves having to deal afterwards with a helpless little girl who begins by thrusting herself forward impulsively and then gets terribly frightened and runs crying to her mother for protection.

97

I discovered the following things about her:

She had never known her father. He had disappeared before her birth and was never seen again.

During her childhood her mother changed her male partners every 4–5 years and looked after the patient in a happy-go-lucky fashion. She now exercised a protective function with regard to the phobia.

The patient had been precocious, had had various relationships with men, but was frigid.

At 18 she married and had a son. This budding relationship collapsed: the marriage was dissolved because of another man and the son died shortly afterwards of an infection.

Since then she had suffered much more from anxiety than before. She was afraid she was going to die of a heart attack or would go mad.

She seemed very infantile, ambivalent in her attitudes, scarcely capable of any firm decision. She was in great distress and was seeking most urgently a vacancy for immediate treatment.

About her anxiety she said something else very important that pointed to a certain degree of insight: "It is as though there were something dangerous in me and I don't know how I should deal with it."

Now there are very many patients who need a vacancy "most urgently" and I had none free. Nevertheless I took her on, remarking that the treatment would not be very intensive at first. In other words, I had allowed myself to be bowled over by her. My unconscious must have responded to her appeal and prevailed upon my conscious mind to give her a vacancy out of turn. If I had been asked then what it was in her that had appealed to me, I should probably have said it was her clinical insight or her need for help, but without being able to formulate the essential thing properly. Perhaps I would have said, all the same, that something spontaneous in her had appealed to me. I might even have added that by "spontaneous" I meant—more precisely—something "animal." But in all probability I would have immediately made light of it again, and an experienced observer would have guessed correctly that the core of the problem must lie there. It took me a long time until I had grasped it, and it will need some patience to follow me on my way.

The course of the treatment was fitful and irregular. Outside it, the patient was very active. To begin with, she did something that looked positive: she finally separated from her divorced husband with whom— and this was typical of her ambivalence and incapacity for decision— she had been living. But she precipitately got engaged to an 18-year-old, broke off the engagement, and immediately afterwards became acquainted with a somewhat older man whom she wanted to marry at once. She was only restrained by the fact that *he* didn't want to. Thereupon she went off for her summer holidays. At the first session after the holidays, in the middle of September, she told me that he wanted to marry her after all. The wedding was fixed for the end of October.

Towards the end of the 29th session she became pensive and said she had a bad conscience about this man. He didn't know, she explained, just *how* neurotic she was. She was also asking herself whether she really wanted to have children or not. He certainly didn't. But it was written in the Bible (of course she didn't believe in God, she said, but she didn't really know): "Be fruitful and multiply!" Couldn't I tell her what she ought to do? I said no, she would have to seek the answer within herself.

At the 30th session she reported that she had had a dream. Although she hadn't understood it, it had made a deep impression on her, and she had even written it down (she had never written dreams before). Unfortunately what with all the upset she had forgotten the piece of paper. So naturally she didn't speak of the dream at first but only of the upset. I sat there and waited, a mixture of analytical patience and all-too-human impatience.

Finally of her own accord she came back to the dream. It had several scenes which the patient described by fits and starts, with repetitions and additions. Then came her own associations. It was all pretty confused, but in retrospect it fitted into a psychologically clear pattern. I reproduce the content here in simplified form, arranged according to themes. I must omit a number of details, important though these are. I am doing the same with my own associations which followed the patient's train of thoughts during the session.

In the dream *the patient had seen a picture in a magazine, with a heading that ran: "Der Tanz der kleinen Nurnen."* The Word "Nurnen" was as consciously unfamiliar to her as it was to me. Her unconscious had coined it. "Nurnen," she said, were goddesses, so that the heading could be translated: "The dance of the little goddesses."

The dream image displayed a striking symmetry. It consisted of 7 rows running from top to bottom. In the 1st and 7th rows (the two outer rows) you saw the "Nurnen," then, towards the center (in the 2nd and 6th rows) came a row of "Stacheltiere [prickly animals] or millipedes" ("that's how they were called"), and then, on either side of the vertical central axis, a blank row, a "no-man's-land." The whole thing was thus arranged like a mirror-image. The "Nurnen" danced from outside towards the center but always slid away from the prickly animals or millipedes and then danced up to them anew (an image rather like waves lapping up against flat boulders, running back and then lapping up again). Such was the dream-image. One "knew" something else: *in the center there would have to be the "Vater" [father]. It was towards him that the "Nurnen" wanted to dance. And while they were dancing the mother died.*

1	2	3	4	5	6	7
N	S	.	V	.	S	N
U	T	.	A	.	T	U
R	A	.	T	.	A	R
N	C	.	E	.	C	N
E	H	.	R	.	H	E
N	E	.		.	E	N
	L	.		.	L	
	T	.		.	T	
	I	.		.	I	
	E	.		.	E	
	R	.		.	R	
	E	.		.	E	

This collective archetypal image of seeking for a center and then sliding away again was repeated in two other scenes in the dream on a personal level: In the first the patient was chatting with the analyst on a camp bed. Then he said, as at the end of a session: "Well, then, that's fine," and disappeared. In the second she was chatting with a girl friend, Gaby, who was described as "young, flighty, and colorless," and who therefore probably represented a shadow component harboring some potential development. Gaby was sitting astride the patient and said: "Stop that, I've got a Tampax in, it's one of my days."

The theme of seeking and being rebuffed or disappointed emerged directly several more times during the session:

a) The patient related that as she was leaving after the last session she thought she would have to turn round and go back to the analyst instead of to her mother who had accompanied her and was waiting outside.

b) She reported a fantasy she had had recently: her son was still living. But in reality it was a woman acquaintance of hers who had got a son, not she herself.

c) She complained about the difficulties she had with her gynecologist (an ingrown pessary needed to be removed) and asked whether she might visit my wife, who has a gynecological practice. I had to tell her that this would not do.

d) She remarked afterwards: "I was just thinking I would like to marry someone like you." She herself knew, of course, that this wouldn't do, either.

Like the "Nurnen," then, she was making one attempt after another at forming a relationship but each time slid away again. In the center stood the "father," but whenever she was rebuffed she switched to the homosexual plane of her girl friend or the analyst's wife.

The most important common factor is perhaps the "son," an attempt at development that miscarries. She must obviously get out of a matriarchal bondage and reach the "father," but the way is blocked. Progression will be possible only via regression to the prickly animals or millipedes. These are wholly undifferentiated, uroboric creatures of an elementary nature. The millipedes may also typify the patient's ambivalence. The prickly animals seem to stand for an encrusted maternal-female element which would have to be released by the "gynecologist." On the archetypal level the image of the "Nurnen" and prickly animals has a transpersonal character. Contrasted with the sexuality in the foreground of the transference relationship it has, with its "goddesses," a religious aspect. The symmetry of the image indicates a tendency towards order and centering.

The session had brought up a wealth of material which could still be interpreted in far more differentiated ways in accordance with its various levels of relationship. The analyst ought to have felt happy. But I was not feeling happy in the least. On the contrary, in spite of the apparently clear connections I felt somehow perplexed and irritated. At the end of the session I told the patient in so many words that there was a problem here but we did not know even what it looked like, let alone how to solve it.

At the same time, once the patient had come back to her dream, the session had got off to a good start. I was glad that she was coming to grips with her problem. I found the material she brought me interesting, and it seemed to me analytically instructive as well. But looking back I would say that all through the session I was somehow split, as if "schizophrenic." One part of me was sitting there quietly, registering and thinking. Another part was intensely absorbed in a subliminal process, getting increasingly excited and anxious, and the first part was registering this too, but—and this was the peculiar thing—as though it really didn't concern him.

Right at the beginning I associated the "Nurnen" with the "Norns," later with "urns": fate and death. These little dancing goddesses I associated with dancing nymphs in wispy garments, seeing them vividly before me: Eros, fate and death. I thought the symmetrical arrangement of the whole was "like a mandala."

But from the beginning this positive, living aspect was contrasted with a negative one, rigid and destructive. Even before I saw the "Nurnen" as nymphs—I shall come back to the nymphs later—and before the patient had mentioned the prickly animals at all, I saw the little goddesses as a row of cold, lifeless beauty queens parading at one of those "Miss" contests. For me the classical goddesses had been frozen and perverted into modern "goddesses." This was due partly to a projective countertransference into the background of which I will not enter here, and partly to a syntonic, empathetic one: my unconscious had, in anticipation, replaced the prickly animals and Gaby by the cold beauty queens. The patient produced spontaneously (I had said nothing about the beauty queens) several confirmatory associations:

a) the "Nurnen" made her think of "Nutten," whores,

b) they were dressed in carnival clothes and

c) finally, when I remarked that we didn't know even what the problem looked like, an earlier dream occurred to her in which two large, cold beauties were angrily confronting one another.

The shadow-side of these emotionally cold, phallic-narcissistic, anti-feminine and perverted women, infantile and shallow, is personified by the young, flighty, and colorless Gaby. Above all, Gaby inhibits the patient's development and rejects her dream-ego. During the session the image presented itself to me in an even sharper, more destructive form: while the patient was describing how Gaby had said "Stop that," there rose up before me a fleeting image in which Gaby was sitting on the patient and stabbing her between the breasts with a knife. The shadow wanted to kill the dream-ego. I registered this image with relative unconcern during the session. Later it will acquire more importance.

A more feeling-toned and rather more disquieting word and sound association that flashed through my mind at the mention of the millipedes and as an after-association to the Norns was: "Yggdrasil, Rata-tösk." My thinking side took it up quite innocently: the World Ash goes together with the Norns, and Ratatösk is the squirrel that runs up and down the ash and at the same time fits in with the millipedes.

For a moment I was really upset on remembering a cartoon I must have seen about 15 years earlier: a man is frightening off his assailant, a snake, by tearing open his shirt and baring his chest on which a snake is tattooed. This was very annoying indeed. I couldn't make head or tail of it, nor could I explain to myself why immediately afterwards I thought of Siegfried fighting with the dragon.

When the session was over I wrote out my report as I wanted to present the case to the group. Something or other was wrong, but I didn't know what. On the morning before the group meeting the case again passed through my mind after I woke up. I was very shocked when I suddenly felt a violently primitive affect rising up in me against the patient: "The fat stupid pig!" I thought. Immediately afterwards it struck me that while working up my notes I had thrust something aside: during the session, I must have felt a vague sadistic pleasure at the image of Gaby stabbing the patient between the breasts. Then, as I was writing my report, the image suddenly changed: it was not Gaby but I myself who was sitting on the patient and stabbing her.

It will now be easier to understand why I had felt so irritatingly perplexed and "split" during the session, and what the peculiar cartoon of the man frightening the snake with a snake meant, also the image of Siegfried fighting the dragon: I was profoundly involved and afraid. "Snake" was pitted against "snake," and "Siegfried" had to defend himself against the "dragon."

We know, of course, that the analyst harbors within him the whole cosmos of the unconscious with all its evolutionary layers right down to the most archaic, and that, depending on the case, now one and now the other layer takes up the patient's problem and reverberates with it. All the same, it scares you when it really happens as it was happening now.

In the group we tried to clarify the background and arrived at the following results:

The problem common to both patient and analyst is a marked ambivalence in the attempt to establish a relationship and in contradictorily defending themselves against it. The relationship is as much feared as it is desired. The image of the "Nurnen" who want to dance up to the "father" and constantly slide away from the millipedes corresponds to the analyst's image of the squirrel Ratatösk, busily running up and down the world ash Yggdrasil and carrying messages to and fro between the eagle at the top of the tree (the father spirit) and the (uroboric-maternal) dragon Nidhögg at the roots. Near the dragon's lair dwell a colony of dwarfs who gnaw the rootlets of the ash to pieces. One of them, Davalin, is the father of the Norns, of fate. (I will add here that the Norns association, which came from me, was finally offered to the patient. She understood it at once and spontaneously answered: "Yes, the Norns, fate! The dream-image is actually quite logical: I dance from outside into a no-man's-land towards father, whom I never find, and at the same time am afraid mother is dying." We may therefore take the association as "correct" in the sense of a compensatory reaction from the collective unconscious.)

Now the important thing about Ratatösk was still not properly clarified in the group and had to be looked up afterwards. A year and a half previously I had read Frau Veszy-Wagner's paper on Ratatösk (*Psyche,* XXIII:3, March 1969) and partly repressed its contents. The paper is called: "Ratatösk—The Role of the Perverted Intellect." (Ratatösk as perverted male corresponds here to the whore as perverted female.) According to Frau Wagner, Ratatösk delivers "distorted" messages. He is the "destructive intellect, devoid of any ethical warmth." "The ambivalent figure of Ratatösk," writes Frau Wagner, "seems to represent in an almost psychotic state an aspect of the psyche that is not yet completely split off. . . . The goal of integration has not yet been entirely abandoned, but all activity in this direction is foredoomed to failure; a frightful lack of coordination seems to prevail among the psychic powers."

If we disregard the countertransference and the total picture we would say: Ratatösk is an amplification of the "Nurnen" and millipedes. The analyst has thus found an image that adequately depicts the patient's uncoordinated thinking, trying to make a relationship and yet almost relationless in its blind activity. But taking the countertransference into account we must formulate it differently and say: the analyst has here portrayed himself as well, his split-mindedness during the session. Under the pressure of emotional tension and the accumulation of archaic impulses or in confrontation with the "dragon" Nidhögg (an obvious but dynamically far more powerful parallel to the prickly animals), the analyst's thinking too has run off the rails and carries "distorted" messages to and fro. Less picturesquely: he has regressed into professionalism, is still maintaining a relationship, but is practically blind to the background clearly being offered to him by the unconscious. His conscious mind does not coordinate any more, while on the other hand it is aware of the challenge to accept the fight with the dragon, and later it does so.

We have said something about Ratatösk and its significance, and we also think that the image of the analyst stabbing the patient helps us to understand that behind the "dragon" an archaic, regressive incest motif is hidden, which holds a great fascination for the libido but has something very frightening about it for the ego. One might think at first of a uroboric incest somewhat on the level of the irruption of the patriarchal uroboros as described by Erich Neumann, and certainly this is right as far as it goes. But since the regression has gone a stage further, the conflict is being played out here more specifically on a uroboric-theriomorphic level which seems to lie deeper in the matriarchal-uroboric sphere. Not only is the differentiation of the sexes uncertain, but man and beast are still intermingled. I mentioned that at the beginning I felt something "animal" in the patient, and at the end I thought: "The fat stupid pig!" This was certainly not meant literally, but we have good reasons for saying: "Well, the unconscious really did mean 'pig'!"

In the group the "nymphs" were associated quite early with Pan, and we believe we have here stumbled on the central archetypal leitmotiv that is also concealed behind the "father" in the patient's dream. Pan, the goat-bodied god from whom the devil is derived, is according to one version the son of Hermes and the goat-nymph Amaltheia; according to another, the son of Zeus and the nymph Kallisto, a companion of Artemis. Kallisto means "The Most Beautiful." She wanted to remain virginal (cf. the beauty queens and the patient's frigidity). It is related that Zeus united himself with Kallisto as a bear, or that Kallisto met Zeus as a she-bear, or that Artemis, on discovering that Kallisto was pregnant, changed Kallisto into a she-bear (she now stands as the Great Bear in the heavens). In both the Amaltheia and Kallisto versions, as in the figure of Pan, there is a mingling of man and beast, the motif of marriage with an animal. This signifies a profound regression in which, however, a tremendously dynamic, intoxicating power may lie in establishing a reconnection with a beast. The cool psychological formula "reconnection with a beast" is doubtless correct but not complete enough to characterize the underlying conflict. It must be expanded to mean: reconnection with a beast including at least the potential surrender of the spirit or of human qualities altogether. Only when this is added can we feel something of the fascination and temptation inherent in the motif; but at the same time we feel the fright and panic fear which arise because so much raw Nature threatens to overpower irretrievably man's spiritually oriented ego-structure and swallow it up for good. Man puts up a desperate resistance, for "bestiality" is counted as one of the most abominable and most primitive of perversions.

That it really was Pan who had to be resisted (and that the amplification in the group was therefore right and worth taking seriously) can be established beyond a doubt in the present case (which was one of my reasons for choosing it). Not only did I recall similar bestial fantasies from my adolescence (they had come up earlier in my own analysis but I hadn't thought about them for a long time); it also happened that at the first session after the group meeting the patient, who had had no contact with me in the interim, brought with her the following, clearly confirmatory dream:

Two dogs, a male and a bitch, ran across the street with their owners (two shadows with their egos). *The male tried to mount the bitch but she bit him off. Then came a fat fleshy man; he looked wild, with a slouch hat and cigar and his coat wide open.* He *mounted the bitch."* —Pan! At a later session the patient brought out, with great resistance, a memory of bestial games with a dog during her childhood.

Then other memories came up in me too, which I had not connected with the case until now. I considered once again what it was about the patient that had appealed to me in the beginning. It must have something to do with my anima and/or with my shadow, I thought. But at first sight she didn't fit in with the anima at all. Then I remembered two girls from my student days who looked rather like the patient and in whom I had shown some interest. Behind them there rose the image of a Polish farm girl whom I had met in my puberty, and behind her again, to my great astonishment, the image of my mother in a quite distinct situation: mother with the gander. He was a pretty vicious gander who would strike out violently at man or beast with his sharp bill (cf. the image of the analyst stabbing the patient). Everyone was afraid of him, only mother could manage him by going up to him and stroking his head. This had made a great impression on me at the time. The image can easily be interpreted in the orthodox analytical way, or else you can think of a kind of "Leda with the village swan." But I think it has more to do with an evolutionarily deeper-lying motif, "The Great Mother as Mistress of the Animals."

Here the circle closes. I cannot describe now the grand, exciting, mysterious, and partly forbidden world of animals that is hidden for me behind this image and that impressed me so deeply as a child. But it is clear enough that the image forms a counterweight to Pan, whose naïve and terrible dynamism, taken by itself, expresses vitalization but does not bring a solution, whereas the image of the Mistress of the Animals represents a fruitful approach to solving the conflict on a plane of consciousness capable of mastering Pan. As a matter of fact, this answer to Pan provided by the unconscious had already been hinted at during the session: in the patient's dream reported above, the mother had died. At the same time I remember the death of my own mother. Later, during the group discussion, another memory came back: before my mother died, I had been seized by a great, deep sadness in a large wood (Pan's haunts). In this memory Pan and my mother were already correlated with one another. — But the mother motif, together with the animal motif and fear motif (phobia, Pan, panic fear), plus a transformation motif that brings deliverance from fear and a renewal, is contained in very condensed form in the image of

Yggdrasil: Yggdrasil means "terrible horse" (Jung, *Symbols of Transformation,* par. 370). "In the wood of the world-ash Yggdrasil a human pair hide themselves at the end of the world, and from them will spring a new race of men. At the moment of universal destruction the world-ash becomes the guardian mother, the tree pregnant with death and life" (ibid., par. 367). In the apparently far-fetched association "Yggdrasil" there was hidden the whole thematic complex together with the outline of a solution.

I have described how the patient's experience reflects itself in the therapist. I shall now present the picture in reverse lest it remain too one-sided, since we are in fact dealing with a *two*-sided unconscious relationship.

I shall choose as an example an unconscious participation in which the patient—altogether apart from certain phenomena that might be described as "neurotic"—reproduced an experience of the analyst's, of which she could certainly have had no conscious knowledge, as a dream-experience of her own.

In order to go on a journey I had to be vaccinated against smallpox. An allergic reaction followed which, like urticaria, could subsequently be brought on by cold and damp. One Wednesday, after I had gone swimming in water that was too cold, my whole body was covered with small, then large, itching bumps, resulting in a really bad circulatory collapse. The patient knew nothing of all this. On the following Monday she reported that on the previous Wednesday she had tried on a bikini in a dream, and had got little pimples all over her body These had turned into large flabby blisters, and she was afraid she was going to suffocate. The fear of suffocation had recurred in a dream on Friday, with the addition: "because she had caught smallpox." She then spent the whole session talking about swimming.

In conclusion I would mention the small matter of names, which though they need not always be omens are often the carriers of meanings or constellate something significant. The patient has two names, one she is called by and likes to be called by, and a "proper" baptismal name. The pet name is "Petruschka," which she associated with "Peter Pan." Her proper name, however, is that of an animal, corresponding roughly to Ursula (the she-bear; see Kallisto above). I also have two names: for a long time I was called "Peter." But my proper name (after my mother's brother) is Rudolf. This comes from the Old High German "Hrodulf" and means "wolfish" or "Wotan's wolf." Thus patient and analyst were connected from the beginning by "Peter" and an animal's name.

Conclusion

The constellation of the countertransference and the way it was handled have here been demonstrated by a case history. Within the analytical process the patient and analyst mutually regressed to an unconscious layer in which "Pan" and "The Great Mother as Mistress of the Animals" confronted one another. The regression was worked through clearly with the help of the group.

Translated from the German by R. F. C. Hull

8

Success and Failure in Analysis
Primary Envy and the Fate of the Good

MARY WILLIAMS, *London*

I am concerned with the roots of an emotion which has many ramifications in later life and becomes attached to objects which are more and more remote from its origin. In borderline states where envy is most conspicuous it seems particularly important to get back to this origin as otherwise the patient's unconscious need to defeat the analyst, or any other helping person, will end in the triumph of the analyst's failure and the patient's pyrrhic victory.

Though envy is common to all men and has a positive social function in ideas such as "fair play" and "equality of opportunity" (Schoeck, 1966), envy has the worst possible reputation. A dictionary definition describes it as "pain excited by the sight of another's superiority or success, accompanied by some degree of hatred or ill-will, and satisfaction at his mortification . . . To regard with malevolent covetousness. . . ."

Envy is usually distinguished from jealousy by belonging to a two-body situation, whereas jealousy identifies the intervening third as the target. It is not surprising, therefore, that its roots belong to the nursing couple and to the infant's relation to its first object, the breast. There is a third in the background of most descriptions who is the one who enjoys the envied object, but in early infancy it is assumed that this is not an identifiable third but consists of contrary experiences of the same object which produce the painful excitement noted above.

I hope to show that primary envy on the archetypal level is envy of the creative functions of the mother archetype in her primary form as bisexual nature goddess. To me, the breast as the first representative of this figure lends itself to a bisexual interpretation, being both soft and round and the nipple hard with erectile tissue when stimulated. The envy of the creative has its counterpart in the fear of the deadly, devouring aspect of the mother archetype, that is, of *her* envy of her creation and wish to reincorporate it.

VIEWS ON ENVY

FREUDIAN VIEWS

The early Freudian work is largely descriptive and the theory confined to the allocation of character traits to erotogenic zones (Joffe, 1969). It was agreed that oral-sadistic and anal traits were present. The descriptive adjectives when put together read like a catalogue of deadly sins. They are: narcissism, hatred of the superior and more powerful object, impatience, possessiveness, avariciousness, anger, greed and covetousness. Abraham's approach was more positive (1924). He noted that admiration and envy were closely linked and that the self was devalued in comparison with the object, sometimes pathologically so. He found that disappointment or over-indulgence in the sucking period led to strong ambivalence and over-developed envy.

It was observed that envy was diametrically opposed to depression, for hope was not lost of one day possessing the envied object. In fact, loss of any kind could not be accepted. The main defenses against loss were projection and denial, and omnipotent and grandiose fantasies. When the envy response failed, pathological depression, psychosomatic symptoms, and paranoid states supervened.

Melanie Klein's notion of envy as innate and its amount constitutional created a furor in the 1930s (Klein, 1932). It was consistent with her assumption of innate "unconscious fantasies," the images of which belong to the life and death instincts. The fantasies of very young children whom she had treated led her to believe that infants could envy the full breast, which appeared to keep its riches for itself, and that rage would induce fantasy attacks upon it with body excreta. Images of the creative and devouring breast-mother are assumed to be operative.

JUNG'S VIEWS

I found only two index references to envy in Jung's works. The first occurs in the paper "On the significance of number dreams" (Jung, 1910–11), in which he uncovered strong unconscious envy in his patient by working out the number symbolism in a dream. The cause was the birth of another child to Jung, which made the score of two to four in his favor. The patient outdid the analyst by including the length of time his wife had been pregnant with three still-births and two miscarriages. The joint interest in this clever game seems to have masked the patient's tragedy of the triumph of destruction over creation. It is an illustration of a pyrrhic victory previously referred to.

The second reference is in Jung's foreword to the *I Ching* (Jung, 1950, par. 980). He describes how he used the oracle to ask how the English translation would be received. He cast No. 50, "The caldron." It contains nourishment. The comrades are envious. Jung comments: "The envious want to rob the I Ching of its great possession, that is, they seek to rob it of meaning, or to destroy its meaning." Of immediate interest is that this symbology is on the nutritional level.

Some work in the last decade, particularly that of Laing, Rosenthall, and Milner, is more helpful in understanding and therefore treating the envious patient and will be used in the discussion of case material.

CASE MATERIAL

GENERAL COMMENTS

I can now recognize that some patients I have seen over the years were —despite very different backgrounds and family constellations—suffering from primary envy, based on a similar view of the mother image. Of diagnostic importance were certain peculiarities the patients had in common. All hinged on the difficulty of taking in anything good or, if they did, of acknowledging it.

1. *Inability to retain an image.* The most striking characteristic was an inability to retain an image, the desired image being a smiling one.

Thus, though some stared, they seemed unable to register *any* feature securely. When they started to be able to retain a "good" image for a short time, lost or panicky feelings supervened when it faded. Tears when shed were likely to come from *one* eye only, an uncanny sight. Covering the eyes, then staring with one of them gave the same impression. The two eyes together tended to dim or scramble the image. Bright light hurt, and they did not like being looked at.

2. *Physical symptoms.* Any receiving organ might be affected, the most common being the eyes, skin and digestive system. Minor eye symptoms included conjunctivitis, irritation of the lids and a blocked tear duct. Tests of vision were unreliable. There were skin rashes of various kinds and/or flushing and sweating. Touch could feel painful.

Symptoms relating to intake and output such as nausea and constipation were common. Patients complained of sensations of spasm or blocking in various parts of the digestive tract and manual evacuation of feces was occasionally necessary. Diarrhea and/or vomiting might follow such symptoms and were experienced as disasters. Most striking was the "gap" between intake and evacuation. Once the food had disappeared, it no longer existed. Feces were dissociated from intake. Feces could be admired products, self-created, but spasm went with the fear that the "crime" would be discovered. The crime was concerned with the stealing and eating of the desired object.

3. *Learning difficulties.* Ambition was common to all and was based on the desire to be "somebody" rather than the "nobody" they felt without "recognition" from others. But learning difficulties led to failure or a result below their potential. Again, the stumbling block was partial or complete failure to take in the desired object. Wanting to be that knowledgeable "somebody" themselves, they did not register the information, yet it could come out later as their own discovery.

4. *Not being able to enjoy.* They all complained about not being able to enjoy anything or, if they did, something happened to spoil it. This is not so unusual, but the enjoyment of observed others was a torment to these patients, particularly loving couples. Only *one* could enjoy. If another enjoyed the same experience, the one felt robbed. Neither could they create anything, for the created took on a life of its own and so it was no longer "their thing." Having children felt like that.

5. *Reversal.* A number of defenses have been mentioned by other writers but the main one distinguishing the envious is that of reversal. The patient analyzes the analyst, who becomes the child who "makes a mess" of the mother-patient and is punished for this and kindred errors. In more anxious mood, the child-analyst is "spared," not bur-

dened with problems, by a kind mother-patient. Such patients often prepared their "work" beforehand, trying to think of all possible interpretations in order not to be humiliated and overcome by the "superior" wisdom of the analyst.

CASE ILLUSTRATION

Mrs. A has been chosen because she was the most afflicted of all. She showed all the symptoms and character traits previously described.

Mrs. A had had several "failed" therapists before coming to me, which she found hard to do as she now suffered from agoraphobia. One of these therapists, a man who had got too involved, recommended me. While with him, she had developed a "blocking spasm" in the bowel which was finally cured, after many specialists had "failed," by a nature-cure place where she was starved. She had now become afraid to eat as well as to go out.

Mrs. A was a handsome, well-fed looking, and powerfully charming woman of 50. She had married young into the upper class to get as far away as possible from her poor and disturbed home, which she never entered again. Both were flying under false colors at the time as gay and sophisticated people, but this front collapsed slowly after marriage. She became the "innocent" child with many mysterious symptoms and he a remote and vaguely depressed man with much guilt about both aggressive and erotic needs which he abjured in order to look after her. Her needs increased rather than diminished until she absorbed his life completely.

The previous treatments had not elicited the rage and despair which was consuming her, but her mother's decline and death, though it did not seem to touch her, coincided with physical attacks on her husband followed by crying fits in which she turned away from him. Her denigration of his efforts to help her increased until he could do nothing right. It was he who finally induced her to seek another therapist and she who hung back.

The mutually accepted story "which accounted for everything" was of a violent and sex-mad father who attacked the mother and terrorized the children. Mother was the pitied victim and "the angel of the neighborhood" though she had one flaw—she was a persistent shoplifter. The other children of which Mrs. A was the youngest had all "gone to the bad."

Mrs. A said she came because of a dream which had frightened her: *she had cut up an old man into small pieces and disposed of them utterly, but a woman neighbor got suspicious and called the police.*

She associated the old man with a doctor who had been kind to her in childhood. He had gently dressed an injured thumb and gave her chocolate afterwards. She was vaguely horrified that it was he. I had to be kind to her too—it worked wonders with her. She then told me how uncaring and cruel her parents had been about the injury. I thought, "So that's what happens to the helpers!"

On the third visit, she told me she could not remember what I looked like nor anything about the sessions. With a great effort, she had remembered coming in the first time, afraid. I had neither gone towards her nor retreated—I had just stood. The phrase "like an empty vessel waiting to be filled" occurred to her. This is what she did for a long time. She could hardly wait to get in and "get rid of it all." I must not move nor say anything, she said, for she dreaded my revenge.

Occasionally, I would repeat something she had said but it was strange to her: she really had got rid of it into me.

The story of her infancy was revealing. Mother had tried to abort her with "steel drops," then had nearly "dropped" her on the stairs because she wanted to finish her dinner. She had made her feed from an abscessed breast because the doctor told her it would draw the poison out. The "good" breast she felt she had never had was imagined as concurrently suckled by her sister though she was already weaned. My interventions were like the cruel steel drops and she felt I only cared about "feeding" myself and had no time for her. She also felt that I used her to get rid of my own poisonous problems, which I forced her to take to do me good, and that I kept the good me to give to others.

Such spoiling attacks were Mrs. A's expression and defense against the image of the envied analyst-mother whom she felt she could never match, and which persecuted her. This she felt about her own mother, particularly in her role as food provider. Mother was an "instinctive" cook, producing marvelous meals which, however, they all had to eat whether they felt like it or not, or they "hurt" her. Mrs. A had become a *cordon bleu* cook in rivalry with her but was much too frightened to do without a recipe. She dared not be creative in case something went wrong for then she could not contain her rage and tears of humiliation.

The eyes as devouring organs are a well-known metaphor but their equation with breasts is not so evident. Eye contact during breast feeding is, however, an observed phenomenon (Gough, 1962), and their confusion would not be surprising. When I recognized this as a feature of primary envy, it was easier to understand certain material. With reference to Mrs. A's difficulty of retaining a good image, she phoned one day highly disturbed because she had had a dream in which she was gouging my eyes out. This reminded her of mother who had worn an eyeshade after a blood vessel burst behind one eye. It linked with the bursting abscess on her breast. Both eye and breast were imagined as "pools of blood" and she was expecting mine or hers to follow suit at any minute. Such fantasies lie behind the need for a smiling image and the panic when it starts to fade.

A year later, she dreamt she was telling a mother with a small girl the way to the eye hospital, but it was the girl she drew aside to tell. The telling involved several changes of underground trains. The girl got very excited and said it was the first time she had been told. Mrs. A said, "but mother must know." She was then telling the mother who apparently did not. Mrs. A's first association was to her several changes of therapists. It seemed that she both hoped that I knew the way to cure her and yet still wanted to prove that she knew and I did not. The girl's excitement meant to her sexual excitement which mother said drove you mad as it had father. It seemed to me that some realization was dawning of the need to repair a damaged view of the mother-child relationship, but she was still fearing the envious excitement of a restored eye-breast would be "too much" for her, as indeed it would if it had its original perfection.

Much later, when resistance to examining the damage to relationships was breaking down, Mrs. A dreamt that her glasses had a clear lens in the right eye and a rose-tinted one in the other so that the two eyes had difficulty in working together. The right eye hurt with all that harsh white light coming in. She equated the right eye with "reality" and the left with "fantasy." I suggested that the two lenses represented the difficulty we had in working together, as she felt my view was harsh and spoilt her hopes of ever attaining the rosy dream breast which, from other material, was an ever-flowing one at her command.

Mrs. A then told me that she actually wore pink-tinted glasses when she went out in bright weather. She so often felt she could "kill everybody" she saw walking about and enjoying themselves in the sun and the glasses hid her anger and her tears. When I said it also protected her from retaliation, she replied, "How could they envy me? I have nothing." The harsh white light meant to her interrogation and torture of innocent suspects, who were made to admit to crimes they had not committed.

A later vignette of the problem was of how Mrs. A shared mother's envious excitement in stealing from shops but with the mounting dread of being seen and caught with the goods, which spoilt it for her. What she envied most was the mother's guiltless enjoyment, which she felt was at her expense. The filled-up shopping bag was referred back to the devouring breast image ruthlessly incorporating its own creation.

Reversing the roles became the unconscious aim, but Mrs. A could only succeed under the cloak of illness because of the dread of retaliation. Hence the need to defeat the helper, for if she failed in this, she felt as if she would have to admit she had stolen the good breast and devoured it utterly so that no trace remained.

DISCUSSION

I agree with Rosenthall (1963), the only Jungian who appears to have written on envy, that the envious are fascinated by the archetype of the phallic mother, a bisexual figure which "has everything" and is characterized particularly by the capacity for orgiastic excitement. He remarks that its character is oral and that the breast-penis equation of Klein is one image of it though bodily experiences of all kinds enter into it. These other experiences I have tried to define more clearly and have shown how they form a continuum with the primary breast experience.

Jung's extensive work (1912) on the dual mother and the hero-ego's battle for deliverance is its mythological expression, as well as Neumann's *The great mother* (1955) in her archaic form as the maternal uroboros, both male and female, creative and devouring, though he, as does Jung, has a womb image. This duality, which is a feature of envious patients and with which they are driven to attempt to deal by splitting, though unsuccessfully, led Klein (1957) to assume that "Excessive envy, an expression of destructive impulses, interferes with the primal split between the good and bad breast." Without this primal split, she says, integration cannot take place as it is based on a "strongly rooted good object" (p. 24). Of this good object, Rosenthall says:

> "it becomes the fascinating and compulsive centre of a psychic universe round which [the patient] unceasingly revolves. If he approaches it he will destroy it or spoil it. . . . But his impulses to possess, devour and incorporate it, remain. . . . Ultimately, the envied object, fascinating, numinous and perfect, becomes, by enantiodromia, dead, malevolent, and persecuting. Then he pours hatred on it, tries to deny, kill it, blot it out, to poison it and deliver it from the earth and from his awareness."

Judging by my material, particularly clear in eye-breast disturbances, enantiodromia is not quite the concept to describe the change. In spite of the apparent split, with the "good" being projected, I believe the vision is essentially a confused one, as in the experience of a persecutory *good* object, and of *painful* excitement. Fordham's work (1957) on ego-development may help here if we presume that the joint parents or the penis-breast is an archaic image of the totality of the self. He supposes that certain pathological states are occasioned by the ego not being sufficiently separated from the self when it is deintegrating. This would result in disintegration of the ego instead of integration. Mrs. A's envious rage might be seen as having this effect. She came to the point of saying, "I can't afford this anger—it's tearing me to bits."

Laing (1961) describes the relationships of the envious patient beautifully: "To make a difference to the other, in the sense of making some impression or dent in a brick wall, becomes his greatest triumph. To allow the other to feel that he or she makes any difference to him in the same sense, becomes his greatest defeat" (p. 73). I often felt that Mrs. A was made of impenetrable material and that my words bounced off the surface, but she was really so permeable that she had to catch the missiles (for that is what they seemed to her), and throw them back hard. If she was dented, she demonstrated my cruelty by showing me the wounds I had inflicted. Laing goes on to say: "Others . . . see that if they give him [the envious one] love he will spurn it (if he feels he is being given anything) or he will despise it (if he feels that the other is dependent on him for receiving anything)" (p. 73).

Marion Milner (1969) comments on this attitude "as having its roots in a defense against the agonies of recognizing dependence on an excruciatingly tantalizing kind of external goodness" (p. 256). She also arrived at the eye-breast equation. Interpreting a drawing which could be of breasts with the nipples cut off or empty eye-sockets, she comments, "it is surely these mutilated breast-eyes in her inner world which make her feel, everywhere she goes, that people are staring at her accusingly" (p. 50). Mrs. A had defended herself against this conclusion.

I learnt that all the things Mrs. A demanded were what she could not endure—kindness, meaning special consideration, explanation, and reassurance. They were "too much" for her and fanned the envious hatred. Laing's explanation of this state comes in his earlier book, *The divided self* (1960). "The abundance *there* is longed for, in contrast to the emptiness *here*; yet participation without loss of being is felt to be impossible. . . . His longing is for complete union . . . but . . . it will be the end of his self. . . . He does not conceive of a dialectical relationship" (p. 97). At these times, Mrs. A felt that only one could survive, and it was going to be her.

Paradoxically, silence, or an absence of response, was intolerable to her. Such patients need to be acknowledged as existing but only in response to *their* initiative. The initiative of the therapist tends to blot them out and sets up furious defenses. Of this Laing (1961) says: "The other who is felt to be unresponsive or impervious to the self-as-agent, and is *in fact* unresponsive, tends to induce by this imperviousness a sense of emptiness and impotence in the self" (p. 72). Mrs. A emptied herself into me while dreading any movement on my part, but passivity was a confirmation of the destructiveness of her hate and of her need. A *lively* receptivity was necessary, with responses of a nature which called for a reply; in other words, a model for a dialectical relationship.

Countertransference affects are likely to be strong in such cases. For instance, I caught myself hating her for "spoiling" my initiative; for trying to force me to admit some monstrous intention from imperceptible clues. At the same time, I found myself envying her for "having everything" as it seemed, which I had not. I also realized a passing feeling of triumph that I had got this material from her, stolen it, as it were, when she was not looking and was the richer for it.

Using these feelings to understand the patient, I could see that her initiative, her approach to the breast, had been constantly negated by a mother who "knew best" and pleased herself, so robbing her of that natural feeling Winnicott (1951) presumes infants have of "creating" the breast (p. 238f). To Mrs. A, the breast was a thrusting and smothering thing which was forced on her. Her monstrous intention was to chew up and devour once and for all this too good and powerful breast which bore down on her; that in fantasy she had done just this as in the presenting dream, and was afraid the police would find it in her feces, hence the "blocks" and denials that she had anything. Her obvious well-being in spite of all the dreadful complaints showed that she had the "good" me breast secreted inside her, only I must not know in case I stopped the supplies angrily and she would die. After she admitted this spontaneously, mourning for the dead and the lost opportunities of relationship could proceed.

REFERENCES

ABRAHAM, K. (1924). "The influence of oral eroticism on character formation," in *Selected papers on psychoanalysis*. London, Hogarth, 1927.

FORDHAM, M. (1957). *New developments in analytical psychology*. London, Routledge.

GOUGH, D. (1962). "The visual behaviour of infants in the first few weeks of life," *Proc. R. Soc. Med.*, **55**, 4.

JOFFE, W. G. (1962). "A critical review of the status of the envy concept," *Int. J. Psycho-Anal.*, 50, 4.

JUNG, C. G. (1910–11). "On the significance of number dreams," in *Coll. Wks.*, 4.

—— (1912). *Symbols of transformation. Coll. Wks.* 5.

—— (1950). Foreword to "The I Ching or Book of Changes," in *Coll. Wks.*, 11.

NEUMANN, E. (1955). *The great mother.* New York, Pantheon/Bollingen; London, Routledge.

KLEIN, M. (1932). *The psycho-analysis of children.* London, Hogarth.

—— (1957). *Envy and gratitude.* London, Tavistock.

LAING, R. D. (1960). *The divided self.* London, Tavistock.

—— (1961). *The self and others.* New York, Pantheon; London, Tavistock.

MILNER, M. (1969). *The hands of the living God.* London, Hogarth.

ROSENTHALL, M. (1963). "Notes on envy and the contrasexual archetype," *J. analyt. Psychol.*, 8, 1.

SCHOECK, H. (1966). *Envy.* London, Secker & Warburg.

WINNICOTT, D. W. (1951). "Transitional objects and transitional phenomena" in *Collected papers.* London, Tavistock.

9

Mandala Symbols and
The Individuation Process

J. W. T. REDFEARN, *London*

In this paper I shall discuss some mandalas painted by a patient of mine. When she painted them she was usually in a state of feeling which although good and helpful involved a certain amount of denial. These good states alternated with bad moods which were associated with strong sadistic impulses. The mandalas manifested these sadistic features but in the form of opposites. I should like to present this material in the light of the contention of the psychoanalyst Clifford Scott (1949), who said, "When Jungians deal with mandala symbols, and when Freudians speak of early stages of ego development, they are both dealing with the same material."

I first wish to explain very briefly my viewpoint regarding tetradic symbolism and the *temenos,* as this influences how I deal with mandalas in my clinical work.

I have no doubts about the universal occurrence and significance of tetrads, but I doubt whether tetrads invariably refer to Jung's four functions. The human mind has a predilection for tetrads, and I think this may explain Jung's schema. However, I do not think Jung's schema always explains tetrads.

The attempt by Marshall (1968) to find correspondence between Jung's functions and some of the factors extracted by Cattell from his batteries of tests was not very successful, and suggests that the four functions are not a major source of variance in peoples' motivation, performance, or outlook.

On the other hand, I am impressed by the sensitive and productive use made of the concept by clinicians such as Baudouin (1957) and Aigrisse (1962). The clinical finding of a rotation of conscious attitude seems to me impressive evidence, although I have never seen a case myself where the rotation was clearly a rotation of the four Jungian functions.

The mutually inhibitory properties of thinking and feeling, sensation and intuition, rational and irrational, subject-orientation and object-orientation, are of course matters of everyday clinical fact. These and many other pairs of opposites may be of great importance in particular cases. So I would not like to be without Jung's "compass," as he used to regard his tetradic schemata. But having a compass, or having to have a compass, is itself only one member of a pair of opposites. The need for orientation, order, or harmony is acute at times, particularly when chaos or disastrous acting-out threaten. The literary critic R. P. Blackmur (1951; quoted by Chouinard, 1971) noticed that in literature, "the more the behavior presses in the more order must be found to take care of it," and this observation expresses the most important feature of tetradic symbols. Jung's theory of the four functions was developed at a time when chaotic psychotic forces were threatening him. Symbols of order and wholeness may play a vital and positive role in an analysis and in the process of individuation, and did in the case I shall describe. They correspond, I often find, with undifferentiated emergent feelings of good mental and bodily states which have aspects of denial and defensiveness as well as aspects of hope, salvation, or independence.

The *feeling* of wholeness, integrity, totality, etc., is very different from the individual's *functioning* as a whole or with his various functions working in harmony. It can be disastrous to confuse such feelings or experiences with individuation.

Turning now to the *temenos* aspect of the mandala, we can I think all agree that a *temenos* of some kind is created when an unconscious element is to be integrated. At least a feeling of safety or security is necessary. The *temenos* may provide this feeling, or it may simply represent it. In other words, the *temenos* indicates a wish for or a feeling of protection. The fact that the wish is possible may be of vital clinical import, but often the pathetic vulnerability of the person having the experience, for example under LSD, is only too obvious to the outside observer.

The feeling of security necessary for the integration of split-off unconscious elements is no doubt provided originally in the child's experience of the holding functions of the mother and the development of the necessary trust so that play and symbolic mental activity become possible. The analytical situation may of course provide such a *temenos*. The circle may represent it and in this case is a mental representation of a hope of safety from eruptive, disruptive, and invasive threats, and of an intact surface and boundary of the self-image. If it occurs during phases of elation, as often is the case, it has aspects of denial and magic, and it is important for the analyst not to be seduced by such material into sharing the patient's inflation. As the same time the precious, personal, and loving-gift nature of such material in the analysis must be fully realized; therefore, the analyst's handling of mandalas and related phenomena in the transference is to my mind of the utmost importance in determining the outcome and duration of an analysis. Interpretation on a purely mythological level, and failure to make links with the transference impulses, bodily feelings, and defenses of the patient would result in an outcome very different from that which is aimed at by London analysts.

The London group may possibly err on the side of skepticism and humor when presented with this sort of material.

I know one London analyst whose patient presented him with a beautiful golden spherical mandala with trumpets radiating from it. The analyst simply said, "That is your timidity." This was true, but it was perhaps too brutal to be taken as typical of the London School as a whole.

To illustrate what I have said I should like now to present some paintings and drawings from a patient who was in her mid-forties at the beginning of analysis. She is very intelligent and is married to a successful civil servant also in analysis. As their children grew up her feelings of support towards her husband's career were replaced by feelings of envy. She resented many homely tasks, withdrew into a self-sufficient shell, and became at times irritable and contemptuous towards her husband. During the first eighteen months of analysis she became more aware of the violent feelings inside herself. In particular, she had voracious and sadistic impulses, in the analytical sessions, towards me.

She began to have horrifying sadistic dreams. In one *a woman and three men were stalking each others in a wood. In order to get out of the wood each had to kill the others—or two had to kill the other two. Then she saw the woman alone, with a man's severed head on the ground. The woman stamped on it and it cracked and squelched.*

She associated the stamping on the head with her sarcastic contempt and irritability at her husband's verbosity. On waking from this dream she had a visual image (Picture 1) of a wavy white band across the middle of the picture, with red suns or explosions equidistant above and below. A peaceful feeling came over her. She said, "It is curious, because the sun things were on their way out of the picture." Then she reverted to talking about stamping on the man's head.

I suggested that she paint the image, and when she brought it along the next time, she said these comets or suns seemed to contain great energy and were whirling around. The line reminded her of a river between green banks, but it was dead—a river of oblivion. It was a picture of primeval innocence, and this reminded her of the four primeval people in the wood. Thus her associations with the picture led back straight to the dream, just as the vision occurred on waking from the dream. This strongly suggests an important relationship between the peaceful feeling of the picture and the sadistic dream.

During the ensuing months more work was done on her sadistic and envious feelings, particularly in the transference. She started a course of study for professional work, but became physically ill. Analysis was interrupted by hospitalization and was affected afterwards by the drugs necessary for her illness. After a period of apathy, however, there was progress in her ability to experience good feelings with me. Increasingly these survived periods of separation. The voracious and greedy impulses were gradually replaced by wishes to be held by me, and on occasions she held my hand and felt full and satisfied. When she was filled with such feelings she would try to preserve them by means of mental tricks, or try to recapture them the next time she came, but these attempts always failed and gave way to desolate emptiness. By this time she was able to experience the feelings outside the analysis, however, and there was a feeling of transformation of herself which was reflected both in an improvement of her physical health and in the production of the first paintings since Picture 1, four and a half years previously. She dreamt of *workmen under her husband's supervision opening up pools of water from an underground lake. There was danger.*

Picture 2 represents the underground lake with two holes out of which a black fountain and a fountain of water issue. The whole scene is colorful, with a "stately pleasure-dome" which reminds us of the comet and its tail of Picture 1. I wonder if the suns going out of that picture somehow foretold her ensuing years of illness and depression. The white line of Picture 1, the firmament, is still present, but the unconscious forces have now been activated—both good and bad products being allowed to emerge in a controlled way. She wanted to paint the opening-up, expanding feeling of the fountain in more detail, and Picture 3 resulted. The fountain becomes an unfolding flower whose stamens became to her surprise the jaws of a crocodile. Here is clear indication of the bodily impulses of biting or tearing contained in the emerging unconscious contents.

A few hours after painting this she felt very jealous and went out while her husband was being charming to others. In this mood she painted Picture 4.

Here the underground waters are still, the rocks have become dead church architecture, and the pleasure dome an empty, black, toothed disc. That night she had the most horrifying dream of all, of *a little girl stabbing her mother repeatedly in the face. The mother's face became an empty skull.*

Thus the fountains, the flower motif, and the toothed circle are associated with sadistic impulses triggered by feelings of being left out or abandoned.

There followed various pictures of stabbing whose horror made her sick. A few days later she brought along Picture 5, which had come to her as a desire to represent opposites combining with the generation of immense blinding energy at the center. It was the center which was the important part for her. She had the feeling of everything having come together inside her. But she also had the insight to say that in a way it was a new sort of protective shell which she verbalized as "You don't have to worry about his snoring because you are whole." She said the feeling was brought about because I had seemed to value her opinion of a mutual acquaintance.

In this picture the rigidity and the teeth are again worth noticing.

She next became preoccupied with infantile blissful feelings, and with the theme of giving and receiving with the hands. In one of her pictures, to her surprise, a large breast appeared (Picture 6).

The hands she drew were always misshapen. She said, "These fingers should be claws." This led me to suggest that there were aggressive impulses in her hands which were being blocked off. She was upset at the idea, but realized she wanted to tear something down before she could be ready to receive. She painted Picture 7, which showed an overturned vessel of milk and a lion clawing at a wall of flesh and producing a stream of blood which mixes with the milk for a cat to drink. The cat is surrounded by a halo, and represented a combination of opposites. The lion reminded her of the girl who stabbed her mother in the dream.

There now followed a series of paintings that involved entwining, giving, and receiving which culminated in a peacock mandala.

One day she remarked how undifferentiated were the good feelings associated with her analysis, and how removed they were from everyday down-to-earth reality and her feelings towards her husband. She felt that I was very skeptical about her having anything good to give to others. Some of these feelings she expressed in her next painting (Picture 8).

The drawing represents four trees with intertwining branches which point inwards. The "rather inadequate roots" are outside, and she felt that was wrong. The branches going through the trunks reminded her of holes in bodies in surrealist paintings and sculptures and of her difficulties in containing her sexual feelings.

I asked her to imagine what the center was like. She said it was not structured, but was very soft, warm, gooey, and delicious. As she said this she felt soft, warm, delicious feelings spreading from between her breasts all over her body. She described them as of a pinky brown color. In view of the wrongness she felt about the tree roots and her doubts about my confidence in her ability to give, I felt it appropriate to point out that there was an obvious food pathway from the center to the "nipples" outside. It will be remembered that she saw the nipples as "rather inadequate roots." She was grateful for this view, which she felt came just at the right time. The feeling of well-being brought about by the spread of pinky-brown feelings over her body survived the weekend's separation, and during this time she painted Picture 9, which was an attempt to elaborate on the flowing sensations spreading from the solar plexus region, schematically the center of the body. The same theme was painted in Picture 10, showing the warm feelings spreading from the center. The pink color is intensified in the form of a cross. Each tree has three branches, two of which intertwine; each central branch subdivides into three twigs, each twig bears three blossoms, and each flower has three stamens, recalling the crocodile flower of the earlier painting. She had the idea also of doing a painting of people in threes being linked through their solar plexuses.

In addition to the overt positive content of this painting it is clear in view of later paintings and development that suffering due to oedipal-based triangular jealousies was being denied, and needed to be felt and worked through during the next months.

This mandala was of course done specially for me, and during the session in which she brought it I did not show sufficient appreciation of this fact. The next session was a moving one for both of us when I admitted this and the feelings of mutuality were restored.

The next crayon drawing (Picture 11) was to celebrate and record these restored good feelings and was meant to express feelings of swirling and combing.

The next weekend was a momentous one for personal reasons; during it, her jealousy of her husband and his other interests and relationships hit her with full force.

While discussing these matters with me she felt opened up vertically down the middle of her body, and also horizontally, thus forming a cross. She had had a dream of this being done in a surgical operation a year after the beginning of analysis.

Her feeling after this session is expressed in Picture 12.

She felt for a time as if she were crawling on the ground—very sensitive, with exposed nerve-endings, yet somehow held and sustained and more alive than ever before. She said she would not like to go back to her previous half-life. At about this time she brought me a Christmas present, a spherical brown and white paperweight made of alabaster. I now felt able to express uneasiness at the munificence of this gift without hurting her feelings unduly. She said she owed me "too much." This was partly connected with her paying me smaller fees than her husband pays his analyst. We discussed this once again and I pointed out the main directions in which her sadism was deflected from me on to others, particularly her husband. We also discussed the tendency of gifts to turn bad if rejected, and talked again about the loving aspect of her sadism, in particular of her anal sadism. The brown color as well as the white in the gift has significance, of course. I also pointed out the real therapeutic effect of some of her sadistic attacks on her husband.

The Christmas break enabled us to analyze further her feelings of emptiness. They were experienced as being surrounded by emptiness, or engulfed by a vortex or pit. The sadistic impulses erupt from this pit of emptiness like lava from a volcano.

The feelings of void were depicted in Picture 13, about which she remarked "The baby is nonexistent. It is not an entity. It is not being held right. There is a feeling of wanting to be held but there is nothing there." This feeling possibly describes her actual experience with her mother. As she painted Picture 13 she experienced the warm, pink feelings and the baby seemed to begin to come to life. (Cf. Picture 14.)

The engulfing void may also be linked with swallowing impulses projected on to the environment. Picture 15, which is another attempt to depict the void, shows the vortex as an open mouth with rosebud lips tipped with black nipples.

The kind of material I have presented is of course familiar to all Jungian analysts, but I should like to stress the following points, which I think are indispensible for success as I understand success.

1. The close link between archetypal content and actual bodily feelings and changes.

2. The close link between the material, the transferences, and the way the material is handled by the analyst.

3. The need for much intensive analytical work and reliable behavior on the part of the analyst before the break-through designated by some as the attainment of the symbolic attitude, in cases where there has been a serious deficiency in early mothering.

4. The need for the defensive aspect of mandalas to be recognized and interpreted. The defenses against "pregenital" impulses were very apparent in the mandalas I have presented.

5. As the patient takes personal responsibility in connection with these archetypal forces and their relationship with his or her own body, the rigid, defensive, formal mandala may be replaced by more direct expressions of body parts, bodily relationships, and feeling states. This may correspond with a dissolution of the persona and the abandonment of long-standing character defenses.

In this analysis there were further cycles of mandala activity. I hope I have presented enough material to illustrate the close relationship between the mandalas and pregenital ego-defenses and fixations— sadistic impulses and their denial.

Success in analysis, in my opinion, has to do with the attainment of natural and well integrated functioning, rather than the attainment of any particular mental state. In a successfully proceeding analysis it is possible to demonstrate

(a) the resolution of oedipal and pregenital conflicts;

(b) the dissolution of the persona, the integration of the shadow, and the emergence of the self;

(c) the dissolution of character defenses and their physiological components.

At the period to which I am referring, this patient's analysis could not be called a success, in that there was still much envy and possessiveness to work through. The period of mandala activity, however, marked a big step in the right direction and involved what I regard as the essential ingredients of success in analysis:

a) separation from parental imagos and the achievement of greater autonomy, without detachment from others;

(b) integration of archetypal, previously unconscious impulses, with their bodily and mental components (this involved the abandonment of the ego-centered attitude);

(c) improvement in physiological functioning, achievement of bodily awareness, body-mind unity, and the synesthetic, symbolic attitude.

REFERENCES

AIGRISSE, G. (1962). "Character re-education and professional re-adaptation of a man aged forty-five," *J. analyt. psychol.* **7**, 95–118.

BAUDOUIN, C. (1957). *Decouverte de la personne.* Neuchâtel, Messeiller.

BLACKMUR, R. P. (1951). "Unappeasable and Peregrine," in *Form and value in modern poetry.* New York, Doubleday.

CHOUINARD, T. (1971). "Eliot's 'œuvre,' Bradley's 'finite centres,' and Jung's anima concept," *J. analyt. psychol.* **16**, 48–68.

MARSHALL, I. N. (1968). "The four functions: a conceptual analysis," *J. analyt. psychol.* **13**, 1–32.

REDFEARN, J. W. T. (1970). "Bodily experience in psychotherapy," *Brit. J. med. psychol.* **43**, 301–312.

SCOTT, W. C. M. (1949). "The psycho-analytic view of mandala symbols," *Brit. J. med. psychol.* **22**, 23–25.

SPITZ, R. A. (1965). *The first year of life.* New York, International Universities Press.

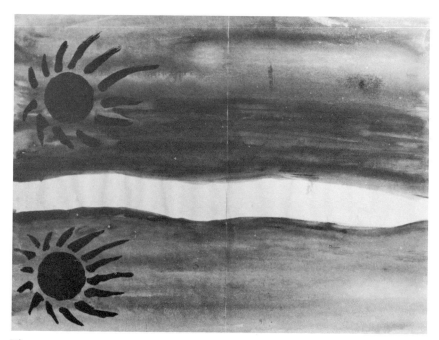

Picture 1

Picture 2

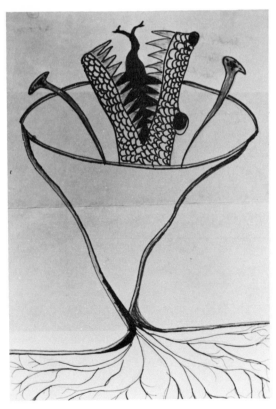

Picture 3

Picture 4

5.10.70

Picture 5

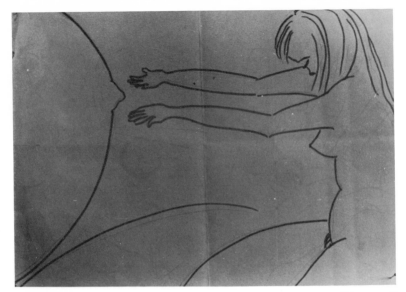

Picture 6

Picture 7

Picture 8

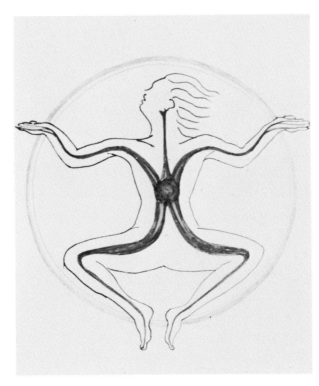

Picture 9

Picture 10

Picture 11

Picture 12

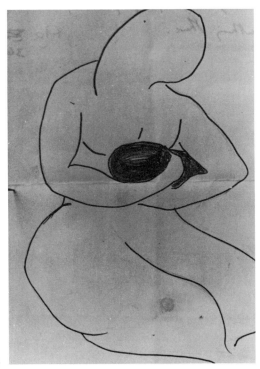

Picture 13

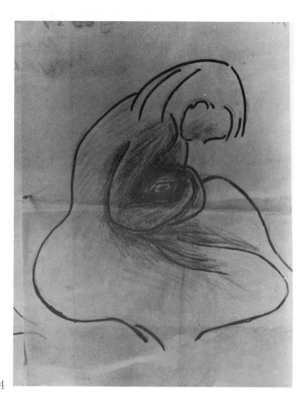

Picture 14

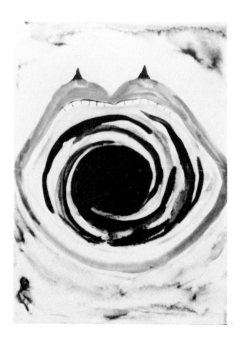

Picture 15

10

What We May Expect of Acute Schizophrenia

JOHN WEIR PERRY, *San Francisco*

During the past decade there has been a trend in psychiatry to consider certain acute schizophrenic episodes as representing not a "mental disease" or "disorder" but a "developmental crisis." This psychosis can be a turbulent "reorganizational process" (Sullivan, 1962) involving an "altered state of consciousness" or "high arousal state" (Fischer, 1971). Even psychoanalytic theory is being adapted to accommodate itself to a concept of psychosis as a "growth experience" (Bowers, 1971; Jackson and Watzlawick, 1963). In the same vein, the diagnostic labelling of schizophrenia is being found to have detrimental effects upon individuals undergoing this crisis, increasing their sense of isolation and disqualification as "abnormal," thereby contributing to their feeling of being "crazy" (Sheff, 1966; Balint, 1957).

In his early work Jung gave clear recognition to the healing potential in the psychotic process and its contents. In 1914 he wrote, "These corrective impulses or compensations which now break through into the conscious mind should really be the beginning of a healing process, because through them the previously isolated attitude ought to be relieved. But in reality this does not happen, for the reason that the unconscious corrective impulses which succeed in making themselves perceptible to the conscious mind do so in a form that is altogether unacceptable to it" (Jung, 1960, par. 458).

In my own experiences of therapy with acute psychotic episodes and by formulations of them, I have found among the various schizophrenias an archetypal process that may be called the "renewal syndrome" (Perry, 1962, 1971). It consists of a profound reorganization of the self, and it has parallels in the rites of the archaic sacral kingship, especially in the ancient New Year Festivals of renewal of the king and kingdom, and of the year and the cosmos (Perry, 1966b).

Following Jung's lead, I think this acute psychotic episode in the form of the renewal process can be viewed as nature's attempt to heal a pathological situation that had prevailed in the prepsychotic personality. In this case, we should think of the "psychopathology" as existing not in the psychotic turmoil itself, but in the prepsychotic state which occasioned the need for so drastic a reorganization of the psyche. Then again, if the acute renewal process turns out for some reason to become abortive in its efforts at reordering the self, it may run into a chronic course and again be termed pathological.

How successful the reorganizational process turns out to be may depend very much upon how it is regarded and handled by those around the patient. If it falls under a psychiatric condemnation as only an illness to be stamped out or controlled by medication, the patient comes to feel himself to be in a "wrong" state that is, so to speak, illegitimate, and then he becomes inclined both to feel and to act crazy. If, on the other hand, the process is held in higher esteem as a turbulent inner journey of some worth, the patient at once feels relieved of the burden of craziness, less isolated, and more able to communicate coherently.

These comments are not made merely of theoretical beliefs about the nature of the acute episode, but rather are the outcome of actual observation, first of my own individual cases in hospital during the 1950's, and then of cases in our current "Agnews Project" in a state hospital, which has been going on during the past two years. This involves an experimental ward of 25 beds, in which a research design seeks to differentiate those who do best without phenothiazine medication and those who do best with it. The milieu is designed to convey to the patient that the psychotic process is of some value, and the staff are trained to handle crises by relating to the patient's needs rather than by controlling his behavior.

In the handling of the acute episode, Ronald Laing's model seems to be built on non-interference on the part of the attendant staff, by setting up a permissive and non-intrusive emotional ambiance for the patient, in which the occurrence of an inner journey is given general respect but not specific attention (Laing, 1967). This seems to me not enough.

I have the impression instead that the inner journey or renewal process tends to remain scattered, fragmented, and incoherent until the point where the individual begins to open up to another person enough to entrust to him his unfolding inner experience. When this happens, the content of his symbolic experience becomes intensified, and thereupon apparently moves ahead in a progressive fashion toward its conclusion. It is often surprising how "psychotic" and yet at the same time coherent the patient's communication can be, providing he feels related to the therapist.

I also have the impression that it is not enough merely to hear the inner experiences of the patient; at certain junctures at least, he needs to be helped to grasp their meaning for his life. As I see it, the archetypal ideation and imagery in the process belong properly to the affect. The images actually turn out to be descriptive of the meaning of the emotional issues in which the patient is entangled, though he is withdrawn from them and is not paying due heed to them. Often enough in the course of interviews with such patients one finds weighty personal problems lurking behind the guise of rather abstruse symbolic talk, giving the impression that such conflicts would not have been revealed at all if one had not probed into the personal associations around the more impersonal symbolic imagery.

For example, an unmarried male Catholic in his early thirties, who was in a profound schizophrenic turbulence, drew diagrams of his journey into death and the underworld and of his rebirth from them, calling them the "four degrees of initiation." In the final one he focused upon a circle that contained an upper white dot and a lower black dot, with a line joining them. He said that the line represented a passage up and down between the head and the heart, the two dots. This, he said, is where his conflict really lay. The upper pole represented the spiritual and the lower one the carnal life. He felt torn between two callings: to be a priest and celibate, and thus a spiritual father, or to be an engineer and to be married, and thus a family father. These were not vague ideals, for he had in fact had several years of Jesuit schooling toward the priesthood, and also had trained and qualified as an engineer. He was a devotee of Our Lady of Fatima, but was also inclined to fall in love, though the romances were disappointing since he tended to be shy and to worship from afar. There had been no other avenue into his personal problems until this moment, and now we were free to discuss some of the major issues of his life in a meaningful way with considerable play of feeling.

Another instance is a married man in his early twenties who was one of the most disruptive patients I ever worked with on the ward. He drew a colorful picture of a cowboy while humming a Western ditty. I assumed he might well by playing with me, but nonetheless I tried to get his associations to the drawing. In the course of a rambling conversation it came out that his grandfather had been such a cowboy—— a blustering, boisterous, swashbuckling character who had died in a barroom brawl at 22, the patient's current age. It was clear that he had identified with this lovable, colorful, roistering personality. The cowboy's son, the patient's father, never knew him except as a legend, and had gone to such lengths to live down his myth that he had become a very conventional-minded policeman—that is, a "law-man," as the classical counterpart of the disruptive cowboy. The drawing then represented the father's father-complex, a repudiated mode of being that was then delegated to the son. In further drawings of this ideation, the grandfather figure went through a death process in an image identical with the dead Osiris (the deceased king and thus the grandfather figure of the realm of Egypt) (Perry, 1966a). The pertinence of the role this image played came into view through a drawing of the marriage of the sun and the moon, labelled "life on the farm." The associations brought to light the painful problem that had precipitated the psychosis: He felt engulfed in his wife's Italian-style city clan, which felt alien to his Dutch heritage. This massive clan backing gave her an unwarranted strength, making him feel devoured and unmanned. The grandfather image was his symbol of manly self-assertion, and his proposed solution to the city-dwelling clan problem was to withdraw into a serene and isolated life in the country where he could feel himself master of his household once more.

To take one more illustration, a young married woman of Mexican descent was engrossed in an array of delusional fantasies about being Queen of the Aztecs. As the great Emperor of the Aztecs her grandfather was seen as maintaining a tyrannical regime, while his four sons, her uncles, were conducting a revolution to overthrow the old man. They would abolish this monolithic dictatorship and partition the realm between them into four equal parts. Unfortunately she was not one to draw diagrams, but the implication was obvious enough that the old emperor was the ruler occupying the center of the realm, and that when the uncles took over, the realm was to be quadrated into equal segments; the mandala-like imagery is there. Also, the theme of the democratizing of the kingship is present (Perry, 1966b), for the uncles were to establish reformed kingdoms that would emphasize fair government, equality, and tolerance. It was not hard to make the transition from this mythlike imagery of kingship and its democratization to the more personal context to which it belonged. This concerned the maternal grandfather, and with a minimum of encouragement the patient began to describe the mother's own tyrannical ways. Soon she was giving a character sketch of the typical controlling and suppressive traits of the "schizophrenogenic mother." The image of the emperor is then identifiable as the mother's father-complex, which colored her dominating animus. Only with the overthrow of this heavy pressure from the experience of her mother would the patient be liberated and could grow into her own way of life.

There are many more instances in my experience with schizophrenic episodes. In all these cases there have been significant junctures when it became apparent to the therapist just how an affective concern is being expressed in symbolic imagery. I like to call them "moments of realization," for at these points the impersonal symbolic image is recognized as having direct reference to a personal emotional issue. When the therapist conveys this recognition to the patient, there is usually a dramatic release of the emotion concerned and an insight into its import. In other words, the affect that is so disrupted in the schizophrenic state becomes restored to its proper context by way of the play of symbolic images in the process. In this regard I have found it helpful, in training ward staff for this kind of therapy in depth, to speak of the archetypal theme as an "affect-image," a term that describes exactly what it is.

However, I have no intention of making this kind of therapy sound like a joy ride by citing these moments of realization. I am only pointing out what I take to be the ideal aim in therapy—to discover the personal context of each impersonal affect-image. I believe it is always there, if we but knew how to bring it to light. But I am reminded by the title of this conference that we are speaking of success and failure in these efforts.

The acute episode consists of an active, absorbing, onward moving symbolic process of renewal, into which the individual is deeply withdrawn; he is held in its grip for a period of six weeks or so. The subliminal process, having usually reached its culmination and goal by this time, releases its overwhelming hold on the patient's attention. With the waning of the acute phase, the period that follows should ideally be a time of assimilating the inner experience and relating it to life. It is often the case, however, that the individual feels demoralized and estranged by his inner experience, and then proceeds to bring into play inappropriately what he has found there. He may be inclined to use it to produce effects upon other people, as a kind of pseudo-relating, or else to spin a veil of confusion behind which he may withdraw. That is, he may make use of the material of the process either to involve or to distance other persons in a primitive mode of relating. In brief, what has been an intensely absorbing intrapersonal experience is now turned to interpersonal use, largely in the form of "playing games" with it. He has learned to play the role of craziness and may them become a chronic "case"—that abortive outcome of the inner process which is all too familiar to those of us who have worked in hospitals and clinics. Watching the process lead into disintegration instead of renewal is an experience of considerable distress for the therapist. He must then throw in all his weight against these defensive tendencies, and must open himself emotionally to further depths of involvement with the patient, in order to turn the trend toward integrative movement within the transference.

But when the outcome of the acute phase is favorable, it seems that there needs to be a period of assimilation of the fruits of the process. Here the task may be partly that of discovering the sense of the symbolic journey, in order that the inner world of meaning recently opened up may be brought to bear upon the broadening of the scope of awareness. All too often one sees the other thing happening: all the wisdom that had made itself evident in the psychotic state becomes closed over and lost upon "recovery."

Even more important than the task of assimilating meaning is that of learning how to live the newly recovered affective life. Affect and image must each receive its due. In this regard, our expectations of what it is to be "normally" adapted to a "normal," conventional, average society must be loosened considerably. Persons who become drawn into this renewal syndrome are characteristically of an unusually sensitive nature, and for them the hurtful emotional surroundings in their upbringing have been unusually damaging. They equate conventional adaptation with the stifling effect of their parents' attitudes which had been so disturbing to their emotional growth. Therefore, as they emerge out of their distrust of relationships and their fear of emotions, they express a justifiable preference for a way of life that emphasizes honest expression of feeling and honest living according to one's own values. The style of living then becomes one of their own making, and they express an abhorrence of the conventional models and goals that now threaten the extinction of their newly won gains.

Our usual "rehabilitation" programs are then anything but helpful to such persons who are sensitively trying to feel out their way into their style of life; all the grooming and coaching to appear normal go exactly against the grain of their further development. On the contrary, there appears to be much more promise of healthy growth into the future if the way of life chosen is unusual, unconventional, and especially if it is creatively original. Anything is in order, it seems, that helps the individual break through the sham of social artifice that makes him feel alienated, and helps him get to the heart of his true feelings and values in his relation to himself and his fellow beings.

References

BALINT, M. (1957). *The doctor, his patient, and the illness*. New York, International Universities Press.

BOWERS, M. B. (1971). "Psychosis and human growth," *Human Context*. London, *3:1*, 134–145.

FISCHER, R. (1971). "A cartography of the ecstatic and meditative states," *Science*, 174, 4012.

JACKSON, D. and WATZLAWICK, P. (1963). "The acute psychosis as a manifestation of the growth experience," *Psychiatr. Res. Rep. Amer. Psychiatr. Assoc.*, 16, 83–94.

JUNG, C. G. (1960). "The importance of the unconscious in psychopathology" (1914). *C.W. 3*.

LAING, R. D. (1967). *The politics of experience*. New York, Pantheon.

PERRY, J. W. (1962). "Reconstitutive process in the psychopathology of the self," *Annals of the N.Y. Acad. of Sci.*, 96, art. 3.

—— (1966a). *Lord of the four quarters*. New York, Braziller.

—— (1966b). "Reflections of the nature of the kingship archetype," *J. analyt. psychol.*, 11, 2.

—— (1971). "Societal implications of the renewal process," *Spring 1971*. New York, Zurich, Spring Publications.

SHEFF, T. (1966). *Being mentally ill*. Chicago, Aldine.

SULLIVAN, H. S. (1962). *Schizophrenia as a human process*. New York, Norton.

11

Analysis in Korea
With Special Reference to the Question of Success and Failure in Analysis

Bou-Yong Rhi, *Seoul*

When we speak of success and failure in analysis, this generally refers to the specific analytical process that takes place in the unique encounter between two people. Analysis, however, goes beyond personal uniqueness. If, for instance, an analysand gives up an analysis at a point when the analyst has the impression that it was a failure, the analysand's unconscious nevertheless continues its activity in one way or another. This may mature his personality, perhaps precisely because he has experienced an analysis for the first time in his life even though it may appear to have been a failure. If, following C. G. Jung, we regard individuation as an autonomous unconscious activity, and also consider the fact that this process of self-realization may last a lifetime, we must admit that fundamentally we do not know how the unconscious is going to complete it, or what role the analyst is playing in the course of the individuation process. The analyst is, after all, not identical with the mythological healer who would be capable of molding every variety of human fate as he wills.

This being so, I think every alleged therapeutic success is accompanied by the shadow of failure, just as every apparent failure carries within it the seeds of light and hope. The sense of failure nevertheless serves the purpose of enabling us to review the analytical process again so that we can realize what we were unconscious of until then.

In what follows I shall report my own experience of analysis in Korea, where I have been practicing since November 1968. I shall describe the difficulties that appeared both before and during the analysis, and try to understand their background. It is not, however, my intention to draw from such relatively short experiences any definitive conclusions about analytical psychotherapy in Korea. Moreover, within the limits of a lecture it is impossible to go into the unconscious processes in detail. I shall therefore concern myself primarily with the following questions:

1. What is the attitude of Orientals to analysis?

2. What is the role played in analysis by popular medicine and its background?

3. What are the special difficulties of analysis in Korea as compared with the Western world?

In order to gain an overall view of the material I would like first to say a few words about the outward conditions of the analytical situation.

The total number of analysands amounted to 23. Besides that, there were many patients with whom I conducted short-term psychotherapy at the psychiatric Polyclinic. Unfortunately, except for a few of these patients, my time did not allow me to work through the unconscious material very intensively. Many patients were unable to undertake the proposed analysis either for economic reasons or because of insufficient understanding on the part of the family. In some cases, however, the main reason could be traced back to their own fear of descending into their inner world.

The proportion of female to male analysands was 12 to 11; the great majority were between the ages of seventeen and thirty—only three were over thirty years old. This fact may be due on the one hand to the possible resistance of older people to a younger analyst, or their resistance to psychotherapy in general; on the other hand, it may be that young people are in greater need of analysis. The duration of the analysis was from three weeks to eighteen months. An analysis lasting more than three months was conducted with 12 patients. Seven of the analysands suffered from a psychotic disturbance of a schizophrenic or manic-depressive nature, and with them supportive medical treatment was necessary; a few had to be confined in the psychiatric clinic. The rest of the analysands suffered from anxiety neuroses, obsessional neuroses, psychogenic reactions, and juvenile delinquency. Thirteen analysands were students, most of them in the top grade or at the University, a fact which may permit one to draw conclusions concerning the role of intelligence or higher social status as a better preparation for analysis. As regards the psychotics, it would be premature to try to assess the clinical results. In the case of the other analysands, we can say that on a purely clinical view four remained unchanged, two were uncertain successes, one deteriorated, and nine showed improvement. The question is whether the clinical evaluation of the latter corresponded with a maturation of the personality.

Consciously, twelve analysands felt the analysis had been a definite help; the rest displayed a variety of different reactions.

Of the original 23 analysands, fifteen broke off the analysis for explicit reasons, but a few did so for no reason in particular. It is of considerable interest to examine more closely the reasons for breaking off the analysis which have to do with the problem of failure.

1. Insufficient inner preparation of analysands for analysis as a way to becoming more conscious.

2. Magical projection on the analyst.

3. Prejudicial influence of collective opinions about psychotherapy and psychic illness in general.

4. Transference and countertransference.

5. Identification of analysis with hospital treatment.

6. Concretistic interpretation of dreams.

A 25-year-old woman journalist rang me up and inquired about "the problem of women today." Later she presented herself in person and asked if she might discuss her personal problem with me. She wanted to "know herself." She said she was often stupid in her relations with other people, etc. But after the fourth consultation she disappeared, leaving behind a note in my absence: "I think I still have many more things to settle before I go to the hospital."

The expression "go to the hospital" was often used by the other analysands. They let it out when they felt they were being degraded into sick people. It is a projection of their own doctor's shadow on the analyst—a projection which must be considered a collective phenomenon in Korea, deriving partly from the popular conception of sickness.

Since the analysands were young and economically as well as intellectually dependent on their parents, discontinuation of the analysis was very often connected with their parents' opinions. Everywhere in Korea there are opinions that exert a strong influence on patients.

A 24-year-old student suffering from obsessional neurosis was talked to both before and during the analysis by many friends and relatives, and particularly by his mother, who all persuaded him that he was not ill if his troubles came from the nerves (from *Maum*, i.e, the soul). He had no need to go to the doctor because after all his soul belonged to him, and he should treat his soul himself. In the end he had to give up the analysis because no one was willing to pay for it. He was very unhappy about this, but later came back for another 6 weeks.

In this vacillation there is hidden a neurotic tendency to do everything perfectly and please everybody. At the same time an unconscious laziness threatens to overpower the ego as soon as other people assert their influence against the need for self-knowledge. This reflects the general attitude of the Koreans to the psyche. The psyche, they think, cannot possibly be a suitable object for treatment, which is contaminated with money. Psychic troubles are plain and simple "psychic" troubles but not a disease. There are numerous other ways of treating a psychic illness in Korea. Besides Western-oriented medicine there is the traditional medicine, including herbal remedies, acupuncture, and magical exorcists mostly from Korean shamanistic circles but also to be found among the Christian and Buddhist sects. For a sick person it is bewildering to have to choose between so many kinds of treatment. The doctor, even if he is a psychiatrist or surgeon with Western training, has therefore also to be an expert on nature cures and related practices. In addition, there is in Korea an unconscious collective projection on to Western medicine of our own still rather primitive, naturalistic way of thinking, which expresses itself in an enthusiasm for modern *physical* kinds of treatment. The psyche, however, is not meant to be an object for treatment by Western methods. Such an attitude sometimes causes great difficulties in getting a neurotic to see a psychotherapist.

When a young man who suffered from psychogenic pains in the chest was recommended by me to try psychotherapy, he exclaimed indignantly: "But, doctor, an illness of the 'nerves' does not mean that the psyche is sick, but merely that there is a disturbance of the nervous system. For instance, two nerve fibers aren't running parallel and are connected up wrongly." The patient added that he thought more highly of Chinese than of Western medicine and that he was fond of herbal remedies.

The affinity of the people for Chinese medicine can be traced back to their belief in the inexplicability of matter. People like mysteries and are afraid that any explanations will do away with them. At the same time, strange concretistic tendencies exist in their unconscious, and this is the shadow-side of the people that was suppressed by the preference for an irrational mode of thinking. For the West it is quite correct to think of consciousness as rational and the unconscious as irrational; but for most Koreans the situation seems to be reversed.

Among the analysands who were unable to terminate the analysis properly I could also observe a special attitude towards the whole question of analysis and particularly that of dream interpretation. The attitude of analysands in a trial analysis is especially remarkable.

A 33-year-old woman analysand was suffering from attacks of anxiety and was unhappily married; she also had an over-protective mother who, instead of fostering her independence, insisted on handing out her own almost fanatical Christian belief as a remedy for the illness. With the courage and exactitude characteristic of her animus, the patient wrote down her dreams and listened attentively to my explanations, but understood them only in a literal-minded way. In her dreams the motif of examinations often appeared; she always did badly or was unprepared for them. Finally she could stand the strain no longer and complained that she was not sleeping well because of her dreams. She knew, she said, that the analysis was a good thing, but she couldn't endure the tension. I terminated the analysis after eight sessions. It seems as though the dream interpretation had only awakened her uncreative intellectual side.

A 43-year-old woman who was occasionally seized by fear of death was brought to me for analysis by her husband after treatment by medication had proved a failure. At the first session she expressed her conviction that I possessed a secret art that would cure her sickness, and said she would like to learn it from me. She complained of her poverty, and excused herself for having to steal my time. This attitude to analysis struck me as unfavorable right from the beginning. At the third session she presented the following dream:

Some women, evidently mudang *(Korean shamans), were walking along a road. They were doing something, and wanted to throw rice cakes on the road, for which purpose they crumbled the cakes into smaller pieces and kept them in their girdles. When they saw me they wanted to give me a cake instead of throwing it on the road. I found this unpleasant and ran away somewhere. Then I came into a forbidden zone. It was large and quiet. After a while the American military came to arrest me and I ran away again.*

We see, then, that there are autonomous activities taking place in the unconscious which are connected with the shamanistic mentality, and it is to this side of the unconscious, obviously corresponding to the religious shadow of the analysand, that the dreamer wants to offer the rice cake as spiritual nourishment. The fact that she finds this unpleasant is an indication that she has remained totally unconscious of the shadow-side. From sheer terror she seeks refuge in the forbidden zone which only privileged persons may enter. The unconscious is trying to tell the dreamer that she ought not to try to stay in the privileged area but should first become conscious of her own shadow-side. As a matter of fact her family was planning to emigrate to America but her illness prevented this. As the dream shows, the analysand is trying again and again to break away from her own culture and to adopt a rational attitude. In other words, she was too rationalistic to make herself conscious of her shamanistic shadow. In other dreams her ailing ancestors frequently appeared, especially female ones, as well as other members of the family with whom she had strong ties. The analysis was discontinued partly at my instigation, in order to give her the opportunity of looking into herself instead of trying to learn my "secret art." With such a very extraverted woman it might have been more appropriate to arrange a shamanistic session and get her to experience the ancestral spirits through the *mudang.*

To become conscious of the shamanistic complex in the unconscious which conflicts with the modern Western mentality is the task confronting many Koreans who identify with the rationalistic attitude. This ancient source of popular spiritual guidance manifests itself in the dreams of some women analysands as a protective, nourishing maternal function. But the protection can also display its negative side by preventing a courageous confrontation with the unconscious complex. This is apparent in the dream of a 30-year-old woman analysand:

I was climbing up a steep clay path with my sister. A group of people barred the way and tried to seize hold of us. Then I saw somebody approaching and quickly went along with him. We found a path that led to a house of mudang. *We stepped into the house.*

For another, 24-year-old woman analysand who suffered from depressions, the *mudang* not only represented a psychic complex in the unconscious but an actual person who exercised a strong influence over her.

As a popular psychotherapist, the *mudang* occupies a not unimportant position in Korea. She can be a fortune-teller and treat sick people by exorcism. Her favorite method of treatment is that of emotional exaltation—intuitive, authoritarian judgment in the name of the gods or ancestors. All this is half consciously or even intentionally emphasized during the shamanistic session.

The analysand we have just mentioned went at the beginning of the analysis to a fortune-teller, who told her that if she got married her younger sister would take her husband away from her and that she herself would immediately die. Nor could her still unmarried older brother expect to remain alive much longer. The analysand was a very reticent and easily vulnerable personality who found verbal communication with the analyst extremely difficult. She presented dreams only sporadically. Almost all of them showed her everyday problems in relation to her women friends and her family. When she developed a violent resistance against me, I found I had to deal actually with my own countertransference.

The analysis seemed to have got beyond the most difficult phase after nearly nine months, when she suddenly mentioned the affair of the fortune-teller. In spite of the analysis, she said, she had not been able to forget his words, and this meant that the analysis had failed. Indeed, the analysis had made his words even more powerful than before, since I had asked her, in an unguarded moment, about the age of her younger sister. Her depression and self-criticism now turned into hatred of me. Finally she gave up the analysis although in the dreams she had at this time there were really positive signs for her further development and no indications for terminating the analysis.

It is remarkable how strong were the traces left behind by the fortune-teller's words and how easily she was influenced by them. Her readiness to believe in magic made her regard the analysis as a sort of counter-magic against the unconscious death- and marriage-complexes which had been further reinforced by the fortune-teller's trifling words.

So far I have given only a rough sketch of the problems that arise in analysis in Korea. Most of the difficulties are due to the culturally conditioned attitude of consciousness and to collective opinions. These, however, cannot be considered as absolute reasons for a failed analysis. Only, compared with the West, we need more time to digest the contents of consciousness before we can plunge into the depths of the unconscious.

In Korea, where all sorts of heterogeneous elements clash together, while the power of tradition is being pushed further and further into the background, it should be the foremost task of analysis to help resolve the dissociated states of mind resulting from this conflict. In my opinion the most unfavorable and most pernicious precondition for analysis is not complete unconsciousness but semi-consciousness.

It looks as if the situation in Korea demanded first of all a clear distinction between good and evil, rational and irrational, consciousness and the unconscious, as a kind of transitional process before setting out on the way of individuation. The distinction between the opposites is already being made in the dreams of young people. The confrontation with the shadow, which so often appears in dreams in the form of the Korean War, hijackings, shoot-outs with spies, and being chased by unknown animals, is sometimes connected with the problem of the mother.

The problem of the mother appears in the dream of a 25-year-old analysand who was afflicted with diplopia (double vision), psychogenic headaches, and a striving for power. In contrast to previous solutions in which machine guns and pistols had figured as weapons of defense or attack, there was an archer who had never appeared in his dreams before:

I was being chased by an animal, perhaps a lioness. I fled into a barracks that was equipped with a few doors. The doors did not close properly. I ran in every direction. Then the lioness turned into two lionesses. It was difficult to hide myself. Now a wildcat ran into the barracks, and I threw it out. An unknown man who was a good archer shot an arrow first at one lioness and then at the other. — There was some kind of contest between the Americans and the English. I took part on the English side. In the end the English side won.

The archer represents the whole-making in the dreamer, uncontaminated by civilization. It is Tao, whereby the destructive power will be overcome.

The unconscious power can be overcome not by rationalistic mechanical means but only by a natural attitude in which the opposites are endured with full consciousness. According to the analysand, he himself appeared in the dream as a child and the archer as a man. The unknown man is thus his hidden masculinity, a hero who was trying to make the dreamer more conscious. About the Americans he commented that there was something optimistic and naïve and rather uncouth in their activity, whereas the attitude of the English was conservative, reserved, and aristocratic. His task is apparently to be found not in any outward activity but in one that is more withdrawn and introverted.

The truly religious attitude in the sense of *religio* (careful consideration) means that we do not seek the reason for failure always in the external world or project our own dark side on outer things, but try to find it in ourselves.

Translated from the German by R. F. C. Hull

12

The Group as Corrective
for Failure in Analysis

C. E. BROOKES, *San Francisco*

My intention is to suggest a basis for the use of group psychotherapy as an adjunct to individual analysis and as a corrective to certain difficulties in individual analysis.

I have practiced group psychotherapy for more than ten years. I did not come to the use of the group setting through any particular orthodoxy. The opportunity for experience with groups was available during my psychiatric training; I found the experience interesting and worthwhile, though not at all to be regarded as an exclusive tool in dealing with the emotional and personal concerns of my patients. By fortuitous or perhaps synchronistic circumstance, my native personality was such that I found the group a generally fascinating and stimulating environment, and I was able to tolerate the anxieties which accrue to group interaction. I simultaneously became interested in the Jungian viewpoint and, most centrally, in the process of individuation. During the course of my training in analytical psychology, I became aware of the rather strong bias against group psychotherapy that marks much Jungian thinking.

This bias I found to be inconsistent with my own clinical experience and with my developing theoretical viewpoint. While continuing my interest in group work, I concentrated more and more on the individual and on the inner journey. I found myself in disagreement with the "groupism" which seems to be implicit in many theoretical justifications of group psychotherapy. Consequently, in the interaction of my therapy groups, I found myself observing phenomena which seemed to encourage rather than hinder the individuation process. Since my observations appeared to be antithetical to much Jungian thinking, and indeed to many of Jung's own comments on the group, I spent some time working out a theoretical basis for my observations. I have come to feel that my experience is indeed consistent with the central ideas of analytical psychology. This paper therefore provides a preliminary theoretical rationale for the use of group psychotherapy as an adjunct to and corrective for individual analysis.

As Jung implied, the conscious and unconscious elements of the psyche exist in reciprocal relationship. This concept seems valid on collective as well as on individual levels, and it seems more than likely that the evolution of the collective psyche is a function of this reciprocity or dialogue, just as the evolution of the individual psyche is a function of the reciprocal relationship between conscious and unconscious. This reciprocity gives an apparently cyclical form to collective as well as to personal psychic events. But the phenomenon of the archetype, with its fundamental significance for psychological and biological life, contributes the dimension of individual and collective potential—a constant "coming into being." To the apparently cyclical picture of psychic change is added the element of movement through time. Stimulated by the inherent tendency of the archetype to manifest itself in symbolic form, the dialogue of opposites becomes an active, evolutionary process.

In the United States the conscious bias in psychology and in psychotherapy until recent times has been extraverted, thinking, and sensate; objectivity and detachment from "contamination" by feeling was the order of the day as psychologists attempted to mimic the traditional methods of the physical sciences, while fantasy and intuition were viewed with suspicion, as if they were somehow pathological. However, in more recent times the polarity between thinking and feeling has begun to reverse itself, simultaneously with the revolution of the younger generation. For some of our young people, consciousness is now dominated by introversion, feeling, and intuition, while thinking and sensation, together with the extraverted dimension, have become aspects of the shadow. The new conscious emphasis on feeling provides an element of immediacy and of *participation* in the experience of oneself and experience with others. The emphasis on intuition provides the element, so highly prized, of the "trip," the "turn-on."

But interestingly enough, although the flow of libido for these young people is now inward and their dominant attitude is now subjective, the presence of others, the presence of groups, is often sought and demanded. Formerly, and in the remaining elements of the old consciousness, membership in groups served the interests of extraversion; it was used as a way of keeping the attention outwards and of avoiding the anxiety generated by shadow questions and concerns. But now, at least with those who appear to be evolving a different form of consciousness, although the turning is inward the demand for the presence of "multiple others" continues.

How might this be explained? It seems quite probable that what we are witnessing is a personal regression, partially in the sense of *abaissement du niveau mental,* but also partially in the attempt to re-establish, in small groups or "cultures," the ritualistic and mythological framework within which the introverted, feeling, and intuitive modes of experience can be given symbolic and personal meaning. The regression, then, is partially in the service of ego-consciousness, and it would be a mistake to construe it simply as a spontaneous lowering of the level of consciousness. Although Jung sees separation from the group, from the collective, as a necessary stage in the process of individuation, he also verifies that the collective is always, as it were, at the elbow of the individual, as an entity against which he must reflect himself and to which he must inevitably and finally relate. Hence, recent events in the evolution of consciousness have demonstrated the internal need for the group—for the culture—as that foundation upon which individuation becomes a possibility and against which it must be reflected. When as analytical psychologists we consider the possibility of using the group setting for purposes of psychotherapy, we must be cognizant that no particular technique should be used to emphasize one polarity of the psyche at the expense of the other. The reciprocity, the dialogue, must be maintained. We must use both group and individual settings as adjuncts.

Jung viewed groups with some trepidation. Although he felt the group was a necessary experience for the individual in the early stages of development, he pointed to the reduction of individual behavior in groups to the collective norm, and with great emphasis reminded us of the necessity of differentiation from the group as a vital aspect of the individuation process. He constantly refers to the phenomenon of the lowering of the level of consciousness in groups. He warns of the identification of the individual with the lowest common denominator of the group. But at the same time he is quite clear on the point that individuation does not mean isolation, and that the individuating person exists in reciprocal relationship with the existing collective. Jung is much clearer on the contribution of the collective to the individual than he is on the contribution of the individual to the collective. The implication is, however, that the reciprocity between individual and collective is a major determinant of psychic evolution.

This leads us to a reassessment of the question of individual membership in a group. The phenomenon of lowering of the level of consciousness and identifying with the group norm is well demonstrated to anyone who works with groups. But also demonstrated is the fact that the group becomes a collective shadow of the individual and therefore representative of the other side of the coin of individuality. The possibility of individuation is identified and given meaning by its shadow opposite: the collective norm represented by the group. Opposites exist in dynamic tension; in one sense they are irreconcilable, and in another sense they are indispensable to each other. Experience in group work teaches that the degree of regression to the collective is a function of the conscious attitude and of the anticipation with which the individual approaches the group. An individual may seek membership in a group in order to experience his individuality. In this instance the relationship with the group is a reciprocal one; the group provides the shadow element against which the individual must both reflect himself and integrate himself in order to further the individuation process. By his own individuation, in turn, the person provides new elements for the group; he creates new symbolic forms of expression for the manifestation of collective archetypal elements; he constellates new aspects of the collective; thus collective psychic evolution proceeds.

Such a situation is very different from that of the individual who returns to a group in order to find in its ritual and in its normative ways of existence a surcease from the anxiety and discomfort which his struggle for separation has caused him. The reciprocal relationship of an individual with a group requires a tolerance for anxiety which can only be a function of the ego. Identification with a group involves a premature abdication of the ego to the collective. On the other hand, it is from the continuing dialogue between ego and collective that the process of individuation arises and the process of collective evolution proceeds. Hence, a certain amount of ego strength is necessary to combat the lowering of the level of consciousness, so that the fundamental work of individuation and collective evolution may proceed, catalyzed by the ongoing dynamic tension between individual and collective, and fueled by the archetypal potential. A so-called therapeutic group setting which allowed a lowering of the level of consciousness would be antithetical to this process. However, a therapeutic group setting which encouraged the reciprocal individual-group relationship would be supportive of individuation and of collective evolution, and would fulfill Jung's criteria for the relationship between the individual and his culture.

The setting of choice for analytical psychology has long been individual psychotherapy. Certain fundamental advantages accrue to this situation. These include an unhindered opportunity for introspective focus, privacy, and confidentiality, the development of transference with its symbolic and healing elements, and, perhaps most importantly, the comfort of the therapist himself. There is no doubt that patients view the one-to-one relationship with the therapist in a unique way. For some, the therapeutic hour becomes a special and secret place, removed from the literal world. As Jung said, a man must have his secrets. A vital and perhaps essential element of the therapeutic transaction is that therapy provides a place where one may share his secret, not so much with the therapist as a person, but rather with the archetype of the self, personified for the moment in and catalyzed by the therapist.

For many patients, however, the individual setting is a place in which to hide. A clinical example illustrates this point. An introverted and agonized young man, whose life combined a grim determination to find his own path of selfhood with an almost incapacitating mental illness which had left him totally isolated, beset by impulses and actions of a bizarre sexual nature, and inundated from time to time with overwhelming depression—this young person described the setting of individual therapy as "a hidden place, a secret place to which I walk from my room through a tunnel of my own making—a tunnel which protects me from the eyes of the world, so that I never need show the evil that is in me to those who would judge me." The fact that this young man was his own worst judge was lost behind his projection of that judgment onto the world of his fellows, from whom he proceeded to exclude himself.

The desire for secrecy, dictated by fear of exposure, is present to some degree in every patient who comes for treatment. This desire to keep secrets, which arises from fear, projection, and self-disregard, is a different order of phenomenon than the secrets of which Jung speaks. The secrets mentioned by Jung are kept to oneself because they involve experiences which radiate the numinosity of the archetype; they are of and from the archetypal level of existence and are therefore kept secret because they are both precious and inarticulate. The numen itself provides the impetus to secrecy; whereas in the example of the young man the motivation is fear and self-hatred. No power, no group, can force the individual to reveal the numinosum to others until and unless he chooses to do so. He shares these secrets with the therapist to the extent that he is able to establish an archetypal transference in a setting of warmth and trust. But the other secrets—the secrets derived from self-hatred—these are fundamentally different. For long ages, the physician has recognized the importance of confidentiality in his consultation.

Any sensitive therapist, however, must sooner or later be struck by the thought that in maintaining the secrecy of the fearful, he is somehow in collusion with an aspect of the illness. The collusion arises from the implication of confidentiality itself. This implication is that the therapist agrees with the patient's view that his secrets are too horrible to be tolerated by his fellow men. Until and unless the patient is able, if need be, to stand before the world, he will remain a victim of the complexes of his own personal unconscious. This victimization denies him the opportunity for contact with the deeper centers of his being and for the possibility of individuation which such contact would provide.

We are now in a position to define a possible source of failure in individual analysis. Failure may derive quite simply from the removed and isolated characteristics of the consultation hour. This removal from the affairs of daily life may perpetuate a tenuousness of the ego which no amount of analysis of unconscious material can correct. This tenuousness is defined by the individual turning against himself those judgmental and valuational functions of his own psyche which would normally operate in the service of his ego and in the interests of eventual individuation. Instead, they are directed destructively against the ego. It is here that a group setting provides a corrective, for any group of individuals is a small culture, and in it the person is confronted with the same fear of exposure from which he seeks to protect himself by means of the one-to-one consultation. In the group he has the opportunity to test his fantasy of the judgments of others against the literal reality of that judgment when it is forthcoming.

There is almost inevitably a disparity between the fantasy and the literal reality; it is only in relation with one's fellows that an awareness of that disparity can be acquired, and the tenuousness of the isolated and fearful ego corrected. The group setting provides an opportunity to work with this problem *in vivo*.

Fear of the judgments of others is often indistinguishable from fundamental apprehensions of exposure and vulnerability to one's fellows. The ego, the sense of separate identity, is always sensitive to the possibility of encroachment upon its integrity, because the personal historical experience of the individual—whatever it is—inevitably constellates archetypal potential along certain lines, and at the expense of other possible lines of development. Thus, the presence of complexes is a human universal. The ego itself, along with other aspects of the psyche, is manifested as a constellated complex, and as such is encroached upon by those internally or externally derived elements which are not consistent with the form of the complex. Apprehension of this encroachment may be said to be the subjective parallel of anxiety. Anxiety itself is a human universal; it varies from individual to individual and from time to time only in intensity; its fundamental quality is universally the same. Fear of the judgments, the actions, the attitudes, the presence of others; fear of the new and unfamiliar—these are with each and every one of us to some degree, because the substance of that fear is built into the nature of psychic life.

Individuation, then, cannot be a categorically different or separate process from the fear of exposure. The two are intertwined and exist in reciprocal and paradoxical relationship as much as do consciousness and the shadow. Individuation proceeds against the gradient of fear and regression; in fact, without the contrast with its opposite, neither process could be identified. In similar fashion, the individual moves and lives in reciprocal relationship between dialogue with himself and dialogue with his fellows. Individuation is not a process of increasing isolation. The dialogue or reciprocal relationship between the individual and his group, as a function of which both individual and group are changed, provides the essential connection between the evolution of the individual and the evolution of the collective; without the individual the collective cannot evolve, and without the collective the individual cannot differentiate and identify himself.

Individuation is marked, accordingly, not just by an internal relating and differentiating; it is marked also by an external relating in the process of which the differentiation is maintained and the collective is changed. For the sake of description, and to provide a theoretical model, we may say that the process begins with the separation of the individual from the collective. This is the stage of which Jung speaks when he stipulates the necessity of disengagement from the group so that a higher level of consciousness can be born. But the next stage of the process is provided by the dialogue which ensues between the differentiated individual and the collective, as a result of which the collective changes. The essence of dialogue is contrast; the very division of the unitary *Anlage* into polarities provides that contrast. The third stage of the process, in which by biological dissolution and death the individual is once again subordinated to the collective, prepares the way for a new individual differentiation and the next stage of the evolution of consciousness.

Human life as we know it is marked by the first two stages of the process outlined above. For the individual, these stages are constantly reflected against the third stage, in which the individual as we know him lives only in and through his unique contribution to collective consciousness. It is a fundamental contention of this paper that analysis can be most successful when it is conducted in a setting which most closely approximates the natural arena of the individuation process. This natural arena contains both the separating out, and the subsequent dialogue between the individual and his group. Hence, it is suggested here that a combination of individual and group psychotherapy provides an optimal setting within which the individuation process may be encouraged. In such a setting, a potential is provided for a reciprocal relationship between the two polarities of conscious human existence: being alone and in relation with the internal collective, and on the other hand being together with one's fellows in relation with the external collective while still separate from it. A basic clinical premise follows: the optimal use of a psychotherapy group involves the development of techniques and attitudes on the part of the therapist which consistently challenge the tendency towards a monolithic and unchanging consciousness. In still different terms, the terms of cultural anthropology, the problem is to produce a small culture which constantly corrects its tendency to become static. The culture must change, and it does so through the resistances of individual members to its invitation to regression.

The preceding exposition provides a theoretical model within which specific techniques for and approaches to the psychotherapy group may be worked out, together with the coordination of group and individual psychotherapy. In this context, it is important to return to the analytical psychologist as therapist. It was mentioned previously that the traditional use of the one-to-one setting in analytical psychology is partially a function of the comfort of the therapist. However well-analyzed, the therapist is a human being who himself demonstrates that psychological vulnerability and fear of openness which we have outlined. At the same time, we may hope, he is a person who has succeeded to some real degree in separating himself out from his group or culture. If such is the case, he is at a stage of development in which he does not hesitate to enter into renewed dialogue with his fellows, because he now knows that he exists and can tolerate the anxiety which accompanies vulnerability. Whether he is primarily introverted or extraverted is not a central consideration, because the individuating therapist now has access to functions which were formerly secondary, or in the shadow. If this has not happened, his view of his own development is erroneous. It is very easy, particularly for us who as analytical psychologists are uniquely prone to such error, to see our separation from the group as if it were the final act of individuation itself. We must guard ourselves as therapists and as human beings against the danger of hiding ourselves from our fellow men. If we cannot be vulnerable in the presence of our patients, we certainly cannot provide them with a model for their development.

There are many therapists who prefer to work with groups exclusively. This is not the bias of analytical psychology. Our bias is much more likely to be unconscious, and to refuse to work in groups. Each of these biases is dangerous, in that the therapist is unconscious and sees himself as conscious, and has found ways to rationalize his position. Each of these therapists avoids the anxiety and the challenge of dialogue and of reciprocal experience. Each has done so because he has chosen one pole of the paradox, and simultaneously denies the existence of the other side of the polarity. Consciousness is a paradoxical phenomenon; it exists only by virtue of the dialogue between opposites: If we choose comfort in our work, we will move to a setting which represents one of these opposites and will deny the other. It is in our own capacity to tolerate what is unfamiliar to us that the possibility of helping our patients arises. It is suggested here that we earnestly consider a paradoxical setting for our work. The paradoxical situation of functioning both individually and with groups provides a fundamental challenge to the therapist. In this situation he must undertake the task of struggling with his own individuation in the presence of his patients, and in so doing he must become a person who can point the way to the path because he himself is truly upon it.

13

The Therapeutic
Community Disease

ROBERT F. HOBSON, *London*

This article is a personal confession. A psychologist, however scientific he might wish to be, is himself a part of his subject matter. Although his tone of voice and literary expression suggest detachment, objectivity, and sublime disinterestedness, every statement he makes is a fragment of autobiography. The psychotherapist brings his whole world into the consulting room, the hospital ward, and the lecture room. But that is not to say that formulations which emerge from personal experiences are merely idiosyncratic. In an attempt to convey something of the atmosphere of the unique human conversations that I enjoyed in a lecture and in discussions at the International Congress of Analytical Psychology, some recorded colloquialisms are retained in this paper (if it can be so called). Yet, I hope that what I have to say has a degree of general significance with at least some relevance to other hospital wards, therapeutic communities, professional bodies, and maybe to the wider society in which we are "living and partly living."

My aim at the Congress was to talk *with* the audience, not to add noise to formulated phrases fixed on a piece of paper. I tried to *do* what I was talking *about*. The process of talking "with," not "at" or "to," is central to my concept of a therapeutic community, and indeed of all psychotherapy. It involves an *exploration in a conversation* which is continually modified by the responses of the other participant or participants—especially by nonverbal signals, signs, and symbols. My hope was that in this *dialectical process* diverse attractive avenues would open for continued dialogue.

A therapeutic community involves the *constant creation and re-creation of a language.* "Language" is a mode of being with people, of living together, and words play a relatively small part. Nonverbal signals are of primary importance in establishing and maintaining interpersonal relationships, and talking *about* bodies is no substitute for talking "bodily." Maybe here lies one source of failure, or damage, in classical psychoanalysis and in many other forms of psychotherapy —an overemphasis upon words, and particularly upon formulated linear interpretations. "Language" involves not only looks, gestures, and touch, but also doing things together with others—sharing common tasks and enjoyable play. The mode in which patients and staff live together—*the language of a ward*—is a potent force for therapy and, perhaps more important, for psychological damage.

Growing up (and we are all still growing up) involves the achievement of a capacity to be alone, and to be together with others. *Aloneness* and *togetherness* are interdependent and are essentially different from *isolation* (or loneliness) and from fantasies and feelings of *fusion* (with which social isolation is commonly associated). I can be alone only in so far as I can be together with others. I can be together with others only if I am able to be alone. That is what it means to become an individual with an identity and to be a member of a community.

In considering the term "therapeutic community" we are assaulted by a plethora of nebulous terms—such as "administrative therapy," "social therapy," "milieu therapy," and "therapeutic community proper." With regard to what are sometimes referred to as "real therapeutic communities" there are wide and, in my view, crucial differences, and yet these are inadequately described and poorly defined. A cursory glance with a critical eye at the voluminous literature (which in this somewhat incautious expostulation I choose to ignore) and an ear to the anecdotes whispered in private groups of devotees suggest that we just do not know what goes on. We know far too little to justify the current "progressive" fashion in English mental hospitals where so-called "community methods" are being introduced widely. There are too many words and too few facts.

I hesitate to add to the verbiage although I have been the founder-leader of a psychotherapy in-patient unit at Bethlem Royal Hospital (called Tyson West Two) for over fourteen years. I do so for two reasons.

1. During the last few years we have begun an *attempt to measure changes in patients and to relate these to therapeutic variables.* However, this difficult research is at a very early stage and I shall merely hint at it in this talk, which must be largely anecdotal.

2. A major part of what I have to say is about failure and damage— a failure to maintain creative conversations, owing to what I term the *Therapeutic Community Disease,* a subject barely touched upon, and nowhere thoroughly explored, in the extensive, largely optimistic, and not seldom apocalyptic, literature in this field. Yet in failure lies the possibility of a different sort of success. It is often in grappling with a failure to communicate that a new language emerges. The disease involves the *failure of a personal ideal.* This can result in cynical dis-illusionment and self-destruction (which I have experienced), but it *can* perhaps lead to exploration of exciting possibilities. Although Tyson West Two closed some weeks ago for administrative reasons, I shall speak of it in the present tense. My meditation is part of a process of mourning accompanied by uneasy apprehension about setting up a new unit.

I recall T. S. Eliot's lines from *East Coker:*

"Our only health is the disease

. . .

Old men ought to be explorers
Here and there does not matter
We must be still and still moving

. . .

In my end is my beginning."

I. AN IN-PATIENT PSYCHOTHERAPY COMMUNITY UNIT

1. DESCRIPTION OF TYSON WEST TWO

There are 19 patients, of both sexes, who are predominantly young, intelligent people with very long-standing, severe personality disorders of a neurotic type. Almost all have had previous therapy of an analytical kind and often with drugs.

It is important that patients make a definite choice to join the community. They see the unit, talk with other patients, and at an initial interview with key members of the staff are informed about the ward in much the same terms as I shall describe it. The difficulties are stressed and no promises are made beyond the statement "there is a chance you can be helped here." (Occasionally "chance" is changed to "good chance.") Since our aim is to modify deep-seated disturbances patients are told that they must be willing to stay at least nine months or a year on the ward. There is a commitment.

Daily on Mondays to Fridays, the patients are divided into two therapy groups, each taken by a junior psychiatrist in training for one hour from 9 a.m. Each patient is also seen individually once weekly by the doctor who takes the other morning group (of which the patient is not a member). Thus, no therapist can speak of "my patient." There is an hour-long group of all the patients taken by the ward sister and her deputy, and a large "ward group" comprising all the patients and all the available staff. This is led by me. At various times the occupational therapist, better termed "activity psychotherapist," is on the ward, and patients are expected to participate in the activities she arranges.

The commitment of the patients to the ward is expectedly shared by the staff, who in twice-weekly staff groups are encouraged to express and understand the feelings they have in response to working in this taxing environment, and to make explicit (in order to attempt to resolve) areas of conflict among themselves in so far as these affect the treatment of the patients. These groups are extremely dynamic, are usually exhausting and often distressing, and can be explosive. In my view they are vital to the functioning of the unit.

Therapy involves specific individual and group psychotherapy, but the techniques are only special instances of the application of psychotherapeutic principles to as many as possible of all the interactions among and between patients and staff. Patients are discouraged from thinking of their individual therapy session as the outstanding event of the week, and on admission they are told "we like to think of your treatment as your whole life here." In the absence of systematic data on the content of all the interactions between the people on the ward, it is impossible to provide a reliable account of what constitutes "the treatment." Therapeutic interventions may be relevant "interpretations" or various types of "holding operations." Apart from occasional night sedation (always Mogadon) and analgesics, no drugs or physical methods of treatment are used.

By *"interpretation"* I mean statements made in order to relieve anxiety and to correct those illusions which prevent a person exploring relationships with others on the unit, whether they be his individual therapist, members of his daily therapeutic group, the consultant in charge of the ward, or other patients and staff members.

"Holding operations" include support, advice, and setting necessary limits by rules which should be as few as possible and capable of being enforced if necessary. In simple language, the *main aim of therapy is the promotion of social learning by revealing disturbances in relationships which occur among both patients and staff and to correct these by the promotion of honest "conversation" in varied settings within the context of a community life.* Patients are required to take part in the quite varied communication situations—two-person interviews, small groups, large groups, as well as community work and play. But there are ample opportunities for them to be alone.

I wish to emphasize again the fact that it is the *total life situation* which is regarded as the treatment—the constant development of a language referred to earlier as a "mode of being with people." Exploration in this broader conversation occurs in the aloneness and togetherness of informal chats, shopping expeditions, and games of Scrabble. The staff as understanding participants are, to some extent, models. But they are changeable models. In an ongoing conversation all participants must be open to change. It is important that the community should remain in close contact with everyday life and that emphasis is laid upon the responsibility of patients both as individuals and as a group to cope for themselves as far as is possible. This raises the thorny question of the nature of authority to which I shall return.

First I wish to mention one relatively "objective" means of characterizing the ward environment as a possible basis for comparison with other wards in which research is conducted—the Moos Ward Atmosphere Scale.

2. THE WARD ATMOSPHERE SCALE

The Ward Atmosphere Scale was developed by Moos to measure the social atmosphere of psychiatric wards by asking each ward member to state, by means of a standardized questionnaire procedure, whether statements about the ward are "generally true" or "generally false." Fig. 1 shows some results in terms of disturbances in standard deviations from the mean of the normative data for each subscale. The stability of such profiles has been shown to be high, as are most of the subscale retest reliabilities (Moos and Houts 1968, Moos 1969).

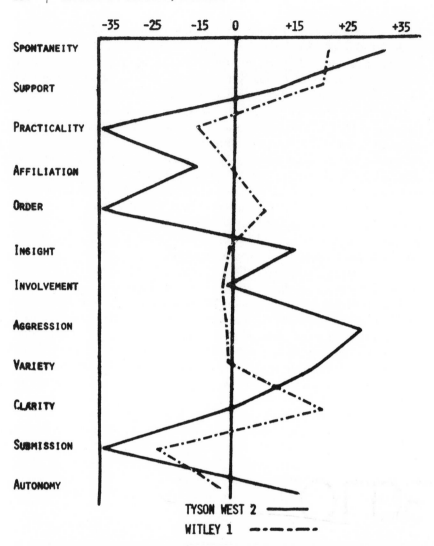

TYSON WEST 2 ⎯⎯⎯⎯
WITLEY 1 ⎯ ⎯ ⎯ ⎯

I shall not discuss this scale in detail but shall cite two examples of items on each subscale in order to give an idea of their meaning:

> *Spontaneity*—"Patients set up their own activities without being prodded by the staff" and "patients are encouraged to show their feelings."
>
> *Support*—"The healthier patients on this ward help take care of the less healthy ones" and "staff go out of their way to help patients."

Practicality—"This ward emphasizes training for new kinds of jobs" and "patients are encouraged to learn new ways of doing this."

Affiliation—"The staff help new patients get acquainted on the ward" and "patients on this ward care about each other."

Order—"This is a very well organized ward" and "the staff make sure the ward is always neat."

Insight—"Patients tell each other about their personal problems" and "staff are mainly interested in learning about patients' feelings."

Involvement—"Patients put a lot of energy into what they do around here" and "the patients are proud of this ward."

Aggression—Is mainly concerned with the open verbal expression of angry feelings, e.g., "patients often criticize or joke about the ward staff" and "on this ward staff think it is a healthy thing to argue."

Variety—"This is a lively ward" and "the ward rules are always changing."

Clarity—"Staff tell patients when they are getting better" and "ward rules are clearly understood by the patients."

Submission—"On this ward everyone knows who's in charge" and "once a schedule is arranged for a patient, the patient must follow it."

Autonomy—"The staff act on patients' suggestions" and "patients are expected to take leadership on the ward."

We are using the Moos Scale in research, correlating it in various ways with measures of change—in patients mainly, but also in staff. In this general account some profiles are used only in order to illustrate one useful way of describing some important features of a ward. I am greatly indebted to Rudolf Moos, who personally administered the Scale with the co-operation of the patients and staff on Tyson West Two.

In Fig. 1 the profile of the unit is compared with one from a liberal admission ward. There are clear differences in these patterns, but these are not so striking as those between Tyson West Two and wards of a more traditional mental hospital. The results were in general what we expected, but we had some shocks—caused particularly by the low score on Affiliation and the relatively low scores on Involvement and Clarity. The surprise is reflected in Fig. 2, in which profiles of patients and staff are compared. It was pleasing to find the close agreement between these profiles, which was especially striking when compared

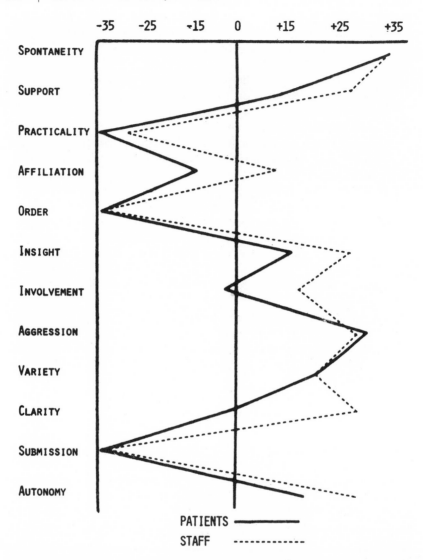

	-35	-25	-15	0	+15	+25	+35

SPONTANEITY

SUPPORT

PRACTICALITY

AFFILIATION

ORDER

INSIGHT

INVOLVEMENT

AGGRESSION

VARIETY

CLARITY

SUBMISSION

AUTONOMY

PATIENTS —————
STAFF -------------

with other wards. This suggests good communication. The staff expected, but did not approve of, the low score on Practicality. But the discrepancies between the judgments of patients and staff on Clarity, Involvement, Affiliation, and Support gave us food for thought—and for subsequent action.

I have given a very brief sketch of the structure, atmosphere, and aims of the unit as it has been in the last few years. This was developed in the light of many vicissitudes, and now I wish to outline a pattern in this evolution—The Therapeutic Community Disease.

II. THE THERAPEUTIC COMMUNITY DISEASE

At the risk of over-simplification, I shall arbitrarily (and perhaps some-what over-dramatically) describe three stages of development of the disease in the life history of a particular type of therapeutic community. It is based not only upon personal experience in Tyson West Two but also upon a good deal of unpublished information about other units of similar, although not identical, type. I shall term these three phases "The Coming of the Messiah," "The Enlightenment," and "The Catastrophe."

1. THE COMING OF THE MESSIAH

A dedicated, enthusiastic leader brings a message of brotherhood in a New Society. Usually he is a sincere idealist with a fascinating charisma. Bringing democratic light into the darkness of a traditional hierarchical mental hospital, he attracts a small body of followers and, at the same time, arouses fierce opposition from the Establishment. When, with the help of a certain shrewd political manipulation, he forms a thera-peutic community, his "mana" increases. Although he speaks of him-self as "just one member of a group" he becomes for his intimates virtually an *incarnation of an archetypal figure*—usually a *Saviour Hero* but sometimes a *Great Mother*. To others he is a dangerous revolutionary or even the devil.

What might have been an ideal is now an idealization.

By an *ideal,* I mean a goal accepted as being unattainable and yet worth striving for with a *realistic recognition of a necessary failure—*very different from the despair of feeling a failure as a person.

An *idealization* involves a splitting between "illusory good" and "illusory bad." The leader and his colleagues collude in an idealization of himself and of the UNIT (now in *very* large capital letters), which is often personified. *The good UNIT is engaged in a battle with the powers of darkness*—the "badness" outside, which is embodied in the rest of the hospital, the traditional psychiatric establishment, or the world at large. The unit is under attack.

It is important to realize that attack occurs in fact as well as in fantasy, e.g., rumors of dreadful happenings (usually of a sexual and aggressive nature), petty administrative interference, and so on. Com-munications are distorted and members of the unit, cut off from their professional colleagues "outside," react by counterattack or by further withdrawal. In the jargon of games theory there is a win-or-lose "zero-sum" game. In cybernetic jargon a "positive feed-back" occurs which increases error and disequilibrium, as contrasted with the "negative feed-back" which restores equilibrium (of which Jung's concept of compensation by the unconscious is an instance). I shall use the term *persecutory anxiety,* by which I mean *a mounting mutual attack associated with illusory idealization and splitting.* It is an interpersonal term. It can occur between individuals or between groups. In the case of a therapeutic community the self-perpetuation of the increasing attack and counter-attack is reinforced by numerous factors, some of which are:

(a) The development of *an esoteric "in-group" unit language.*

(b) *An exhilarating sense of cohesion* not unlike that experienced by some of us in small ships during the war. This "cohesion" is to be distinguished clearly from the differentiated aloneness-togetherness mentioned earlier.

(c) The *striking improvement in the symptoms* of many patients—for the time being.

2. THE "ENLIGHTENMENT"

"Enlightenment" (note the quotation marks) occurs as some of the above-mentioned processes are recognized. The danger to which experienced analysts are prone (not only in their own professional societies) is to formulate prematurely and, not seldom, pretentiously, forgetting that what is unconscious *is* unconscious.

With dawning recognition that *an egalitarian "democratic" ideal has thinly disguised a destructive power-game,* there is now a good deal of talk about the "badness inside" and debates occur about definitions of "role," "status," and "authority." The sickness lies not in what is talked about but in how the conversation develops. A sign of great danger is a tone of voice implying a subtle satisfaction: *"now* we know ourselves."

This rationalizing tendency only serves to exacerbate the persecutory situation. There are, however, potential positive possibilities as well as greater dangers of disintegration, in that during the "Enlightenment" the persecution occurs within the unit group where it can conceivably be dealt with. *Rivalries and destructive alliances* (e.g., patients versus staff, or sub-groups of each) can lead on to the next stage.

3. THE CATASTROPHE

The unit can disintegrate and collapse with very serious consequences. The existence of Tyson West Two has been maintained—at a cost. This cost (which at my age has now become too great for me) could be conveyed only by telling many stories, and I can only make a few broad generalizations.

Serious psychological breakdowns occur especially in prominent members of the staff. Imagine the situation of a leader. His charisma has been wearing thin. Suddenly he sees anew his Brave New World, established with personal emotional sacrifice, devoted clinical work, and complex political maneuvering. It is an illusion. The image of the unit, and of himself, is shattered. He experiences in his body the destructive impact of the split-off "shadow" which he has done his best to recognize. Maybe this does not happen to properly analyzed leaders. It can be avoided if the leader leaves soon enough to spread the gospel honestly elsewhere before moving on once again. Perhaps these days we know enough to prevent it—but this I doubt.

The continued persecuting situation can be damaging to patients and staff in ways too diverse to be elaborated here. Recurrent disturbances occur within the group, often with the *extrusion of members*, patients, or staff, who "act out" the unresolved persecution and destructiveness. Relief follows—but only for a time. The ritual of the "scapegoat" needs to be repeated.

One, among many other less obvious but perhaps more serious effects, is a chronic state—a narrowing of the lives of staff members as well as long-stay patients, who become devoured by the dragon UNIT. Then, they remain relatively out of touch with the rest of the world in a state of what can be termed "incestuous regression" (a metaphor—not a defined technical term). It is an important fact that there can be profound effects upon families, who can suffer either intolerable involvement or envious exclusion.

III. COMMITMENT AND SKEPTICISM

I suggest that there are five questions which are worth asking about any unit, whether it be a therapeutic community, a ward for chronic patients, a day-hospital, or any other treatment situation in which two or three are gathered together. Although they cannot be answered, they can be used to help in *formulating limited hypotheses,* which can be tested by correlational methods or by more strictly experimental investigations in which variables are manipulated and predictions made. Furthermore, such testable questions can be teased out from implicit or explicit value judgments. My first question relates directly to this last problem.

1. WHAT IS THE IDEOLOGY OF THE UNIT?

The structure and functioning of any unit reflects the *Weltanschauung* of the leader. In some communities the political-religious nature of the founder's ideology is evident—as in my own case. During hard times, when I have doubted whether patients were being helped at all in a strictly psychiatric sense, I have had to fall back upon an ideal that it is a "good" thing to attempt to promote honest relationships between people, respecting them as persons and not only as things. It is important to bear two points in mind.

(i) The ideology which is concealed is often the most dangerous. Value judgments are implicit in every psychiatrist's work—in diagnosis, in treatment, and in therapy. Notions of "sickness" and "health" necessarily imply moral (although not necessarily moralistic) values. Once I was a Christian revolutionary. Now I regard myself as a relatively enlightened radical.

(ii) A man's stated beliefs are seldom an accurate indication of what he does in fact. My unconscious values *are* unconscious.

2. WHAT IS THE NATURE OF AUTHORITY?

Where does the power lie and how is it used? It appears easy to contrast a legalistic, hierarchical, doctor-orientated system under its untouchable high-omnipotent superintendent, with a unit in which patients make decisions about admissions and discharges and openly attack the consultant as a "thick-headed bastard." Yet it is relatively simple for a subtle leader to use (consciously or unconsciously) an egalitarian appearance as a disguise for an intensely controlling manipulation of patients and staff.

There are marked differences between so-called therapeutic communities in methods of control or leadership and in the extent to which the status and roles of staff are blurred. On Tyson West Two physical violence is expressly forbidden and is a reason for immediate discharge. The "democracy" ultimately depends upon physical power.

I shall make a few bald statements about authority in Tyson West Two which arise from my experience—remembering that "experience" is often that which confirms a man in his mistakes.

(a) Tyson West Two is not a democracy—although I hope that it approximates to one. It is not a democracy because the government, which ultimately is me, cannot be elected out of office.

(b) Although roles overlap much more than in most units, we try to make these as explicit as possible. Nurses are not doctors, and neither nurses nor doctors are patients (not during working hours that is). In any case, democracy is not the same as egalitarianism. In Tyson West Two an effort is made to allow everyone to have a say on any matter, and, ideally, weight is given to all views. But everyone does not have equal powers. Decision-making is complex and space does not permit a description of detailed ways in which this is done in varied situations.

(c) I do not yet understand the function of *authority* in a non-authoritarian setting which aims to promote patient responsibility. I believe that although it can arise in a group it needs to be *invested in leaders,* and I suspect that this requires an "open" nonexclusive relationship between a man and a woman. As far as possible they will be "instrumental leaders," being sensitive to and expressing the needs of the group, but they must have clearly defined executive powers in order to set *limits* if necessary. The only sanction is discharge. In Tyson West Two this has been used rarely—as the result of physical violence, persistent refusal to take part in therapeutic activities, and repeated self-mutilation or suicide attempts. Much could be said about the latter. The fact is that since we (maybe the royal "we") have clearly said "Thou shalt not cut thy wrists or take overdoses," these activities have virtually ceased.

3. WHAT SPECIFIC TREATMENTS ARE USED?
4. WHAT ARE THE NEEDS OF THE STAFF?
5. WHAT ARE THE NEEDS OF THESE PARTICULAR PATIENTS?

The last two are large questions which would take another long paper to answer fully—and that would still leave the very large query about how we can make an objective assessment of results. I will conclude with a few further general remarks about the Therapeutic Community Disease, wishing to convey a profound skepticism (not cynicism) about the increasing fashion in England, and making a plea for a committed exploration of an important and exciting area in psychiatry while remaining in "uncertainties, mysteries, doubts."

"Our only health is the disease." In Eliot's words, "the wounded surgeon plies the steel," and as we recognize the sickness, in ourselves and in our society as well as in our patients, there is a hope of promoting a creative process. In maintaining an ideal (not an idealization) of *an aloneness-togetherness group—an integrated whole of differentiated individuals*—the symptoms of the disease, if detected early enough and appropriately responded to, have healing possibilities. The disease recurs, in miniature, over and over again. All its stages can be seen in our group session. But states of *disintegration and isolation* or of *cohesive collective fusion* can sometimes be converted into the creative alternating phases of *relative disorganization* with *re-organization* that I have described in previous papers on group therapy (Hobson, 1959, 1964).

Despite many failures, some apparently striking successes urge me on to pursue the investigation of a possibility—the possibility that a psychotherapy community unit if suitably developed could be most suitable for the resolution of persecutory anxiety which, associated with prolonged hostile dependency, is notoriously difficult to analyze in relatively closed two-person situations. I do not *know* if this is so. Partly as a result of the disease, the structure and functioning of the unit have greatly changed during fourteen years, and (in the continuing tradition) history, legend, and myth are vital factors. But we lack hard facts. Treatment needs to be guided by careful research. We can only make haste slowly.

I do not expect a quick cure—if indeed there is one. My speculation is that a community such as Tyson West Two attracts people who express a partially concealed sickness rooted in the values of our modern competitive-acquisitive society. Perhaps the structure of the unit makes this disturbance more evident. The unit can reinforce the splitting, but in the failure to achieve an ideal there lies a possibility of a creative success in treatment which could have very wide implications. Some might well see the main features of the disease in our analytic societies.

"Old men ought to be explorers."

REFERENCES

Hobson, R. F. (1959). "An approach to group analysis," *J. analyt. Psychol.*, 4, 2.
—— (1964). "Group dynamics and analytical psychology," *J. analyt. Psychol.*, 9, 1.
Moos, R. H. (1969). *Ward Atmosphere Scale: preliminary manual.* Stanford: Stanford University School of Medicine.
—— and Houts, P. S. (1968). "Assessment of the social atmospheres of psychiatric wards," *J. abnorm. Psychol.*, 73, 595–604.

14

Family Therapy:
When Analysis Fails

GEORGE H. HOGLE, *Palo Alto*

Thirteen years ago, at our first International Congress, one of our promising younger members gave an earlier paper on "group analysis" (Hobson, 1961). I have thought over for a long time the impassioned plea to the assembly then, following that paper, of one of our most distinguished and creative colleagues, Dr. M. Esther Harding. She said approximately: "Let us not dilute our energies by entering into these newer fields of therapy. Let us maintain the pure culture of what Jung has taught us." I mourn her loss and regret I shall not have the opportunity of a response from her.

By "pure culture" analysis, I have always assumed that it was a prolonged, introverted transaction of the patient with himself and his analyst. It did not include working through current relationship problems of the patient and certainly did not include seeing other members of the family separately or jointly. For the introverted analyst with the introverted patient, the "pure culture" is a most natural process and has worked well in reorganizing the psyches of many such analysands.

Unfortunately, however, a failure may occur when this introverted approach is used where the patient problem has to do predominantly with external relationships, or if the patient is so extraverted that his problems manifest themselves to him and he deals with them mainly in extraverted ways.

Now, I had reacted with some dismay at Dr. Harding's plea because I, as a Jungian analyst, have spent a fair part of my time in these newer fields—group and family therapy. I have drawn comfort and support, however, from one of Jung's basic principles: that the life aim of a person should be the search for his unique essence and the attempt to manifest it. Or, as many young Americans, who are increasingly being attracted to Jungian ideas, express it: "Doing your own thing." For long, I had assumed that the individuation process, the goal of analysis, was essentially an introverted one. I have come to realize that for extraverts, a large part of their individuation process will be an extraverted one, although it is to be hoped, of course, that they will come to realize the importance of, and become much more familiar with, their own inner workings as well.

My practice as a Jungian analyst and psychiatrist has been near San Francisco, California, in an extraverted university community. Although I had some general psychiatric referrals, most patients who came to me wanted to be treated by a Jungian in solving some problems or said they wanted to have a Jungian analysis. Early in my practice I found that I all too often engaged in what I later saw as a kind of stereotyped response to such new referrals. If they asked for individual Jungian treatment, then the "pure culture" is what I tried to give them, without realizing there might be a more appropriate treatment mode, like group, couple, family, or even behavioral therapy.

In fact, the first private patient I had was a 34-year-old, extraverted male gynecologist who had previously participated with his wife in a Jungian-oriented religious discussion group. Now he felt that a Jungian analyst could best understand and help him through a very difficult marriage problem. His wife wanted a divorce. He did not—instead he wanted to find out what was "wrong with himself" and try to change. After first hearing of the difficulties in their relationship, we set off earnestly to analyze the vivid dream material he presented over a period of three months. I did try to counsel him, in as nondirective a way as I could, how to deal with his wife, although in my own life experience and in my analytic and psychiatric training, like most analysts. I had had no specific experience in handling major marital problems. Not surprisingly, he became increasingly dissatisfied and finally stopped seeing me. Shortly thereafter, his wife divorced him amidst much bitterness, and he rightly felt that I had not really understood or helped him.

It took me some years to determine what I might have done otherwise. In retrospect I could have referred him to a marriage counselor, who need not really have been Jungian and who could have seen him and his wife together, with the purpose, first, of determining whether their marriage was viable and really desired by both of them, and second, of either helping them get on with improving their marriage, *or* working out as constructive and bitterness-free a divorce as possible.

Another patient who frustrated the usual analytic approach was a gifted 28-year old female composer and wife of a physician who came to me through her reading of Jung. She was introverted, low on feeling, had many big, vivid dreams, actively imagined, and spontaneously took up drawing her dreams. Try as we would to analyze this material, there constantly intruded, like an unwelcome guest, the very painful aspect of life with her husband, who was apparently an insensitive, immature, extraverted young doctor. The contrast of her very positive feelings toward her understanding therapist with those toward her husband widened the gulf in her marriage. Although I felt that analysis precluded intervention in relationship problems, as well as not feeling myself competent in this area, I finally felt I had no other choice. After some individual sessions with her husband and jointly with her, it became patently clear that they heartily disliked each other, yet had not considered parting because the idea of divorce was anathema for them. After reconsidering that old assumption, they decided that divorce would serve their lives much better after all than staying together. Although she was then ready for and needful of individual analysis, she had used up her own savings and refused to go on with an unimpeded analysis because she could not pay.

These two cases pointed out to me the essential importance of a careful evaluation of the family relationships and problems prior to beginning therapy in earnest, in order to determine whether dealing with relationship should take priority, and if so to see a couple together in the beginning or to refer them to someone else who was qualified. Since relationship and communication problems almost invariably arise during analysis, this would also indicate a desirability for more explicit and formal training of analysts and psychiatrists in the dynamics and therapy of marriage and the family. In our loyalty to the principle of the *individual* inner search, how often may we Jungian, Freudian, and other therapists have also been destructive of patient relationships and, at the most or at the least, used up effort, time, and money with well-meaning but off-the-mark analysis.

Initial stereotyped responses by the analyst no doubt derive from the old one-to-one medical model in which the wise doctor diagnosed and then helped root out the disease in the individual who sought his help. Jung, as a strong introvert, maintained this model and developed a highly introverted psychological approach, which has attracted predominantly introverted followers. I have found by inquiring from a number of you the personal discomfort experienced in dealing with more than one person at a time in a consulting room. In addition many of us have been trained in psychiatric institutes, often Freudian-dominated, with further emphasis on the one-to-one model. Some of us, perhaps the extraverted ones, got caught up to some degree with group therapy. Actually, any kind of systematized, specific training in marriage and family dynamics and therapy has emerged only in the past fifteen years, although social workers and marriage counselors have been active in this area for decades.

We may not have acknowledged as openly and emphatically as we should the not infrequent hazards and disadvantages of the one-to-one model. The powerful dyadic analytic relationship may compete profoundly with the marital one. This may be complicated by the actual or imagined formation of a kind of alliance against the spouse. The patient is protected by the non-directive, understanding approach of the analyst during the sessions, in which some secrets and certainly much other material are presented but never shared with the spouse. Few individual patients can resist the temptation to try out therapy on or against the husband or wife waiting at home, often with negative results. If denied access to the analyst, the spouse has no way of dealing with conflicts or possible distortions arising through the analysis, and may become increasingly resentful of the patient, the analyst, and analysis generally, sometimes alienating the spouse from therapy himself and certainly complicating the marriage.

Even with a meticulously careful handling of marriage problems while analysis is under way, a patient may mature and progress psychologically beyond the spouse, increasing the emotional gulf between them and putting the spouse at a further disadvantage. During analysis, moreover, the patient learns to communicate with and better understand his own psyche, and he learns how to relate after a fashion to his analyst. If he has not had help with relationship problems, however, he is likely to return home after the sessions communicating and behaving with the spouse in the same old patterns, many of them inappropriate.

The classical way of dealing with some of these difficulties has been for the spouse of the patient to be in analysis at the same time with a colleague with whom one can confer. In fact, I was the Jungian colleague to whom a male spouse was referred by an analyst who had been seeing his wife and his mother in analysis for some time. This man, an extraverted physician, came to me with some reluctance. He worked halfheartedly at a reductive analysis and at a few odd dreams, but mainly he wanted to complain of all the ordinary tensions of his marriage to a difficult wife. We two analysts attempted some therapy of the relationship with each spouse individually. Our occasional conferences by phone or at the end of some Society meeting, although helpful, were irregular and inadequate. During the second year, therapy with this man dwindled away and by common agreement we finally stopped, feeling that not much more could be effected. The basic problem for him and his wife, which was never solved at any depth, was (as George Bach describes in *The Intimate Enemy*) how they might fight creatively and negotiate effectively in the service of their relationship. He and his wife had achieved some insight into their own and each other's behavioral patterns, deriving from childhood, but were unable to help themselves to implement these insights by changing the nature of their encounters with each other.

In a marriage of any duration, unconscious "rules" of habitual interaction become established and a kind of homeostatic mechanism occurs to maintain these unwritten rules. If this pair could have been in couple or family therapy with the children, the therapist in time would have discovered their "rules," which often had unfortunate consequences. He could then have helped the family be aware of them and find alternate ways of behaving and communicating. The first priority and limited goal, then, for this couple well could have been direct help in therapy together for their foundering marriage. Then, if either of them individually wanted to go further on the road toward introverted individuation, this could have been attempted with far less distraction from the constant marital conflict and the ineffectual attempts at solution.

In the case just mentioned, both analysts were cooperating basically in trying to assist in the relationship problems. There are times, however, when therapeutic failure is compounded by disagreement between the two analysts as to where the therapeutic emphasis should be. An introverted colleague analyzed for some years an introverted/thinking young physician. Although the individuating process seemed slow, there was profound commitment on the part of both analyst and analysand to the journey. The extraverted/sensation wife in a depressed state was referred to me by her husband; she could talk only of her difficulties of living with a husband so different from herself. She had come to resent the feeling of exclusion from his analysis and the enormous amount of libido, money, and time going into his analytic sessions and the writing down and studying of his numerous dreams. The husband evidently reported little of his wife's disturbance to his analyst, who was surprised and incredulous to hear from me that things were so bad.

Finally, after I reported her very disturbing dreams and suicidal thoughts, he began to deal more intently with marital problems, but their magnitude was so great that I felt they demanded joint sessions, which my colleague resisted. The wife limped on in the relationship, trying out another analyst, a female, who found a similar frustration in dealing with the wife alone. The analyst of the husband had an honest difference of opinion in that he believed the undisturbed continuation of the husband's analysis was more important and the relationship problems could be dealt with well enough on an individual basis.

After a number of such cases, I began to wonder whether the introverted "pure culture" approach needed specific supplementation. With family therapy training I felt that I added valuable therapeutic philosophy and skill for myself and my patients to my own Jungian training and experience. Now Jung described marriage as a psychological relationship; he outlined its complexities, pitfalls, and possibilities; he stressed the need for developing consciousness and perseverance during the transitions of the maturing marriage. He pointed out how the psyches of the children are as much affected by the unconscious aspects and interactions of the parents as they had been by those of their parents before them. What a pity that neither he, Freud, nor many other of our mentors until recently saw the possibilities of dealing with unconscious as well as conscious material in the therapeutic setting of the married couple or the whole family. As analysts, we use the transference and counter-transference between ourselves and the individual as important therapeutic tools. Yet in a family there also develops the richest possible variety of unconscious manifestations and behavior, which can also be allowed free play, observed, and dealt with therapeutically in the presence of all the members. It is, of course, quite a different role for the therapist. What is emphasized is not so much that the analyst contains the patient within his *temenos* and is the patient's sole companion on his inner journey; rather, the couple or family have their own *temenos* and journey together, and the therapist accompanies them as a trusted companion.

In couple therapy, the husband and wife can share also in a limited amount of each other's reductive analysis, come to understand and deal with the differences in each other's psychological types and functions, learn to make more meaning out of each other's dreams, and become more conscious of various projections. They may also learn that their various ways of being different are not grounds for hostile judgment but are to be acknowledged as uniqueness in the other and coped with. They may learn the various non-functional ways of communicating and interacting and know they have other options of behavior.

I would add to Jung's statements about marriage that it is a setting in which there is as great a potential for psychological growth and individuation of both partners as any other, including analysis. For the potential to be achieved, however, it requires that the two people love, and like, each other enough to work through the times they hate each other—which calls for a sustained and functioning dialogue in which both take part. Couples often arrive at terrible impasses because they have never achieved much of a dialogue at all, and instead withdrawal and devitalization take place. Let me repeat one is unlikely to learn in individual analysis the art of creative fighting with one's spouse and children. It requires working through the conflicts as they happen for two people to come back together in real closeness. It is in this affectual oscillation that insight and growth may take place, through separation and coming back together again.

Patients sometimes come to analysis in a depressed state and in a marriage afflicted by alienation, devitalization, and withdrawal. Many husbands or wives may resort to another kind of vital encounter—a love affair. Either kind of encounter may cause a marriage to break up or, interestingly, may add enough to the individual's life that a moribund marriage may hold together. Therefore, when an unhappily married person presents him or herself for analysis (or starts an affair) this would seem a time for a serious evaluation, in depth, of the marriage relationship—with both partners, and sometimes the children, included. If it is discovered that there is no real love on the part of one or both partners and/or that there is a major mismatch of the two people and no desire even to work on the relationship in therapy, then they can be helped to the decision of divorce. Remaining in couple or family therapy can be of enormous value in accomplishing a constructive separation, divorce, and settlement. In fact, crucial therapeutic opportunity may be lost when couples break up in bitterness that haunts them and the children for years. In order to keep the couple going in therapy, when there may be much bitterness, it is of the utmost importance that the therapist avoid taking sides or forming a coalition with either spouse.

As I thought over my cases, I decided to make a simple statistical summary of all the patients I have seen during my ten years of private practice, which incidentally has been on a half-time basis. (As with a number of California colleagues, the other half has been in teaching medical students and supervising the training of psychiatrists and other professionals such as social workers and nurses.) I have had significant therapeutic involvement of any length of time with only 126 individuals. Of these, 70 started in individual therapy, of whom half were married. In 20 of these 35 marriages, relationship problems were so significant that I finally felt I had to see the spouses and some of the children a few times. The earlier ones usually ended as abortive attempts to help solve the marital and family problems. I now consider that fifteen of these twenty cases were failures because of the emphasis on individual therapy or analysis.

If I had it to do over again, I would recommend from the outset extended couple or family therapy for about one-fifth of the individual patients I have ever treated. Parenthetically speaking, as an analyst, of the remaining 50 individual patients, I have had only 24 in "pure culture" analysis of any intensity and duration, or about one-fifth of my practice—a common experience, I have found, with a number of younger colleagues who are extraverted, as I am. We have a mixed bag of types of referrals, often who are extraverted themselves. The other 26 in individual therapy were mostly unmarried, and although they benefited reasonably well, I believe they could have gone further towards individuation by the addition of intensive group therapy experience.

Of those in analysis, after an extended time four went on successfully into couple therapy. Individual treatment seemed right at first, and the relationship problems emerged later for solution. Two of these were' married couples, and the other two were single young sons in analysis who brought their widowed mothers into couple therapy for a time and then resumed individual therapy.

Since I had my own family therapy training I have started out therapy with thirteen couples or families—cases in which this has seemed the therapy of choice. There has not been any one unalloyed success, mainly because one or both of the partners were resistant to change and/or hostile to any kind of psychotherapy. Four such couples dropped out of treatment after a few sessions, much to my own relief as well. In one of these couples, the wife did go on with analysis, and with real benefit.

In order to meet the needs of those who are referred to me, I now undertake an initial screening and try to make a selection of the most appropriate type of therapy. Sometimes this can be decided straightway, sometimes it may take several weeks of sorting out. The first decision is whether couple or family therapy should be the choice. I have found it important at the beginning to see the spouse, or parents, in at least one separate and one joint session, and not rely on a report (possibly distorted) by the referred patient about the nature of the functioning of the family relationships. If couple or family therapy seems indicated, there is still the problem whether the other member or members are motivated for therapy and will cooperate. If not, individual or group therapy may be the only resort for the person originally referred.

In regard to referrals of disturbed teenagers or younger children living in the home, I have found that family therapy which includes the young person is most frequently the treatment of choice, possibly followed by group therapy with his peers or individual analysis or play therapy .Often a disturbed child can be helped only after the disturbances in communication in its home environment are remedied. Bringing the parents together in the treatment situation with the children allows the therapist to see a truer representation of what goes on at home than when parents are counselled separately by auxiliary personnel. In fact, treating the family at home some of the time can be beneficial. There was most dramatic help when a female family therapist colleague actually lived with a family for a period of a week or so.

To return to the screening procedure, if family or couple therapy is not indicated, the patient enters some kind of treatment without his family present, that is, individual or group therapy. In determining whether to take a person into prolonged introverted analysis, I have come to think he has to be a rather special individual, with a real capacity for introversion.

In another paper at this Congress, Dr. C. E. Brookes presented some valuable guide lines in recognizing the traits of a potentially individuating person:

Offers some openness to his or her own unconscious material.

Seeks and uses aloneness for assimilating experiences.

Searches for personal meaning.

Has some capacity for self-awareness and self intervention in behavior.

Is goal-directed and has the ability to change goals.

Wants to grow and is disturbed enough to want to change.

Has a certain tolerance for his or her own anxiety.

Has a sense of personal significance.

Chooses people and situations rather than being passively chosen.

I would add to the list an environmental condition: that the person not be in a situation where there is too much conflict and duress from immediate relationships.

If many of these guide lines are not fulfilled, the substantial commitment implied by deep analysis would seem too great. Limited goals with a consciously more limited kind of psychotherapy would make for better use of the analyst's time and effort. Group or family therapy could have such limited goals. Or either kind can serve as an intensive, meaningful link in the chain of individuative processes for the creative or potentially creative person. For example, developing a sense of personal significance and the capacity for assertiveness by a passive individual of low self-esteem can often best be accomplished in a group or family therapy setting. He needs the presence of others besides the therapist to discover how he may "count himself out" in many ways and to have the practice with others of "counting himself in." Others who have a problem of aggressiveness learn about that and have to restrain themselves, thus allowing the less assertive to grow. In a family setting, some members actually can learn how to communicate verbally for the first time in an effective way—how to argue creatively, to negotiate fairly, in other words to make known their own wants and stand up for them. Parents, we hope, will learn that they cannot preserve a mythical *status quo* of child behavior as the children reach major turning points in their lives. Family members will discover that individual differentnesses can be unique and valuable assets, rather than obstacles to be punished or suppressed by one or two members always speaking for the others. In many families, critical comments are threatening and taken as attacks, so that perceptions are often distorted, denied, or obliterated. The members can learn a new kind of culture whereby open, non-attacking negative "feed-back" is considered not as a threat but as a gift. They can also learn how important it is to give honest positive "feed-back" when it is felt but often not expressed. Finally, within the family where communication is blurred as to who is supposed to get the message, what the message is, and whether it is congruent with the affect, there is the opportunity to point out when these happen and opportunity to try over again with improved clarity.

The therapist tries to act as a good model on his own, by communicating with clarity, specificity, directness, congruence, and brevity. He will not only make and encourage ego-esteeming messages to all members but also will encourage critical response, which can be accepted constructively rather than as a hostile attack. He will value the contributions of each member as unique, even the smallest child. He will help each to express his own pain more appropriately and perceive and appreciate the pain of the others. The members will learn the value of completing a transaction rather than interrupting it or leaving it hanging. They will learn—let us hope—that differentness can lead to growth rather than be a barrier to understanding. They will learn to argue and negotiate as equals, so that the wants of each are considered in all decisions. Reductive analysis and dream analysis may take place in each other's presence. These can enhance individual and mutual insight, understanding and closeness. If the therapy has been effective, everyone will have grown in his own self-concept and self-esteem, and each will have learned a better way of fulfilling his own life wants and fitting them in more creatively with those of others, both in his family and outside.

In conclusion, I would like to say that for ultimate success in treatment, the quality of initial screening and the choice of treatment are just as important as the quality of the treatment and the therapist himself. "Pure culture" analysis, perhaps our most precious and unique offering, can well be saved, moreover, for those with the creative potential to use it to the full.

REFERENCES

BACH, G. R., and WYDEN, P. (1969). *The intimate enemy.* New York, Morrow.
BROOKES, C. E. (1973). "The group as corrective for failure in analysis." In this volume.
HOBSON, R. F. (1961). "An approach to group analysis." *Current trends in analytical psychology,* Ed. G. Adler. London, Tavistock.

15

Psychotherapeutic Success With "Hippies"

WILLIAM WALCOTT, *Pasadena*

The phenomenon of long-haired, bearded, scruffy young men and their young women—the so-called "hippies" is far too conspicuous in California to overlook. On the highways, in the cities, and even in their ghettoes and communes, these children are wayfarers in an alien soil, devotees seeking the true prophet. Where they journey, singly or in twos or threes, they encounter the fear, hostility, and abuse reserved for pilgrims in a foreign land. Their invasion of many of our consulting rooms forces us not only to acknowledge their existence, but to re-examine our shibboleths, as well as our concept of progress or success. Most importantly, this examination of the cases of several young people will show, I believe, the inherent difficulty of our judging the psychic development or health of anyone who lives in a world or culture or *Weltanschauung* different from our own.

In the time provided, I will offer my observations of twelve young

178

people or pilgrims known to me who were "into" the New Culture. Besides showing how they compare with others of their kind, I will attempt to assess their "success" in Jungian-oriented psychotherapy.

During a period of five years, from 1965 to 1969, but especially during the last twelve months of that time, I experienced an amazing influx of young people in my private practice. Why I chose 1969 as an end point is not particularly important, except that at the end of that year I happened to look into my files and to count the number of youngsters from age thirteen to twenty-six that I had seen during the previous few years: thirty-five. What really piqued my curiosity was the question: of these, how many so-called hippie youngsters had I seen? How were they different from the others, and how had they fared with psychotherapy? Among those thirty-five were some who used marijuana, some who used Seconal, some LSD users, one addicted to heroin, and many who used no drugs. Also, there were some who wore outlandish dress, had beards, long hair, were barefooted or were notably unkempt, and many who dressed quite conventionally. Some ventured ideas about God, worried about fulfillment and goals, while others talked about boy friends or girl friends, popularity, intolerable parents, intolerant teachers. In short, I seemed to be seeing two distinct groups of youngsters.

Thinking of three particular cases, I decided that their most distinguishing characteristic, which seemed most distinctly in contrast with the average youngster I had known, was their religious-psychological orientation. By this I meant that their interest, their attention, and their concern was concentrated on psychological matters, on both their own psychology and psychology in general, and on religious questions of meaning and purpose. Soon the names of three other youngsters of similar outlook came to mind, and then three more when I checked through my files. Because I was so familiar with them in many respects, I added three more young people to the group of nine even though they had not been in therapy with me. There were, then, twelve young people, mostly girls, from fifteen to twenty-six who, in my view, belonged to a single group.

The orientation of the remainder seemed to correspond to the typical adolescent stage of psychological development, the same now as it was twenty years ago or more, according to the textbooks. These were primarily ego-centered, concerned with status, popularity, material acquisitions, and so on. On the whole, their involvement in psychotherapy was superficial, at least by analytical standards. For one thing, they seldom if ever volunteered dreams. Mostly, their goal—or their parents' goal—was symptom cure. For example, òne thirteen-year-old girl, physically and socially precocious, was referred because of psychosomatic gastrointestinal complaints. Her concerns were how to hold onto a boy friend, tolerate her father, and live with a mother who was sexually promiscuous and an excessive drinker. Of those who were intellectually endowed, their attitude toward education was somewhat passive and uninterested—that is, what they learned seemed not a part of their lives. In general, this group had no argument with collective morality and goals, though this is not to say they always abided by them. In sum, their outlook and aspirations were centered on sociability, freedom from tension, material gain, and heterosexual success; aspirations, I would say, representative of adolescents in general.

Untypical adolescents were the group of twelve youngsters of religious-psychological orientation. Both religion, in a broad, all-inclusive sense, and psychology, generally and personally, were of special interest to them. Their outlook expressed concern about human welfare, individual freedom, world peace, human dignity, and love between men. Some of them began as innocent, naïve "flower children" attending love-ins at Griffith Park in Los Angeles. Their naïveté soon vanished when they saw their fellows beaten by police clubs at those gatherings. In fantasy or for real, all sought a Rousseau-Waldenesque flight to nature or flight from urban turmoil, impersonality, and repression. Most were attracted to eastern mysticism, divination through Tarot cards, the *I Ching,* and palm-reading; many were drawn to Jung and his affirmation of the individual and the human spirit; lately, the teachings of Jesus often came to the fore. At one time or another, all raised the issue of meaning either to contradict something I had said or to assert their own philosophy. They exhibited a deep concern for psychological growth, not merely symptom cure. Most of all, they wanted to overcome the confusion that pervaded their lives, their lack of goals, or their failure to achieve meaningful relationships.

Curiously, these twelve youngsters came from intact families, that is, families in which both parents lived together in the home. This contradicts newspaper and magazine articles and hearsay accounts which offer convincing evidence that members of communes, hippies in ghettos, and the street people are preponderantly from broken homes. Besides the relative stability of these twelve youngsters' homes (if parents living together can be accepted as a criterion of stability), many of the parents had had some amount of psychotherapy or analysis (parents of five children had some Jungian analysis). In most cases the family religion was Protestant. With respect to social-political outlook, the parents of at least half of the youngsters were of liberal persuasion; the rest were either conservative or of opinion not known to me.

The youngsters' education was above average when compared with all of the other young people in my practice during the same five-year period. Ten of the twelve were either enrolled in or had completed high school or college; the other two dropped out of college before earning a bachelor's degree. Altogether, their average time in school was thirteen and a half years. Again my experience differs from the popular press: the common belief is that the long-haired, hippie youngsters are school drop-outs.

Nine of the twelve left home for one of several reasons. (Parenthetically, I will add that subsequently the other three have left home.) The two motives for leaving home I have classified loosely as conventional and unconventional. The conventional included getting married, going to college, or finding separate living accommodations and regular employment. The unconventional implied a search for a radically different kind of life from what they had known in their homes. This meant anything from living with a partner as though married to living as a vagabond on the streets or in communes. Some of those who left home in the conventional (read "parentally approved") way, sooner or later took up the unconventional way of life typical of long-hairs and hippies. The important point here is that one way or another almost all of these young people wanted and achieved lives independent of their parents. The three who stayed home (to leave later) were high-school students, under eighteen years of age. Of the rest only three left home unconventionally; most of the others left originally for college. In working with these people, one seldom gets the impression that they were running away from home, the sort of motivation one is accustomed to, for instance, when dealing with people who were married too early. It is much more accurate to say that they were running toward, not away from, something. More than half of these youngsters, once on their own, were financially free of their parents; their subsistence varied from working part-time to living like pilgrims of old, relying upon the bounty of the land and the generosity of the native populace. Several frankly acknowledge begging and rummaging in the back of supermarkets for discarded food; one girl lived in a community of forty which grew its own vegetables in the summer and supplied its needs in the winter from supermarket discards. In short, these young people were mostly independent of their parents.

The twelve young pilgrims under study were sophisticated about the goals of psychotherapy; several, even about Jungian analysis. Or let me say that once most of them grasped the Jungian view of the psyche, they felt they had come to the right place. When working with adolescents, I judge therapeutic involvement on the basis of how much initiative or responsibility a youngster takes for the hour, and whether or not he volunteers life material, fantasy and dreams, paintings done at home. Even the youngster who is passive in the therapeutic relationship but interested and reasonably cooperative would represent positive involvement compared to the uncooperative youngster who sullenly waits for you "to do something." Of the nine pilgrims whom I saw for psychotherapy, eight sooner or later achieved maximum involvement in the process and the ninth only slightly less in my judgment because she did not volunteer unconscious material at any time. This compares with the fact that only one other youngster in my practice during that five-year period consistently volunteered dreams or fantasies after being asked once or twice. However, most of the non-pilgrim young people were active participants in therapy, welcoming their sessions, and usually taking initiative for their hours. Though these findings seem to contradict my hypothesis that psychological interest, as well as religious, distinguished the pilgrims from other youngsters in my practice, the difference in therapeutic if not life goals was the significant factor. With respect to psychotherapy, the pilgrims were more inner, self-oriented; the others much more outer, socially, collectively oriented.

One cannot speak of the New Culture, hippies, or the young generation in general without mentioning the use of drugs. In California, at least, the use of some kind of drug by young people between fifteen and eighteen years of age, if one believes the reports from the commercial media and the children themselves, seems close to universal. Conservatively, the actual number of children who use drugs occasionally probably comes to around seventy-five percent. This, at any rate, is my personal guess; but my guess is as good as the next person's. What drugs are being used, whether marijuana, barbituates, LSD, or something else, is an even more difficult question to answer. All of the pilgrims had used marijuana in some degree and were continuing to smoke it at least occasionally when I saw them. Not as many were using harder drugs occasionally. My guess would be that at least four of the twelve had at one time lived what is called a drug-oriented life. Before, during, or after their therapy, at least four gave up the use of all drugs except an occasional social puff of pot if anything. I have included these sparse items in the spirit of information, knowing fully well that I know too little to say more. Several of my California colleagues, namely Dr. Thomas Kirsch and Dr. Ernest Rossi, are far more knowledgeable on this subject than I and have made their reports. With respect to the youngster seeking higher and higher states of consciousness, not unlike the pilgrims of this study, Dr. Rossi says many use drugs as a means of achieving "instant individuation," an apt term indeed. Only one pilgrim, and one for whom therapy was unsatisfactory, never gave up the notion that drugs could serve the purposes of consciousness better than psychotherapy. However, the notion of "instant individuation" is a very provocative one and deserves further study as it concerns psychologically-religiously oriented youngsters.

When Jung wrote in *Aion* that the problem of the Aquarian aeon will be the union of opposites, he certainly hit the mark squarely with the pilgrims, if one limits his meaning to emotional and physical union or love. A year or so of love-ins (the motif of the flower child exemplifying peace and love) was always in the background of the twelve pilgrims. For all of them, extending love and affection to everyone meant personal sexual experiences which ranged from superficial and momentary to deep, lasting marriages, both legal and not. Yet the suggestion that sexual congress is a criterion of a more than average desire to form a human relationship is admittedly invalid. In fact, only four of the thirty-five youngsters known to me during that five-year period experienced no sexual relationship. I did attempt to rate heterosexual relationships (not necessarily physical) in terms of depth and superficiality. By superficial, I meant no relationships or few and far between, though sexual intercourse might have occurred. Some people, adults and young people alike, seem capable of only sexual relationship and have practically no other company with the opposite sex. But any relationship that involved serious feelings according to the person, or regular dating or companionship over a period of time, or living together, or being married at one time or another—I considered these levels of relationships more than superficial. My general impression was that pilgrims were desirous of developing relationships based on openness, honesty, and love, and that it was as important that they be capable of loving as that they attracted another's love. On the whole, other youngsters I had seen in my office took a more conventional view of love, that is, they loved love, wanted to be loved, wanted to experience love, but seldom looked beneath the surface of what the relationship meant. And, though the pilgrims were generally serious about relationship and its responsibilities, they did not let such feelings interfere with physical pleasure.

To turn to the original question of this paper, success or failure of hippies in Jungian-oriented psychotherapy, you can see that I have stacked the deck, or so it may be argued. By definition, the pilgrim group was composed of those youngsters who were most involved in therapy, most interested in psychological growth, and most intrigued by the contents of the unconscious. But the question still remains: did this group benefit from Jungian psychotherapy?

In my opinion, even several years after most of the analyses terminated, it is too early to judge. Let me take one example that will serve for all. Sarah, I'll call her, consulted with me for over two years. Her concerns were about lack of feeling, isolation, and fears of relationship. She used drugs moderately, quit school after high-school graduation (though accepted by three colleges), became alienated from her parents, had one sexual affair, and, living at home a year, depended almost entirely upon her parents for her support. She brought in dreams regularly, associated to them, initiated discussion of them and other inner and outer matters in her life, and developed warm, affectionate, trusting feelings toward me. Although she improved in her self-concept, she remained unsure and overly critical of herself. We terminated regular appointments when she left home to go to college. She corresponded and, as of this writing, has moved from her dormitory to live with a male student off campus. In her last letter she wrote: "Bob and I have realized a lot about each other and ourselves. We're not officially in love anymore. In fact we realize that we both made many mistakes by living together. Right now we are still friends and still have a lot to grow with each other. It's good to realize the limits of another person and your own and to be able to live with them without judging." According to her letter, she probably won't remain in college much longer. "I am now certain that it is the woods I want and I can do well without the city. This is not to say that the city and its people are 'unnatural' or bad as compared with mother earth, but I now know that it is no use torturing myself trying to fit in with the society when there is a way of life which is more real to me." How does one assess the success or failure of psychotherapy in nine cases (remember, three were not in therapy) such as this one?

Time alone will judge, because I believe these children are being prepared for an unforeseeable future. Pilgrims that they are in a foreign land, they seek goals that we can barely comprehend and are only barely able to accept. From my experience, analytical psychology, in terms both of viewpoint and of method (or lack of an approved method), stands a far better chance than other schools of psychology in helping these young people. This is because we respect not only the individual way of life, we respect the integrity of the human spirit that can manifest itself in the most curious and mysterious of ways. In the final analysis, one can only hope that he has helped the individual achieve his destiny; that, of course, is the true measure of success.

16

The Archetypal Foundation of Youth Protest as a Cultural and Individual Phenomenon

Mario Moreno, *Rome*

For some time now, those that have a psychotherapeutic practice have more frequently been accused of limiting themselves to "readjusting the neurotics and some psychotics to the least evil in order to send them back to live a frustrating and destructive social life," or "reinserting the maladjusted into the system" (Altan, 1968, pp. 332f.). One may immediately point out that this accusation does not concern analytical psychology in so far as it is the psychology of individuation, understood as a process of differentiation that has as its aim the formation of the individual personality. Yet I remember at the 2nd Congress of Analytical Psychology (Zurich, 1962), when Dr. Whitmont intervened during the discussion of Henderson's paper entitled "The Archetype of Culture," and alleged that "as analytical psychologists we are in need of a more positive approach to the social attitude" and that "there has been a tendency among ourselves to regard the external collective as nothing but a dangerous and stupid beast." Whitmont added finally: "As with the collective psyche, so also in respect to its corresponding external counterpart, the social group collective, a merely placating or propitiating attitude is not enough. Individuation calls for a more positive orientation, a searching for the creative value, the gold hidden in the dark *prima materia* of outer, no less than the inner collectivity" (1964, p. 15). I perfectly agree with Whitmont and hold that just as the individuation process implies the maintenance of a dynamic equilibrium between pairs of opposites that establishes itself between conscious and unconscious elements of the collective psyche with which the ego has a dialectic relationship, a particular consideration of the cultural, social, and political problem is also necessary since it is increasingly proposed in the psychotherapeutic relationship. I further maintain that in some cases the success or failure of analysis may depend on a more or less adequate consideration of this problem. I personally have become interested in the phenomenon of youth protest because of my psychotherapeutic practice. Analytical psychology's experiences create an awareness not only of the dialectical nature of authentic interhuman communication, as a practice in which reciprocal relations are relived and modified, but also of the reciprocal conditioning that exists between man and society. This experience may also particularly increase the understanding of human phenomena not only at an individual level but also at a cultural one. Thus it allows the intuitive collection of the structuring functions of the human psyche through which man becomes both a social and historic being and of which the social function is the superstructure. From my experience I have tried to lay down the archetypal foundation of the phenomenon of student rebellion in an essay entitled "Psychodynamics of protest" (1969). I would like to explain briefly here the conclusions I have reached, in order to illustrate how the analysis of this cultural phenomenon may prove useful in psychotherapy. I would also like to underline that the conclusions which lead to the psychoanalytical and sociological analysis of student rebellion, in the wider context of the youth problem, do not seem capable of offering a valid interpretative hypothesis of all the aspects that a phenomenological analysis of this rebellion brings into evidence.

From a psychoanalytical point of view, one can perceive in this phenomenon only a repetition of the oedipal struggle against paternal authority. One then considers the cultural commitment of youth—as regards the adolescent accentuation of instinctive unconscious demands

—as a defense mechanism in the form of intellectualization, to use the term proposed by Anna Freud.

From a sociological point of view though, the various hypotheses that have been suggested may all be due to a lack of models, whatever the reason for such a lack may be. In fact *anomia* has been mentioned, as well as alienation from work, a cultural lag in the sense of a hiatus between the technique and the moral concept of life, excessive desire for choices, and failure of the educational function of the family. From various points of view, all these phenomena indicate the depth of the crisis which society and contemporary culture are undergoing and their incapacity to supply valid models and values. Members of the younger generation are naturally the first to suffer these crises and to react more or less adequately to them.

At the recent International Congress of Psychoanalysis (Rome, 1969) A. Mitscherlich introduced a debate on the subject of "Protest and Revolution." No really illuminating indications emerged from this debate. Much of what was said was a repetition of the conclusions drawn from sociological analyses of the behavior patterns of young people in present-day society. It was stated that "in their protests and their withdrawal into the world of hallucinogenic drugs, youth rejects the consolidation of their personality in whatever role society offers" (Mitscherlich, 1969). This was related to the "increasing process of concentration of power and production, the increasing dependence of the individual on anonymous organization, and the request for conformity concerning ever more numerous aspects of private life and the assumption of a political role." It was concluded that "probably one of the most deeply felt narcissistic wounds at present is the increasing difficulty of self representation in the given work conditions." Mitscherlich pointed out that: "the profoundly anxious restlessness that can be felt beneath the youth protests has its roots in the frustration experienced in a world where self-realization is seriously hindered by a compulsive tendency towards conformity, widely organized by mass culture." The specifically psychoanalytical considerations on this occasion were not any different from those which I have already mentioned. It was said that "the reactions of the young rebels derive part of their virulence from the emotional confusion that characterizes adolescence," that "these young people are searching for new ways of self-expression," trying to live according to a provocative ego ideal, but that "the way they do it has clear neurotic features and carries the signs of acting out behaviour" (ibid., p. 27). At the end, P. Kuiper stated that the struggle of the young against paternal authority, which is gradually waning both in the family and in society, could be unconsciously determined by the desire for a strong paternal authority.

In my phenomenological analysis of student rebellion based on documents and statements involving French, German, Italian, and North American students, I seemed to find at the base of it an authentic aspiration to renew the social world that goes far beyond university or school reform and manifests itself as anti-authoritarianism, as a tendency towards the integration of excluded social components, as a need for redemption from repressive schemes of sexuality, and at the same time as an anarchic attitude.

My interpretative hypothesis of the phenomenon of youth protest as an expression of the emergence of the *puer aeternus* archetype in our contemporary culture is based on the phenomenological comparison of student rebellion and of this archetype as described by Jung.

In order to understand the significance of the emergence of the *puer aeternus* archetype in our culture, it would be opportune first to consider the significance of its activation in the unconscious of the single individual. To be able to do this we need to refer to a scheme of the psychological development in which to place the phenomenon.

Jung, as we know, never formulated a systematic theory of psychological development. This task was undertaken by Neumann, based on the ingenious intuition of the relationship existing between archetypal images and stages of development of the ego consciousness, both in the history of humanity as well as in the single individual.

In one of his recent essays Edinger has displayed in synthesis the stages described by Neumann (1954), uroboric, matriarchal, patriarchal, and integrative, pointing out that: "these stages are, so to speak, successive way-stations that we return to again and again in the course of a spiral journey which takes one over the same course repeatedly but each time on a different level of conscious awareness" (1968, p. 17).

In the stage which Edinger calls integrative, a new change is necessary to recuperate the psychic elements excluded from the previous unilateral and incomplete patriarchal phase. According to Edinger the dominating archetype in this phase is the one he calls the transformation archetype. The theme of the birth of the hero or *puer aeternus,* he says, belongs to this archetype: "this image expresses the emergence of a new dynamic content in the personality presaging decisive change and enlargement of consciousness."

We may say, therefore, that the activation of the *puer aeternus* archetype in an individual existence, in relation to the events of the personal history and cultural influences, corresponds to the demands of the passage from a patriarchal stage to an integrative stage. The *puer* tends to determine a new attitude of the ego, renouncing the security offered by conventional patriarchal schemes and exposing oneself to the unconscious, to the dangers of regression and matriarchal bonds. The aim is that of redeeming lost elements which are necessary, in so far as this recovery represents a decisive step towards the psychological integration and reconciliation of opposites.

In "The Psychology of the Child Archetype" Jung said that "the child motif represents the preconscious, childhood aspect of the collective psyche" (1959, par. 273). Its emergence therefore is conditioned by the fact that previously a dissociation occurred between the present and the past states. "For instance, a man's present state may have come into conflict with his childhood state, or he may have violently sundered himself from his original character in the interests of some arbitrary persona more in keeping with his ambitions. He has thus become unchildlike and artificial, and has lost his roots" (ibid., par. 274). The *puer* archetype therefore has a compensatory function: "Our differentiated consciousness is in continual danger of being uprooted; hence it needs compensation through the still existing state of childhood" (ibid., par. 276). Another essential aspect of the archetype mentioned by Jung is its character of futurity: "The child is potential future. Hence the occurrence of the child motif in the psychology of the individual signifies as a rule an anticipation of future developments, even though at first sight it may seem like a retrospective configuration. . . . It is therefore not surprising that so many of the mythological saviours are child gods. This agrees exactly with our experience of the psychology of the individual, which shows that the 'child' paves the way for a future change of personality. In the individuation process, it anticipates the figure that comes from the synthesis of conscious and unconscious elements in the personality. It is therefore a symbol which unites the opposites; a mediator, bringer of healing, that is, one who makes whole" (ibid. par. 278).

In Jung's statements about the *puer* archetype, we can grasp positively a psychological moment of radical renewal, spiritual rebirth, and transformation of the psychic cosmos. From there we can move our attention to the cultural plane in order to ask whether there really are conditions favoring the activation of the archetype at present, and whether the narrow analogy between the phenomenology of this archetype and the phenomenology of student rebellion may be interpreted as a sign of the emergence of the *puer* archetype in our culture.

Jung has, in a certain sense, already replied affirmatively to the first question when he wrote a propos of the *puer* archetype: "we may perhaps extend the individual analogy to the life of mankind and say in conclusion that humanity, too, probably always comes into conflict with its childhood conditions, that is, with its original, unconscious, and instinctive state, and that the danger of the kind of conflict which induces the vision of the 'child' actually exists" (ibid., par. 275). And still more explicitly: "the sort of situation that produces the 'child' as the irrational third is of course a formula appropriate only to a psychological, that is, modern stage of development" (ibid., par. 288).

In other words, the patriarchal character of our culture in its present crisis gives the essential premise for the activation of the archetype. The determining factors are so numerous and so obvious that it is unnecessary to dwell on them at length. On the philosophic plane empiricism and rationalism dominate; mechanical and deterministic science promote an alienating technological development; an authoritarian and repressive morality based on a sense of guilt persists on the ethical plane; on the social plane there is either a competitive capitalist economy or a socialism that denies some of its own theoretical premises; and on the psychological plane, what prevails is individualism based on will power. In "The Undiscovered Self" Jung pointed out that in our culture there is a unilateral development of consciousness, and simultaneously, a progressive loss of contact with the unconscious. He wrote: "The forlorn state of consciousness in our world is due primarily to loss of instinct, and the reason for this lies in the development of the human mind over the past aeon. The more power man had over nature, the more his knowledge and skill went to his head, and the deeper became his contempt for the merely natural and accidental, for all irrational data—including the objective psyche, which is everything that consciousness is not" (1964, par. 562).

The determining elements of a crisis in patriarchal values and attitudes are also numerous and are contributing towards a disintegration of the present cultural canon. Modern art is characterized by symptoms of such a disintegration. For a long time in the figurative arts as well as in literature, schools, traditions, and laws of composition have been "contested" while an increasingly exasperated search goes on for what is spontaneous, authentic, essential, and related to the unconscious. On the philosophic plane it is Kierkegaard and other phenomenological-existentialist scholars who are involved in protest against the anonymous world of the general rule with its unauthentic dispersion into everyday banality. Dilthey's doctrine states the methodological irreducibility between natural and spiritual sciences, while Freudian psychoanalysis points to alienation in the instinctual sphere as one of the essential causes of modern man's troubles; and on the social plane Marxism denounces the class-structured society and work alienation.

To Erich Neumann goes the merit of demonstrating, in a particularly convincing way, how a certain culture—while in its historical balancing phase—finds itself balanced between two great collective systems. One of these is made up of archetypal elements that are operative in the collective unconscious of the single individual, while the other system consists of the values of the cultural canon operative on the plane of collective consciousness. In "Art and Time" (1959) he speaks of the cultural canon as the group of collective values that uphold the system of a culture during its historic evolution. Neumann wrote in *The Origins and History of Consciousness*: "The collective transmits to the maturing individual, as cultural possessions in his world of values, such contents as have strengthened the growth of human consciousness. . . . 'Heaven' and the world of the fathers now constitute the superego or conscience which, as another 'authority' within the personality, represents the collective conscious values, though these vary with the type of collective and its values, and also with the stage of consciousness which the collective has reached" (1954, p. 364).

When the equilibrium between the archetypes and values of the cultural canon is broken—that is, when the culture is no longer balanced between the collective unconscious and collective consciousness—then, according to Neumann, a disintegration of the cultural canon occurs, while new archetypes emerge from the collective unconscious to form the basis of the new cultural canon. Neumann in fact admits a genetic correlation between the collective unconscious elements, archetypes, and the elements of the cultural canon in its historical evolution. The activation of a certain psychic, transpersonal, archetypal substratum gives rise to the movement of various creative men, unknown to each other and therefore incapable of being motivated to reciprocal influences, in the same direction. They follow an impulse of which they are unaware rather than a pre-established program. This *Zeitgeist* phenomenon, generally seen first in artistic and philosophical fields, gradually extends to all modes of cultural expression, including social and political behavioral patterns.

Having recognized the patriarchal character of our culture and stated its critical situation, we may affirm that the essential premises exist for the emergence of the *puer aeternus* archetype from the collective unconscious. In the first place it manifests itself in the anti-patriarchal, anti-authoritarian, anti-traditional, innovative, and revolutionary aspect. Youth is opposed to old age, the childhood world to the adult world, the rational to the abstract, the irrational to the concrete, and so on. The other essential aspect of the archetype is turned towards the future: the integrative aspect. It proposes the redemption and recuperation of everything that the present culture has rejected or repressed. The "shadow" of a patriarchal culture such as ours includes numerous elements that are not subordinated to a model of virile dominating behavior: for instance, instinctiveness, especially in its "pregenital" narcissistic components; and sensibility, feeling, irrationality—the "female" world in general as an antithesis to the rational control of directed thought and the world of "virility." Closely linked to the integrative is the religious aspect, which derives from the archetype's function of sponsoring, as a conciliator between the opposites, a new unit of the personality, the self. The emergence of the archetype, in fact, points to the possibility of overcoming the paralyzing split between consciousness and the unconscious, the possibility of restoring the culturally alienated unconscious and creating a new equilibrium favoring the activization of the archetype of the self, which tends to organize all the components of the psyche in a structure transcending the ego. Through the above considerations, which are founded on the lessons of Jung and other members of our school of analytical psychology, I believe it possible to relate the phenomenology of student rebellion to the cultural emergence of the *puer aeternus* archetype. This rebellion is, as I have said, anti-authoritarian, anti-exclusive, and sexophile. This seems to correspond perfectly to the anti-patriarchal and integrative aspects of the archetype. Perhaps the link between the religious aspect of the archetype and student rebellion might appear less easy to apprehend. It seems to me, however, that the enthusiasm and ardor of student action, the spreading of the phenomenon from an élite to the student mass, bear witness to a transpersonal element rich in numinosity and capable of involving the single individual—even inflating him with the zeal of a neophyte, savior, redeemer, of one who maintains that he has something to say. On the other hand the coincidence of the archetypal phenomenology with the characteristics of student rebellion is not limited to positive aspects.

On the individual plane the *puer* archetype may manifest itself negatively by inflating the ego or overwhelming it with its own heroic contents, thus inducing the individual to identity with it. M.-L. von Franz has provided an excellent description of this condition, which she calls the *puer aeternus* neurosis.

She says that in general there is "a tendency to lead a provisional life while one is fantasying a 'real' creative life to come, but the latter is never searched for." She adds: "Messiah-illusions frequently also play a role, be it that one actually hopes to redeem mankind as a new saviour or at least one believes one will soon be able to announce 'the last word' about philosophy, art or politics. Reality as it is is felt to be unbearable, the routine of everyday life which demands so much patience, and long-lasting efforts towards a goal, are avoided. Everywhere in the job, in the women with whom one lives, in colleagues, one finds things to criticize which serve as an excuse for indolently cutting off the relationship." Von Franz notes further that "the *puer aeternus*-obsessed frequently have no feelings of social responsibility, but they love drunken ecstatic revolutions for their own sake wherever they may lead" (1964, p. 150).

Jung, for his part, had pointed out two forms of inflation which von Franz cites: "the colossal pretension grows into a conviction that one is something extraordinary, or else the impossibility of the pretension ever being fulfilled only proves one's own inferiority, which is favourable to the role of the heroic sufferer" (1964, p. 180).

The anarchic character of some student protests and certain inflationary student attitudes, both in the victimistic sense as well as in the pretension of being something extraordinary, seem to correspond arrestingly to the negative and infantile aspects of the *puer* archetype.

Finally, von Franz also points to the possibility of a negative involution of the *puer* neurosis. She writes that sometimes the *puer* "in a sudden crisis discards all his former ideals and either shrivels up into a cynical little bourgeois or becomes a criminal through suddenly giving way to his formerly repressed realistic side, which leads to a short-circuit reaction" (1964, p. 142).

Now I would like to outline two cases which to me illustrate quite clearly the link between the cultural phenomenon of student rebellion and the individual problem structured by the *puer aeternus* archetype. These cases demonstrate that sometimes a clear grasp by the analyst of the link between his own political position and the individual exigency becomes essential for the success of an analysis, at least when the analytical relationship becomes symmetrical and constellates an individuative problem.

Paul is thirty and for some time has successfully devoted himself to the same commercial work as his father. While at the university, he was a brilliant student with many cultural interests and stimulating plans. He was politically involved in a student group of the extreme left and took active part in student strikes. In the same period he had many relationships with girl students but never became sentimentally involved. As soon as he graduated, however, Paul decided "to be concrete and not to lose time," and he took up the same work as his father—work which beforehand he had despised—and began to work intensely. His father is a "great worker" who prefers "to die on his feet" rather than remain inactive as doctors have advised him since a heart attack. He is the owner of an old firm and is intent on safeguarding its good name. Paul increasingly revalues his father: in the past he had reproved him for an extramarital relationship which had made his mother suffer, and was very irritated by an often too servile attitude towards his clients while being too brusque with his employees. He identifies more and more with his father, especially since his own marriage and the birth of the first son. He too, in his occupation, even at the cost of economic sacrifices, defends his reputation as a serious honest person. He is scrupulous in his work and is in fact tending to become as apprehensive as his father. Paul is therefore a confirmed business man, a good father, and an integrated bourgeois. Little remains of the typical *puer* of his university days—only a very controlled passion for gambling, some "not too compromising" female friendships, and the apparently unjustified idea that he is destined to die young. Otherwise, his *puer* phase is completely obscured by the identification with the patriarchal cultural canon.

A few days after the sudden death of a relative who was a happy person, always ready to enjoy life and seeming to be perennially youthful, Paul began to show signs of neurasthenic illness that soon developed into hypochondria. Very soon an obvious link shows itself between the appearance of the symptoms and Paul's work activity: the symptoms precisely tend to hinder the work activity and to defend the *puer* demands, both the most regressive ones such as the return to maternal protection as well as the integrative demands of lost values. Paul's problem is obvious in one of his first dreams: *"I arrive in a dirty squalid village. I go into an old hovel where I find a very beautiful intelligent half-caste child who speaks in a surprisingly mature way for his age and with an aristocratic accent. He has very little to eat. On one side is the child's father, an ugly unpleasant man who seems overbearing."*

In this "stable of Bethlehem" setting Paul finds the "divine child" who is half-caste, perhaps because he is relegated to the shadow or perhaps because of the union of black and white, but a child that has all the attributes of this archetypal image: beauty, intelligence, and nobility. Besides the *puer* stands a tyrannical oppressive father who at the same time is the concrete realistic side of Paul himself who desires power. The elaboration of this problem is, however, very complex: in an initial phase a positive maternal transference allows the nourishment of the *puer*. Paul reassures himself, improves clinically, partially liberates himself from the worry of work, takes up reading again and meets old university friends. Yet subsequently Paul begins to contest my role as analyst, my belonging to the "establishment," my "patriarchal tolerance," the political point of view he supposes me to have. The interpretation of this behavior as a negative paternal transference, projection of the aggressive power-seeking shadow, is partly accepted.

Paul however continues to contest my supposed political position still more pointedly and with less distortion in his projection.

As soon as I realize that his suppositions are correct, even though judged negatively as an expression of opportunism and need for security, I decide to speak to Paul about my political position. I explain in synthesis to Paul that I personally am trying to safeguard my individuality and freedom from every identification with values of the collective consciousness, and from time to time I use those choices that favor the integration of new values arising from the collective unconscious, without the implication of an alienation from conscious values, but simply presenting to me a possibility of dialectic comparison.

Paul reacts to my explanation with the following dream: *"I am alone in my room and hear children's voices in the next room. I go and find two children I don't know. One is very talkative and noisy and asks me to play with him. The other is calmer and smiling, sitting at a table drawing a compass card. The first child moves away and then I ask the other if he wants to go out for a walk with me. He accepts willingly."*

It seems to me that my talk with Paul, which brings into evidence the link between my political position and the individuative problem, worked as a spiritual recall. In the dream, the *puer* manifests itself in two aspects: one, more infantile and extravert, that asks to play; the other, more engrossed and introvert, that designs a compass card. It is this second child that Paul accompanies, and it seems a reasonable guess to see in him a prefiguration of the self.

The second case is that of Frank, 32 years old, the only child of a left-wing intellectual couple. Of the two parents it is the mother that is politically more active, whereas the father has become increasingly absorbed in his studies and in the family circle is criticized for being less concrete and politically lukewarm. Frank is intelligent, artistically gifted, and cultured. He divides his time between political and artistic activity. Slowly, however, he has to admit to a great difficulty in realizing his revolutionary artistic projects, not only because of external obstacles but also because of his "laziness," which hinders him from devoting the necessary continuity to his artistic activity. So at about 30 he found himself as a party official weighed down by work from which he derived no satisfaction.

Since his adolescent period Frank had been surprised by his homosexual fantasies concerning contemporaries whom he despised both politically and as men; he regarded them as aggressive individuals, conservative and ambitious with a desire to dominate others. These fantasies of his were always controlled, and at the same time he had various comradely affectionate relationships with girls for whom he never experienced an authentic erotic response. His relationship with a girl of bourgeois origins, who wants to marry him, gives rise to a serious depressive crisis. Frank is anguished by the idea of marriage, yet for the first time he feels sentimentally attached to a woman whom he does not want to lose. In these circumstances Frank turns to the analyst. The analysis brings out Frank's mother complex and the necessity to integrate the virile shadow that is projected into the partners in his homosexual fantasies. He rapidly becomes aware of his problem but nevertheless is incapable of taking any decision as regards his work, his artistic activity, or his sentimental relationship.

A dream unexpectedly clarifies the situation revealing a counter-transferential problem. *"I am at home where the analyst is speaking to my mother. She says that A. is a little bourgeois who wants to dissuade Frank from his political and artistic choices. The analyst does not explicitly approve of this but smiles benevolently. I am quite amazed and also a little anguished."*

What the mother says in the dream corresponds to what she actually thinks of her son's relationship. Personally I have never approved of such attitudes, but I must admit to being notably fascinated by the many *puer* aspects of Frank's personality. His intellectual vivacity, anticonformity, political commitment, artistic sensibility, and intuition may possibly have induced in me a protective sympathy which echoes the maternal position and hinders his evolution. On this occasion I realized that a possible projective identification of mine impeded my understanding that, above all, many of Frank's attitudes were not the result of his identification with the *puer aeternus* archetype, but most likely the effect of the education he had received in an atmosphere where these attitudes were already part of the collective consciousness. Many of Frank's ideas and points of view were, in effect, products of cultural stereotypes, and therefore he has to be helped to differentiate himself from the collective consciousness in which he has always lived. This dream was undoubtedly the point of departure for a global revaluation of Frank's psychic situation. At this meeting I am unable to dwell at length on his further evolution. I would like to refer merely to a later event that represented the final positive turning point in his analysis.

One day Frank came to his session and asked me to consult the *I Ching* with him; I had never spoken to him of this work, but he had heard from a friend of his that a Jungian analyst sometimes used to have his patients consult the *Book of Changes*. I did not resist his request because I intuitively felt that it might acquire a particular significance for Frank, that is, the possibility of an experience that would allow him access to a deep potentiality of his psyche.

He was most affected by the reply of the *I Ching* as regards his relationship with the girl and brought this dream to the following session: *"A young man, whom I recognize as myself, wants to free a girl held prisoner in a tower, perhaps because she has committed political crimes. A strange character appears at the tower door, an old man, something between a high priest and a court dignitary: he has a short sword with which he wounds my forehead. Immediately afterwards, however, he offers me the key to the room in which the girl is locked."*

It would be possible to speak at length on the symbolism of this dream; it seems sufficient to me, however, to say that the old man with the golden sword is already a personification of the self that now guides Frank's evolution, wounding him on the forehead so as to free him from the cultural conditioning of his thought and offering him therefore the possibility of a meeting with his anima.

The theme of this Congress concerns the problem of the success and failure of analysis. I have tried to show how in analyzing young people the positive or negative result may be conditioned by—among many other factors—the possibility of an exact evaluation of the dynamic significance that in each single case is attributed to the phenomenology of the *puer* type. Such an evaluation, freed from every counter-transferential distortion, may allow the analyst to favor the use of the *puer* dynamics in the individuative sense.

REFERENCES

ALTAN, C. T. (1968). *Antropologia funzionale*. Milan, Bompiani.

EDINGER, E. F. (1968)."An outline of analytical psychology," *Quadrant*, New York, 1, 17–20.

FRANZ, M.-L. VON (1964). "Religious aspects in the background of the puer aeternus problem," in *The archetype*, ed. A. Guggenbühl, Basel and New York, Karger.

JUNG, C. G. (1959). "The psychology of the child archetype." *C.W.* 9, I.

—— (1964). "The undiscovered self." *C.W.* 10.

MITSCHERLICH, A. (1969). "Introduction to debate on protest and revolution." *Int. J. Psycho-Anal.*, 50, 25–30.

MORENO, M. (1969). *Psicodinamica della contestazione*. Turin, ERI.

NEUMANN, E. (1954). *The origins and history of consciousness*. New York, Pantheon/Bollingen; London, Routledge.

—— (1959). "Art and time," in *Art and the creative unconscious*. New York, Pantheon/Bollingen; London, Routledge.

WHITMONT, E. C. (1964). Discussion of Henderson's "The archetype of culture," in *The archetype*, ed. A. Guggenbühl, Basel and New York, Karger.

17

Images of Success in the Analysis of Young Women Patients

FAYE PYE, *London*

This paper is an attempt to examine the psychology and analysis of young women patients and to estimate the outcome of their analysis. Attention is given chiefly to a group of patients who appear to represent a cultural type, but whose psychology shows certain features that may be common to many women in Western society today. All the patients referred to live in or near London.

It is suggested that the term *success,* applied to analysis, must be taken to mean *the most desirable outcome,* and that the criteria by which this outcome can be judged cannot be formulated in terms which are only intellectual. The criteria correspond to complex images in the mind of both analyst and analysand, and are a product of the personality, life experience, and values of each.

Further, although the outcome of each analysis must be considered in relation to an individual person, the analytic undertaking is contained within the general process of historical and cultural change. Criteria of success will be influenced by transpersonal values such as the purpose and meaning of life, the nature of man, and the identity of male and female; and also by the social and symbolic forms in which these values can be fulfilled. Images of success in analysis will therefore be concerned with the way in which the unique individual is able to develop, adapt, and integrate within the particular cultural circumstances of the times.

It is now commonplace to speak of the rapidity of change in our century; but it is also an indisputable fact, constituting in itself a "particular cultural circumstance." In the analytical setting, this appears as a pair of psychic opposites which might be formulated as on the one hand *rootedness in eternal forms and values* and on the other hand *flexibility in change*. In the final outcome each analysand must come to terms with this pair of psychic opposites. But it is especially and acutely relevant in the analysis of young women patients. It is as though the psyche of the individual woman actually consisted in this inner opposition: rootedness in eternal forms and values, and flexibility in change.

The individual woman seems to be impelled by an inner drive to find an integration and adaptation in which both poles of these opposites are fulfilled, not only psychically but also in the life. The ego, supported by the animus, is oriented towards adaptation to cultural change, and indeed even to the cultural cult of change: the same ego, polarized by the archetype of the feminine especially in its aspect as mother, is orientated towards what is unchanging and resistant to change.

Jung (1961, par. 668) noted as early as 1913 the point of psychic conflict at which woman seems to stand in history. Neumann (1954, p. 171) also formulated the situation historically when he said, "Whereas man's ego and his consciousness have changed to an extraordinary degree during the last six thousand years, the unconscious, the Mother, is a psychic structure that would seem to be fixed eternally and almost unalterably. . . . The mother image is less conditioned by the temporal and cultural pattern."

Analytic theory has long been aware of an element active in the psyche of woman which disturbs the relation of her ego to the feminine archetype. Freud postulated "penis envy," Adler "masculine protest," and Jung "animus identification." Toni Wolff (1956, p.8) in her *Structural Forms of the Feminine Psyche* wrote that "our present time offers widest scope to the Amazon structure." Neumann (1954, p. 126) seems to imply that the ego is in itself masculine. He says "Ego consciousness stands in manly opposition to the feminine unconscious."

In the psyche of young women today, this inner opposition appears to have reached a further stage. There is now a generation of young women who have grown into adult life since the Second World War, in a society in which the specific values, creativity, and numen of the traditional pattern of feminine life have been challenged and depreciated perhaps as never before. They have experienced only a technological society, in which the cult of change and the means of change are consistently presented as the highest value and achievement of mankind. It is necessary to mention only a few factors to illustrate the assault on feminine values: the insecurity of the family and dispersion of the extended family; the technological invasion of the home, especially in the preparation of food; effective contraception, sexual promiscuity, easy abortion, the population explosion; the depersonalization of sexuality in education, the press, literature, and advertisements; the educational emphasis on logos at the cost of eros; and the new role of women as wage-earners in industry and profession. More recently "Women's Liberation" has entered the field. It is not really surprising if this generation of young adult women manifests in an extreme degree the intrapsychic conflict between rootedness in eternal values and orientation towards change. In so far as she "never is not-a-woman," as Erikson puts it (1968, p. 290), she is confronted by a traditional feminine identity which on the one hand gets an enormous amount of attention, and on the other hand is progressively whittled away.

It is from this generation of young women that there comes a type of patient that occurs with sufficient frequency perhaps to represent a cultural group. It is possible to give a descriptive profile that is in the main applicable to them all.

They come from stable homes, in so far as the parental marriage has remained intact, and from various levels of the middle class. They have never known poverty or social discrimination. They have passed through school to the latter teens, and afterwards to an institution of higher education in preparation for a socially recognized profession which they practice.

They give a history of a relatively sheltered and conventional family life in which mother has been a homemaker and has not gone out to work: She has also been the decision-maker in the family and the dominant partner in the parental marriage. Father has been introverted or retiring and yielding; he has been passive within the family, and perhaps emotionally dependent, but he has not been ineffectual in the world or as a breadwinner. The daughter's tender eros-attachment has been to the father, while her relation to her mother has been intensely ambivalent. At the same time father has been held in some contempt as weak or pitiable.

These young women seem to have been driven into life by an anxious inner intensity. They have been oriented in relationship towards men, and have tended to regard peers of their own sex as rivals rather than friends. At an early age they have plunged into sexual experimentation with something like heroic determination. But their experience has been without emotional depth or satisfaction, haunted by the secret worry that they were not adequate as women. It has been as though they were in search of the proof of their female identity at the level of the body. They have been preoccupied with an ideal of self-development and self-validation which precluded emotional involvement and commitment and therefore always left them with a sense of emptiness.

Their attitude towards marriage and motherhood is one of anxiety, as an experience that they must at all costs not miss, but also as a threshold that they dread to cross because it leads into what they feel to be bondage, submission, and a loss of individuality. Their attitude to their career is also one of anxiety, as an enterprise they cannot forgo but which they also cannot wholly embrace for fear that it will lead them away from marriage and motherhood. They give the impression that they cannot tolerate the idea of commitment on either count, because what they really want is total commitment to each of two opposing principles: as it were, to lead two different lives at once. It is as if they wanted to be both man and woman at the same time. It is a psychic situation that might at one time have been resolved by the social sanction to "choose marriage or career." But for their generation this resolution of the psychic conflict is lacking.

Erikson (1968, p. 282) has described a normal early phase in the life of a young woman in which she ventures into the world, as he puts it "with a bearing and a curiosity which often appears hermaphroditic if not outright 'masculine.' " He describes also "the singular loveliness and brilliance . . . one of these esthetic phenomena which almost seem to transcend all goals and purposes and therefore come to symbolize the self-containment of pure being" (ibid., p. 283).

This description of the youthful anima, which includes a kind of psychic bisexuality, is typical of these young women. They do not in any sense appear unfeminine: quite the contrary. It is rather that they are impaled on an ideal of wholeness which they cannot relinquish.

There does not appear to be anything exaggerated in the personality or constitution to account for the difficulty. They are so to speak "ordinary" young women in the best sense who would be acceptable in any circumstances. They do not have an animus that is in competition with men. They are attractive and intelligent but not intellectual, and they are neither exceptionally talented nor crippled by any defect or handicap. It is difficult to avoid the impression that had it not been for the confusion of ethics and mores in the permissive society, and the expectations that it provokes, they would not have been thrown themselves into early promiscuous experience and might have made an unproblematic transition. On the other hand, perhaps the ground of disturbed feminine identity was laid early by an imbalance of male and female attitudes in the relationship between the parents, later reinforced by the collective confusion of norms.

They come to analysis for a variety of overt reasons, characterized by moods, anxiety, a growing sense of inner isolation, and a confusion of goals and purposes. Underlying all the overt reasons and symptoms is the psychic opposition between rootedness in *unchanging feminine forms and values* and participation in *the male world of change.*

There are several significant features common to all the analyses. In the early stages totality symbols appear, exemplified by the following dream: *"I am standing in a great stone circle, like Stonehenge. The figure of a man falls out of the sky right into the center of the circle. As he reaches the ground I begin to walk out of the circle towards a house that stands outside it. It is a large old house which is all in darkness. A new wing has been built onto it."*

These totality symbols might appear to have, but do not in fact have, the character of a premature individuation process. The movement is away from the totality symbol rather than towards it, in the manner of the dream. There are several ways in which it seems appropriate to estimate such symbols, perhaps all of which are relevant. First, they may be uroboric forms preceding the separation of the opposites. Secondly, they may be attempts, which have failed, to resolve the psychic opposition by transcending the conflict. And thirdly they may represent an activation of the self in preparation for a psychic integration which is not only new in a personal sense but also new in a cultural sense, since it will represent a resolution of the conflict between rootedness and change. The not-infrequent occurrence of the hermaphrodite symbol may have a similar significance.

The archetype of the mother is of course a major feature, and the negative mother image is invariably confused at first with the personal mother. The analyst is involved in the whole range of the positive-negative projections. But the developmental process is not wholly contained within the consulting-room situation. Either before she comes to analysis, or during the course of it, the patient establishes a relationship with a young man in her peer group to whom she is loyal and together with whom she acquires a recognized social status among their fellows. Her experience in the area of

(1) work,

(2) the personal relationship, and

(3) analysis

together become inter-related aspects of the psychic developmental process. It is as if work were the experimental field of the ego in its male capacity, related to the world of change; the peer relationship the experimental field for the specifically feminine eros; and analysis the field of integration in which the values of what is changing and what is unchanging can be brought together to find their appropriate place.

In the course of time it becomes possible for the patient to risk the commitment of being simply human and female. The inflatory identification with totality falls away, and the negative projects are withdrawn from the parents.

The healing outcome of the analysis is preceded by intermediate forms of integration. The following dream is an example: *"There is a room extending from my bedroom which was not there before. It is a kitchen but it is also a living-room. There is an old-fashioned range, primitive farmhouse furniture, some Victorian pieces, and also some modern chairs."* Here old and new, what changes and what is unchanging, are brought together in the kitchen, the feminine place of transformation.

The transformation which constitutes the healing outcome is peculiarly difficult to describe. Although certain features are common to all the analyses, the final outcome is necessarily very individual and also in some respects subjective. In general terms it might be said that the patient has experienced the transpersonal numen of the feminine which before had been eclipsed. She therefore has a sense of belonging in the generations, in the female line of her own ancestors. This in itself changes her attitude towards the meaning and value of the family. But she has also learned through experience that, in Dr. Esther Harding's words, "submission to the Eros law entails discipline just as much as does submission to the conventional code" (1970, p. 229). She now has within herself an authority on the basis of which she can define an attitude towards the opposites of rootedness and change, such that she does not need to identify heroically with either. As an individual woman she has psychic ground to stand on and is confident of it. She is capable of both commitment and detachment in relationship and in work.

This does not mean that the tension of these opposites is forever resolved, only that her ego is now able to contain them. The test will come when she herself becomes a mother. Only then will it be known whether the outcome of her analysis was in the fullest sense successful or only relatively so.

Nevertheless, from the point of view of the patient and the analyst, to have arrived at this outcome is to have arrived at a position that is satisfying and desirable. The patient is aware that she has matured, has gained insight, has become confident as a woman and is free from symptoms. She has improved her relationships and her outer life has moved forward. The analyst knows that a deep reorientation has taken place, that the patient's ego is established in her feminine identity, and securely related to the unconscious and to the outer world.

But still, for cultural rather than personal reasons, a doubt remains —the test will come when the patient is herself confronted with motherhood.

The intensity of the intrapsychic conflict of woman is most clearly manifested in relation to her role as mother. There is an indefinite variety of ways in which this is expressed, giving the impression that the woman's individual ego desires to be committed to the world of change and struggles desperately to come to terms with the massive power of the maternal archetype, which seeks to mold her life and identity in ways that are unchanging. Certainly there are women who can adapt without conflict to their mother role and find it fully creative and satisfying. There are others who integrate their motherhood effectively with activities of another kind. And there are yet others who in the absence of a family of their own express their maternal nature in their work. But there are also "casualties," and many situations of great stress.

Not every ego is strong enough to stand the tension of the psychic opposition. An unmarried girl may deliberately incur a pregnancy and insist on carrying the child to term in the absence of family or support. A young married woman may abandon her home and child to return to her career. Another may abandon a successful career and contract an unsuitable marriage in the desperate need for a child. Women today may escape *from* motherhood or *into* motherhood. Women with stronger egos, in situations in which there is an established home and young family, may heavily overburden themselves with double responsibilities and activities, feeling an imperative compulsion to fulfill both poles of their personality at the same time. These are all young women, in whom it might seem not too much to expect that they could wait a while for complete fulfillment.

To conclude: In view of the intensity and prevalence of intrapsychic opposition in the personality of woman today; and in view of the importance to mental health of the childhood relation with the mother; and in view also of the population explosion and all its possible implications—it seems that there are several peculiar problems for the consideration of analysts in the outcome of the analysis of a young woman patient:

not only

(a) what kind of adaptation and development has the patient made in her individual personality and circumstances?

and not only

(b) what is the relation of her ego to the maternal archetype in so far as it will affect both her own stability and her capacity to fulfill her possible role as mother?

but also

(c) if the time is to come when childbirth will be necessarily restricted, what are the ways, if any, in which the creativity of woman can helpfully be directed into other channels? Can it be that, for reasons known only to the collective unconscious, woman's present problem of intrapsychic opposition is already a means directed towards that end?

REFERENCES

ERIKSON, E. H. (1968). *Identity; youth and crisis.* New York, Norton; London, Faber.

HARDING, M. E. (1970). *The way of all women.* Revised ed., New York, C. G. Jung Foundation/Putnam.

JUNG, C. G. (1961). "Some crucial points in psychoanalysis: a correspondence between Dr. Jung and Dr. Loÿ," *C.W.* 4.

NEUMANN, E. (1954). *The origins and history of consciousness.* New York, Pantheon/Bollingen; London, Routledge.

WOLFF, T. (1956). *Structural forms of the feminine psyche.* Zurich, C. G. Jung Institute.

18

La Relativisation du moi comme critère de succès de l'analyse jungienne

GEORGES VERNE, *Paris*

CLINIQUE EXPÉRIMENTALE ET WELTANSCHAUUNG

Étant entendu que, dans mon language, le succès de l'analyse concerne moins ses résultats thérapeutiques que l'accès de l'individu à sa propre authenticité. . .

Étant entendu que l'on ne peut proposer, ni se proposer, l'individuation comme un objectif, conventionnel ou disciplinaire, il demeure que le succès de l'analyse signifie, dans l'optique jungienne, la *réalisation existentielle du Soi.*

Son échec, l'incapacité à atteindre cet objectif, à réaliser cet état.

Cette entreprise que JUNG, comme chacun sait, a appelé individuation, peut être considérée sous l'angle strictement clinique, ou sous l'angle thématique de la *Weltanschauung.*

Il est recommandé, je le sais, de s'en tenir aux "cas cliniques" et d'éviter ainsi d'intellectualiser un vécu, de l'enfermer dans le cadre

206

rigide—et insuffisant—de règles preéétablies. C'est ainsi que JUNG nous enseigne, lorsque nous abordons un "cas" quelconque, de commencer par oublier ce que nous savons ou croyons savoir. . .

Le conseil est judicieux: mais il me paraît également recommandable de garder présente à l'esprit cette évidence que, fût-elle implicite, notre conception du monde demeure toujours à l'arrière-plan et ne cesse d'induire notre compréhension et notre interprétation du problématisme proposé: le freudisme, par exemple, qui se flatte de ne connaître aucune *Weltanschauung* et entend amener la résolution de la problématique dans le seule analyse du *hic et nunc* de la situation . . . est, en fait, téléguidé par un dogmatisme rigide, intransigeant et excluant, un véritable système métaphysique à l'aide et au nom de quoi le *hic et nunc* est interprété.

De la même manière, il n'est que de lire la littérature jungienne pour se rendre compte que, tout en traitant volontiers de "cas cliniques," la plupart des auteurs les comprennent, les décrivent et les exposent comme des applications, voire des démonstrations du "système" jungien: la *Weltanschauung* jungienne demeure, explicitement ou implicitement, la clé de compréhension du problématisme envisagé.

Au demeurant JUNG l'a souvent dit, nous ne pouvons nous passer d'une conception du monde: "En même temps qu'il se crée une image du monde, l'homme qui pense se transforme lui-même" (1).

Ou encore: "Celui qui entreprendrait de décrire le processu d'individuation, à l'aide seulement de cas cliniques, devrait se contenter d'une mosaïque de pièces et de morceaux, sans commencement ni fin" (2).

Or, il se trouve que la *Weltanschauung* jungienne repose sur quelques postulats précis, qui se retrouvent sans cesse et conditionment la suite du propos. . .

JUNG l'affirme, le but de l'existence est la conquête de la conscience: "Le principal travail du héros est de remporter la victoire sur le monstre de l'obscurité: c'est la victoire attendue et espérée de la conscience sur l'inconscient" (3).

Sur ce chemin, il semble que l'humain ait une suite d'étapes à accomplir, dont la première paraît être la conquête du Moi.

LA CONQUÈTE DU MOI

Je serai bref à ce propos: le Moi naît par différenciation à partir de l'inconscient collectif, dans le vécu existentiel. C'est une réalité à trois dimensions, dont on pourrait proposer la définition suivante: une *instance psychique se sentant, puis se sachant exister une singularité au sein d'un ensemble.*

Si nous reprenons la formule proposée par FORDHAM (4):

$$\text{Soi} = (\text{Moi} + \text{ombre archétypale}) + (n-1) \text{ archétypes,}$$

on en déduira aisément la formule du Moi:

$$\text{Moi} = \text{Soi} - ((N.\text{ombre archétypale}) + R(n-1) \text{ archétypes}),$$

N devant être entendu comme négation et R comme refoulement.

Le Moi est un archétype parmi les autres, mais un archétype privilégié, quant à la date de naissance tout au moins . . .

Qu'il s'agisse des archétypes, de la "matrice biologique" ou de "l'ordre vital" cher à FREUD, nul ne nie cette genèse: une différenciation, directe ou indirecte, à partir d'un "donné" inconscient.

Cette instance originale, née l'indifférenciation originelle, dans l'expérience prométhéonne de l'insulte et du défi, connaît la séparation comme premier vécu.

Livrée à l'ambivalence du besoin et de l'agression, sa nature demeure d'exister une différence dans la multiplicité, un mais un du multiple. A la fois sujet, dans la mesure où il est un par rapport à quoi l'autre se situe et se définit: et *objet,* dans la mesure où il est un du multiple, qui le situe et lui assigne son rôle et ses limites . . . il est l'acteur et la proie des tensions des oppositions.

Sa fonction est de préférer et d'exclure: s'il ne l'assumait point, il demeurerait dans l'indifférenciation.

Rien n'est plus démonstratif, en ce sens, que de voir comment FREUD a conçu le Moi, non pas comme le centre de la conscience, mais comme une instance introduite par la conscience, pour faire barrage aux perceptions venues de l'intérieur et pour permettre le seul accès à la conscience de la réalité extérieure, considérée comme le critère du réel.

Le Moi freudien naît par cette préférence et cette répudiation et son modèle nous permet de comprendre parfaitement la fonction limitante du Moi: une option parmi des paramètres contradictoires et une identification au pavamètre choisi.

Or, cette préférence et cette exclusion sont l'architecture même de la névrose, puis de la psychose; et, si la fonction du Moi est, caricaturalement parlant, de créer la névrose, en quoi sa naissance et son accomplissement sont-ils nécessaires?

C'est que la névrose n'est que le prix payé pour une conquête magistrale: celle de la conscience.

La conscience, en effet, naît d'une inadéquation, elle ne commence qu'avec la proposition concomitante des contradictions et la prise de conscience des oppositions d'appelle de Moi.

Devant son impuissance à les assumer, il lui faudra, dans un premier temps, choisir: et, s'il est bien ainsi le héros dont la totalité attend l'émergence de ses brumes, la victoire lui est d'abord promise. Mais la mort demeure l'accomplissement de son destin car, s'il a dû préférer, il ne pourra accomplir.

Le Moi apparaît ainsi comme le critère immédiat à partir de quoi va se situer une maturation psychologique à un moment donné:

Sommes-nous en deçà du Moi, dans un état encore d'indifférentiation d'avec les sources originelles?

Sommes-nous en état de plein épanouissement du Moi, d'identification à lui et de négation de tout ce qu'il n'est pas?

Avons-nous déjà su prendre de la distance par rapport à lui, qui ne représente plus, tout en demeurant le centre de la conscience, qu'un élément de la totalité?

Sommes-nous au-delà de lui, avons-nous ou allons-nous accéder à la "conscience du Soi", à travers le dépassement et l'abandon des formes et des modes fragmentaires qui avaient permis son émergence. Le héros est-il prêt à mourir, son oeuvre accomplie?

C'est là, probablement, l'une des questions majeures de l'existence . . .

A cette question, la réponse freudienne est sans ambiguïté:

"Ainsi se réalisera le but essentiel du traitement psychanalytique: le renforcement du Moi, sa maturation. *Was Es war, muss Ich werden:* ce qui était ça, doit devenir le moi" (5).

A son tour, la réponse jungienne est tout aussi précise:

"Le but de la psychothérapie est une métamorphose, une transformation interminable, dont le seul critère est une diminution de la prédominance du Moi" (6).

Ainsi passons-nous d'une identification au Moi à une relativisation du Moi. Et on comprend que JUNG ait été moins occupé du transfert que FREUD: car le problème n'est plus, pour lui, de permettre au Moi, par déplacement de l'égocentre et sa projection sur un support fantasmagorique, de se construire par identification à lui, puis par désidentification de lui. Mais, à partir de là, de reconnecter ce Moi à ses sources profondes.

L'INDIVIDUATION JUNGIENNE

Il n'est pas tellement simple de réaliser quels sont les élément permanents qui sous-tendent ce que JUNG a appelé l'individuation: d'abord, parce qu'il parle notre langage, qui suppose un certain nombre de conventions tacites par rapport à quoi nous n'avons que peu de distance et qui nous paraissent l'évidence; ensuite parce que, dans une large mesure, il a tout dit, y compris les choses les plus contradictoires . . . ce qui n'est pas forcément une critique.

Mais l'individuation est moins une théorie qu'une expérience, qui se manifeste à l'individu par la révélation de son sens: "C'est le moment d'élection où l'homme se sent devenir conforme à lui-même" (7). Au delà la signification, elle est sens en elle-même, un sens vécu comme une expérience de la totalité, comme les retrouvailles du Moi avec le Tout.

JUNG a souvent tenté de décrire cet état et, comme toute description de cet ordre, la sienne est davantage métaphorique qu'abstraite:

"Le Soi . . . est l'expression la plus complète de cette combinaison du destin que l'on appelle individualité . . . lorsqu'on en arrive à sentir le Soi comme quelque chose d'irrationnel, comme une existence indéfinissable à quoi le Moi n'est ni opposé, ni soumis, mais plutôt relié et autour de quoi il tourne comme la terre autour du soleil . . . alors on a atteint le but de l'individuation" (8). Ou encore: "Si l'inconscient peut être reconnu comme un facteur co-déterminant avec le conscient, et si nous pouvons vivre de telle manière que les demandes inconscientes soient prises en considération aussi loin que possible, alors le centre de gravité de la personnalité totale change de position. Il ne se situe plus dans le Moi, qui demeure simplement le centre de la conscience, mais en un point hypothétique entre conscient et inconscient. Ce centre nouveau pourrait être appelé le Soi" (9).

C'est, en somme, le sentiment "d'avoir été remplacé, sans avoir été déposé, comme si la direction de la vie se faisait désormais à partir d'un centre invisible" (10).

Le processus est donc apparemment simple: l'individu cesse de s'identifier à son Moi, qu'il a eu tant de peine à conquérir à partir de l'inconscient collectif et, du même coup, cesse de s'identifier à sa conscience actuelle, puisque le Moi en est le centre.

Bien que cette désidentification, pour un Occidental tout au moins, ne soit pas une mince affaire, la reconnaissance des systèmes autonomes fragmentaires inconscients est cependant le premier pas vers leur intégration, vers l'individuation: elle n'est possible que par la médiation de ce que JUNG a appelé l'animus et l'anima et se fait sous l'impulsion de la fonction transcendante, dont l'ambition est la réconciliation de l'extra- et de l'introversion, "l'union des contraires à mi-chemin" (11), qui "sont susceptibles de trouver leur accord dans une certaine moyenne, dans un certain compromis" (12). "L'entéléchie du Soi est faite d'une voie de compromis infinis, où le Moi et le Soi se tiennent en équilibre, pour que tout aille bien" (13).

Ainsi l'individuation apparaît-elle comme une désidentification de la conscience actuelle et une rencontre avec l'inconsciente, prélude à son intégration dans une conscience supérieure. Et, dans la mesure où le Moi demeure le centre de la conscience, comme une *relativisation du Moi actuel,* pour la conquête de son élargissement.

Car le but ultime demeure l'accès à la conscience totale, "cette énorme entreprise dont la nature a chargé l'humanité et qui réunit les cultures les plus diverses dans une tâche commune" (14) . . .

LE COMPLEXE DE NICODÈME

Cependant, à travers la description jungienne, se manifeste un certain nombre de paramètres permanents qui peuvent paraître comme allant de soi, mais dont l'adoption est lourde de conséquences . . .

En effet, dès l'instant que l'on établit:

—que le Moi est le centre inamovible de la conscience

—que le but de la vie est la conquête de la conscience

—que cette tâche ne peut être enterprise "qu'en demeurant fermement établi sur notre sol", le long "d'un chemin qui n'exige point le sacrifice de notre propre nature, ni ne nous confronte avec la menace de voir nos propres racines arrachées" (15).

—que la conscience est inconcevable sans ego, qu'une condition de mental sans ego ne peut être, pour nous, qu'inconsciente; que les états mentaux qui "transcendent" la conscience, perdent la conscience dans la mesure même où ils la transcendent; que l'on ne peut imaginer un état mental conscient qui ne se réfère pas à un ego et que, tant qu'il y a conscience de quelque chose, il doit y avoir quelqu'un de conscient (16) . . .

—que tout ce qui n'est pas l'ego est donc inconscient, bien que l'ego puisse en avoir conscience,

—que la conscience est, avant tout, celle de "l'extérieur",

—enfin, que "la rencontre entre la conscience individuelle, claire mais étroitement limitée et le vaste domaine de l'inconscient collectif est dangereuse, car l'inconscient a une action résolument désintégrante sur la conscience" (17),

—si, en substance, le but suprême demeure la conquête d'une conscience totale liée au Moi, sans la remise en cause de ce qu'il a acquis, mais avec la seule connaissance qu'il n'a pas encore tout acquis . . .

Alors, il faut convenir que la *Weltanschauung* jungienne est une éthique du Moi conscient et qu'elle entend demeurer fixée à ce stade de l'évolution, tenu pour une fin-en-soi.

Bien entendu, il n'est pas question de tenir pour un résultat achevé le Moi actuel, clair mais étroitement limité: il convient, au contraire, de prendre conscience de ses limites actuelles et, par le fait même, de ce qui lui manque, les contenus inconscients "introvertis". Il imparte même, au delà, de conférer à ces contenus une dignité égale à celle du consciente et, mieux, de les amener à la conscience, pour les intégrer à elle. L'alchimie du Soi est une entreprise d'intégration de l'inconscient au conscient, de l'ombre à la lumière, de l'intérieur à l'extérieur (18).

Mais cette prise de conscience, cette concession de considération, cette intégration, demeurent finalement des décisions du Moi et ne dépendent, en dernière analyse, que de sa bonne volonté: la fonction transcendante, elle-même, ne peut que venir proposer au Moi son propre élargissement; il demeure que le dernier mot restera à l'ego, un ego dont il est clairement établi qu'il n'aura à renoncer à aucun de ses privilèges fondamentaux. Ce qu'il sait est acquis, il ne reste qu'à acclimater ce qu'il ne sait pas encore; bien entendu il faudra, chemin faisant, jeter du lest: et ce lest, c'est la croyan ce de l'ego qu'il sait déjà tout.

Sans épiloguer sur le point de savoir si ce n'est pas du "wishful thinking" que d'imaginer que l'on peut recevoir ce qui est contradictoire de ses privilèges, tout en refusant d'y renoncer autrement que dans une attitude précaire et "politique" de compromis, excluant tout espoir de dépassement—puisque l'un des interlocuteurs est, à la fois, juge et partie—il faut convenir que semblable position risque d'amener une attitude perfectionniste et bien-pensante du Moi, instance ultime de décision: à la limite, le Soi risque fort de meurer mon Soi, "my enigma" (19) et l'ensemble de l'opération de se figer dans une attitude d'idéal du Moi.

La conclusion paradoxale en est une infatuation de l'ego, dans les meilleures intentions du monde, une identification de l'ego-pour-soi, sinon à la vérité absolue et universelle, du moins à la possibilité de la connaître et de la vivre par son propre progrès: c'est là, me semble-t-il, le trait fondamental de l'attitude du Juste.

Et c'est pourquoi je pense que l'on pourrait appeler cet instant de la promotion psychique que JUNG décrit sous le nom d'individuation, où se pose la question du choix entre l'élargissement et le dépassement du Moi, et l'option finale pour son élargissement, le complexe de Nicodème.

LE DÉPLACEMENT DU CENTRE DE LA CONSCIENCE

Mais le but de la manoeuvre n'est point la perfection du Moi: peu importe que mon Moi soit "parfait" si, dans son imperfection, il s'est accompli assez pour prendre conscience de sa contingence.

Ne convient-il pas, en effet, que le Moi qui a pris conscience de ses limites, réalise en même temps que son rôle n'est point de se borner à les repousser? car, aussi vaste que soit un domaine, s'il demeure bordé de frontières, il reste un enclos limité?

Ne convient-il pas qu'il réalise que ses limites ne sont pas seulement des limites actuelles, mais des limites fonctionnelles et que sa fonction, précisément a été de limiter, de préférer et de nier: et que tel a été le prix payé pour la conquête de la conscience?

Ne convient-il pas, maintenant, qu'il accepte de perdre ses formes et ses modes en même temps que sa souveraineté, pour permettre à la conscience de s'épanouir sur un plan ultérieur, que lui-même n'atteindra jamais?

Mais comment, l'en convaincre?

On ne l'en convaincra pas. Et c'est là, précisément, le rôle de l'intuition, fonction irrationnelle de projet, d'arracher le Moi au sentiment de sa légitimité et, provisoirement, de le déposer. Ainsi la fonction transcendante pourra-t-elle accomplir son oeuvre de promotion de niveau.

Et, si le Moi peut alors prendre conscience que cette déposition provisoire était nécessaire et que, pour un temps, ce ne sera plus à lui d'être le critère du juste, alors "il y aura plus de joie dans le ciel pour un pêcheur qui se repent que pour quatrevingt-dix neuf justes qui persevèrent" (Luc 15:7).

Mais, bien sûr, tout ceci suppose que la conscience puisse exister sans les formes et les modes du Moi, au-delà d'eux. En d'autres termes, que le Moi n'est pas le centre inamovible de la conscience; et je promets beaucoup de joie à quiconque essaiera de faire accéder l'Occidental à cette "évidence", qu'il refuse et nie avec passion: car l'identité de l'ego et de la conscience fait partie des conventions implicites du consensus occidental, au point que toute notre psychologie est une psychologie du Moi.

Du moins pouvons-nous savoir qu'une tradition plusieurs fois millénaire le soutient et nous pouvons, au moins, essayer de comprendre ce qu'elle veut dire et, même, essayer de rapporter ce qu'elle dit à nos propres connaissances occidentales actuelles.

JUNG est fort ambigu sur ce point: ne dit-il pas, par exemple, que l'expérience du *sammadhî* est un retour à l'inconscience? (21). Mais ne tente-t-il pas, aussi, d'identifier son processus d'individuation à ce que DORN décrit comme l'union à *l'unus mundus* et aussi à l'expérience du *satori* zen?

Il ne me paraît pas que cette ambition soit légitime: car le propre de l'état de *satori* ou de *sammadhî*, comme l'*unio mystica* est précisément la conscience, mais libérée des qualités fragmentaires du Moi, alors que JUNG insiste sur la responsabilité encore accrue de la conscience liée au Moi: "Avant tout, la conscience fait l'expérience d'un élargissement de son champ . . . et . . . le conflit jusque-là inconscient est amené à la surface, chargeant la conscience d'une lourde responsabilité, dans la mesure où c'est d'elle que l'on attend, désormais, la résolution du conflit" (22).

Étant moi-même Occidental et, par conséquent, victime de mes préjugés, j'ai tendance à me poser la question: "Mais alors, une conscience de qui?"

Je crois que l'on peut répondre qu'elle est précisément la conscience de ce que JUNG appelle le "facteur subjectif" réputé inconscient et dont la conscience ne pourrait s'acquérir qu'au prix de l'abandon du Moi: c'est une aura de conscience de l'inconscient collectif en lui-même, sans rêves, sans images et sans symboles, ce que le Zen appelle la conscience du Vide, notion, au demeurant, reprise du *Tao*.

Le problème est donc de savoir si cette "conscience de l'inconscient collectif" est une régression à partir d'un Moi qui n'a pas su ou pu se conquérir, ou l'accession à une conscience ultérieure.

Dans le premier cas, les formes inachevées du Moi ne manqueront pas d'être projetées, comme en "flash-back," dans cette expérience régressive de submersion de la conscience liée au Moi, par les systèmes autonomes: c'est le domaine pathologique de la schizophrénie.

C'est aussi le cas de certains mystiques, chez qui l'expérience apparaît alors comme une brutale projection de conscience sur les systèmes autonomes et une identification à eux: c'est ce que m'évoque, par exemple, les expériences rapportées du "face à face" avec Dieu . . .

Plus loin, c'est encore le vécu du retour à la mère primitive la mère primordiale, l'engloutissement, comme le disait JUNG, par le nombril: et si le retour à la claire conscience, centrée sur le Moi, ne se produit point, la promesse de la déréliction psychotique.

Mais l'expérience peut être aussi celle de l'accession à une conscience "ultérieure", des archétypes en tant que tels, au delà d'un Moi qui a su se construire, puis se dépasser: c'est ce que le Zen appelle la conscience du *satori*.

Bien sûr, on peut se demander ce que signifie cette expression "d'archétypes en tant que tels": c'est pour répondre à cette question que j'ai cru utile d'introduire les notions d'*homo*- et d'*hétéro*- *polarité*. Ce n'est pas le moment d'aborder cet aspect des choses; disons simplement que, dans mon esprit, ces deux réalités constituent les archétypes fondamentaux du fait de la vie, qui la fondent et qui la relient à ses sources cosmiques.

L'extra- et l'introversion jungiennes en sont la traduction au niveau des attitudes existentielles, c'est partir à d'eux que se conquièrent la conscience et le Moi préférentiel et c'est à leur conscience, enfin, que permet d'accéder l'expérience du *satori*.

Bien entendu, de même que dans l'expérience d'individuation, nous échapperons difficilement à la tentation de tenir cet état pour une fin-en-soi: aussi est-il difficile, à ceux qui l'ont connu, de ne voir en lui qu'une (!) nouvelle étape provisoire, prélude à une nouvelle actualisation du Moi au niveau ultérieur, permettant de nouvelles intégrations qui eussent été impossibles a Moi précédent . . . mais promises également a même dépassement.

C'est, en somme, une amplification de ce que FORDHAM a décrit, sur un autre plan, comme le processus d'intégration-déintégration (23).

Bien entendu, ceci suppose que nous soyions capables, un jour de quitter les rivages connus sans déchirement ou, pour reprendre les termes de l'humour jungien, Mayfair, son téléphone et son J & B.

Si le Moi tourne autour du Soi comme la terre autour du soleil, le problème se pose de savoir si, tout en sachant que le soleil est le centre du système, nous allons vouloir demeurer sur terre—et garder ainsi le Moi comme centre de la conscience—ou accéder à la conscience solaire, la conscience centrée sur le Soi: mais alors, bien sûr, ce ne sera plus le Moi qui y accèdera.

Nous avons parfaitement le droit d'entendre demeurer sur terre et de nous satisfaire de la conscience que notre Moi a de la totalité: la sagesse des nations, qui n'a pas hésité à attribuer un Moi à Dieu, nous y convie. Nous deviendrons ainsi des hommes pleins de sagesse et de culture, de redoutables connaisseurs de la représentation symbolique . . . de ce symbole dont la fonction, précisément, était de nous suggérer qu'il est ou qu'il existe d'autres réalités que celle que nous connaissons et que lui-même n'est pas cette réalité, mais sa représentation en forme de monde.

Mais, si notre demande nous pousse irrémédiablement vers l'autre côté du voile, il faudra nous décider à abandonner la sécurité des signes connus et accepter de perdre, dans la foi de devenir d'être et de redevenir.

"L'homme est déjà ce qu'il deviendra encore" (24).

Contrairement aux craintes jungiennes, je crois que nous ne risquons pas grand'chose—à la condition qu'elle ne soit disciplinairement forcée, cad prématurée—dans cette entreprise de schizophrénie aseptique: car nous sommes faits de soleil autant que de terre et, en déplaçant de l'une à l'autre le centre de la conscience, ce n'est jamais que la vérité et le sens plus profond de la vie, qui se dévoileront.

*   *   *

On mesure quelle est l'importance de la relativisation jungienne du Moi, au moment de l'affrontement et des retrouvailles de deux mondes; au moment où l'Occident est confronté avec la nécessité de se dés-identifier d'un Moi qu'il a su, collectivement, si magistralement con-struire et sur quoi il a bâti toute sa psychologie . . .

Où l'Orient découvre la nécessité d'affirmer le sien que, dans l'euphorie d'un dépassement prématuré, il avait, peut-être, quelque peu négligé de construire: et c'est là, peut-être, l'un des sens de la Révolu-tion Culturelle.

Mais pour nous, analystes d'Occident, la première tâche paraît de savoir d'abord reconnaître la demande de notre interlocuteur . .

En ce sens, la structuration d'un Moi peut parfaitement représenter un succès analytique: et ce serait bien regrettable d'utiliser alors le matériel onirique qui ne manquera pas d'apparaître—car toute étape est sous-tendue et rendue possible par le projet de celle qui va la suivre—pour vouloir entraîner plus ou moins de force, vers l'aven-ture de la relativisation, un ego qui ne s'était pas encore construit.

Plus loin, ce que JUNG a appelé individuation représente aussi un succès de l'analyse, au niveau ultérieur, si la demande de l'analysand était ou devenait celle des trouvailles du sens de la reconnection de son Moi à la totalité.

Mais plus loin encore, si le projet de l'analysand s'avère être le dépassement du Moi, il nous faudra alors éviter la tentation de le réduire à celui de la relativisation: nous aurons ainsi l'occasion d'ap-précier si nous sommes prêts à accepter la mort provisoire de notre premier héros . . . fût-il relativisé.

Mais est-ce encore de l'analyse? De même que du langage naît le silence, l'analyse ne serait-elle pas, parvenue à ce point, la rampe de lancement vers une autre aventure?

LITERATURE

The textual references are given in square brackets.

FORDHAM, M. (1957). "Ego, self and mental health," *Brit. J. Med. Psychol.* **33**, 4. [23]
—— (1960). *New developments in analytical psychology.* London, Routledge. [4]
JUNG, C. G. (1959). *The archetypes and the collective unconscious, C.W.* 9, I. [3]
—— (1966a). *Two essays on analytical psychology.* 2nd ed. *C.W.* 7. [8]
—— (1966b). *The spirit in man, art, and literature. C.W.* 15. [11, 12]
—— (1967a). *Symbols of transformation.* 2nd ed. *C.W.* 5. [17, 18]
—— (1967b). *Alchemical studies. C.W.* 13. [9, 10, 14, 15]

—— (1969a). *The structure and dynamics of the psyche.* 2nd ed. *C.W.* 8. [1, 16]

—— (1969b). *Psychology and religion: west and east.* 2nd ed. *C.W.* 11. [6, 7, 13, 21, 24]

—— (1970). *Mysterium coniunctionis.* 2nd ed. *C.W.* 14. [21, 22]

NACHT, S. (1964). *Le masochisme.* Paris, Payot. [5]

SCOTT, W. C. (1949). "The 'body scheme' in psychotherapy," *Brit. J. Med. Psychol.* **22**, 3/4. [19]

The Relativization of the Ego as a Criterion for Success In Jungian Analysis

EXPERIMENTAL CLINICS AND WELTANSCHAUUNG

In the Jungian view a successful analysis means that an existential realization of the self has been achieved. Analysis fails when that objective cannot be reached, nor that state attained.

Individuation, as we know, was the name Jung gave this enterprise, this undertaking; and it can be considered from the strictly clinical point of view, or be seen from the broader thematic angle of the *Weltanschaaung,* the world view.

I realize that it is advisable to speak only of case material and thus to avoid intellectualizing a lived experience, enclosing it within the rigid—and inadequate—framework of pre-established rules. This is why Jung teaches us to approach any case by first forgetting what we know or think we know.

This is judicious advice, but it seems to me equally advisable to keep in mind the obvious fact that, though it may be implicit, our conception of the world is always there in the background to condition our comprehension and interpretation of the proposed set of problems. Freudianism, e.g., which prides itself on having no *Weltanschauung* and proposes to resolve the problem pattern completely in the analysis of the here and now of the situation, is in fact remote-controlled by an excluding, intransigent, and rigid dogmatism, a true metaphysical system with whose aid and in whose name the here and now is interpreted.

Similarly, we have only to read Jungian literature to realize that, though they willingly treat case material, most authors understand, describe, and present these cases as applications, indeed as demonstrations, of the Jungian "system." The Jungian *Weltanschauung* remains, explicitly or implicitly, the key to understanding the problems the authors see.

And, as Jung has often put it, we cannot do without a conception of the world: "With the picture that the thinking man fashions of the world he also changes himself" (1969a, par. 696).

Or again: "Anyone who attempted to describe the individuation process with the help of case-material would have to remain content with a mosaic of bits and pieces without beginning or end . . ." (1970, par. 792).

The fact is, Jung's *Weltanschauung* rests on a few precise postulates which recur constantly and condition the entirety of his work.

Jung affirms that the purpose of existence is the victory of consciousness: "The hero's main feat is to overcome the monster of darkness: it is the long-hoped-for and expected triumph of consciousness over the unconscious" (1959, par. 284).

On this path, it seems that the human being has a series of stages to accomplish, and the first of these appears to be the conquest of the ego.

THE CONQUEST OF THE EGO

I shall treat this only in brief: the ego is born through differentiation out of the collective unconscious, by participating in existential experience. This is a three-dimensional reality for which the following definition might serve: *a psychic entity sensing itself, then knowing itself to live as a singularity in the midst of the "set."* If we recall the formula proposed by Fordham (1960, p. 250):

$$\text{self} = (\text{ego} + \text{shadow archetype}) + (n - 1) \text{ archetypes},$$

we can readily deduce the formula for the ego:

$$\text{ego} = \text{self} - ((\text{N. shadow archetype}) + \text{R}(n - 1) \text{ archetypes})$$

N being understood as negation and R as repression.

The ego is one archetype among others, but a privileged archetype, as least in regards to its date of birth.

Whether we speak of the archetypes or of the "biological matrix" or of the "vital order" dear to Freud, no one denies this genesis: a differentiation, direct or indirect, starting from an unconscious "given."

This original entity, born out of the primordial nondifferentiation in the Promethean experience of insult and defiance, knows separation as its first lived experience.

Delivered over to the ambivalence of need and aggression, its nature remains that of living a difference within multiplicity, being one, but one of a multitude. At once subject, to the degree that it is one with respect to which the other situates and defines itself; and object, to the degree that it is one of the multitude, which situates it and assigns it its role and its limits. It is the actor and the prey of the tensions of opposites.

The ego's functions are to prefer and to exclude: if it did not assume these functions it would remain in a state of nondifferentiation.

There is no better demonstration, in this sense, than to see how Freud conceived of the ego, not as the center of consciousness but as an entity introduced *by* consciousness to serve as a barrier against perceptions coming from within and to allow consciousness access only to external reality, the latter considered as the criterion of actual reality.

The Freudian ego was born through this preference and this repudiation, and its model enables us to understand perfectly the limiting function of the ego: one option among the contradictory parameters and an identification with the chosen parameter.

Now, this preference and this exclusion are the very architecture of neurosis, and then of psychosis; and if the function of the ego is, to employ a caricature, the creation of neurosis, what is the purpose of its birth and accomplishment?

Neurosis is nothing but the price paid for a masterly conquest: the conquest of consciousness.

In point of fact, consciousness was born out of an inadequacy; it begins only with the concomitant proposition of contradictions; consciousness of these opposites is called the ego.

Faced with its impotence in coming to terms with them, it must, for the time being, select: and if it is in fact the hero whose totality awaits emergence from the mists, it is at first promised victory. But death remains the accomplishment of its destiny, for if it has been obliged to prefer, it will not be able to accomplish.

So the state of the ego seems to be the immediate criterion to be used to determine psychological maturation at any given moment:

Have we an insufficient ego, still keeping us in a state of nondifferentiation with respect to the primordial sources?

Are we in a state of full flowering of the ego, of identification with it, denying all that it is not?

Have we already learned to take our distance from it so that, though it remains the center of consciousness, it now represents only one element of the totality?

Are we beyond the ego, have we acceded or will we accede to consciousness of the self, by transcending and abandoning the forms and fragmentary modes which enabled it to emerge? Is the hero ready to die, his task accomplished?

Those are, without doubt, the major questions of existence.

To those questions, the Freudian response is without ambiguity: "Thus will be accomplished the essential goal of the psychoanalytic treatment: the reinforcement of the ego, its maturation. *Was Es war, muss Ich werden*: What the id was, must the ego become" (Nacht, 1964, p. 164).

In its turn, the Jungian response is just as precise: "The goal [of psychotherapy] is transformation . . . an indeterminable change, the only criterion of which is the disappearance of egohood" (1969b, par. 904).

Thus we pass from an identification with the ego to what I might call relativization of the ego. And we can see why Jung was less concerned with the transference than Freud: the problem for Jung is no longer to enable the ego, by a displacement of its center and its projection onto a fantasy support, to build itself by identification with it, and then by disidentification from it. It is rather, by starting with it, to reconnect the ego to its deepest sources.

JUNGIAN INDIVIDUATION

It is no easy matter to define which are the permanent elements that subtend what Jung has called individuation; first of all, because he speaks our language, which presupposes a certain number of tacit conventions with respect to which we have little distance and which appear to us as taken for granted; then, because to a great extent, he has said everything, including the most contradictory statements. This is not necessarily a criticism.

But individuation is less a theory than an experience which is manifested to the individual by the revelation of its meaning: It is the moment of election when people feel that "they came to themselves" (Jung, 1969b, par. 138). Beyond mere signification, individuation is pure meaning in itself, a meaning lived as an experience of totality, like the reunity of the ego and the whole.

Jung often tried to describe this state and, like all descriptions of this order, his is more metaphorical than abstract:

"The self . . . is the completest expression of that fateful combination we call individuality," when one succeeds in "sensing the self as something irrational, as an indefinable existent, to which the ego is neither opposed nor subjected, but merely attached, and about which it revolves very much as the earth revolves around the sun—thus we come to the goal of individuation" (1966a, pars. 404–5). Or again: "But if the unconscious can be recognized as a co-determining factor along with consciousness, and if we can live in such a way that conscious and unconscious demands are taken into account as far as possible, then the centre of gravity of the total personality shifts its position. It is then no longer in the ego, which is merely the centre of consciousness, but in the hypothetical point between conscious and unconscious. This new centre might be called the self" (1967b, par. 67).

It is, in sum, the feeling "that we have been 'replaced,' but without the connotation of having been 'deposed.' It is as if the guidance of life had passed over to an invisible centre" (ibid., par. 77).

The process is thus apparently simple: the individual ceases to identify himself with his ego, which he took such pains to conquer and win out of the collective unconscious; and, at the same time, he ceases to identify himself with his present consciousness, since the ego is its center.

Although this disidentification, at least for a Westerner, is no small task, the recognition of the unconscious fragmentary autonomous systems is nonetheless the first step towards their integration, that is, towards individuation: it is possible only through the mediation of what Jung has called the animus and anima, and is achieved under the impetus of the transcendent function, of which the ambition is to reconcile extraversion and introversion, "the union of opposites through the middle path" (1966a, par. 327), can "unite in a mediatory meaning" (ibid., par. 311). "The entelechy of the self consists in a succession of endless compromises, ego and the self laboriously keeping the scales balanced if all is to go well" (1969b, par. 960).

Thus individuation emerges as the process of disidentifying from present consciousness and encountering the unconscious, the prelude to its integration in a higher consciousness; and as relativizing the present ego, in order to achieve its broadening.

The ultimate goal remains access to total consciousness, "the tremendous experiment of becoming conscious, which nature has laid upon mankind, and which unites the most diverse cultures in a common task" (Jung, 1967b, par. 83).

THE NICODEMUS COMPLEX

Through Jung's description, however, there are manifest a certain number of permanent parameters which may appear axiomatic but whose adoption has considerable consequences.

In fact, as soon as we establish:

—that the ego is the unmovable center of consciousness,

—that the goal of life is the conquest of consciousness,

—that this task can be undertaken only "by remaining firmly established on our own soil," along "a way that does not require the sacrifice of our own nature and does not confront us with the threat of being torn from our roots," (ibid.),

—that consciousness is inconceivable without an ego, that a mental condition without an ego, for us, can only be unconscious; that the mental states which transcend consciousness lose consciousness to the degree that they transcend it; that we cannot imagine a conscious mental state which has no connection with an ego, and that, as long as there is consciousness of something, there must be someone conscious (Jung, 1969b, par. 474),

—that everything that is not the ego is thus unconscious, though the ego might be conscious of it,

—that consciousness is, above all, consciousness of the external,

—and finally, that "the meeting between the narrowly delimited, but intensely clear, individual consciousness and the vast expanse of the collective unconscious . . . has a decidedly disintegrating effect on consciousness" (1967b, par. 46)

(if, substantially, the supreme goal remains the conquest of a total consciousness related to the ego, without a reconsideration of what it has acquired, but only with the knowledge that it has not yet acquired everything)—

We must then admit that Jung's *Weltanschauung* is an ethic of the conscious ego and that its intention is to remain fixed at this stage of evolution, taken as an end-in-itself.

Naturally, there is no question of taking as a final result the present ego, clear but narrowly limited: on the contrary, what is required is to realize its present limits and, in so doing, to become aware of what it lacks, the unconscious introverted contents. Even beyond this, we must confer upon these contents a dignity equal to that accorded to consciousness and, better still, become conscious of these contents so that they can be integrated into consciousness. The alchemy of the self is an undertaking of "integrating the tendencies of the unconscious into the conscious mind," (Jung, 1967a, par. 683), of the shadow into the light, of the interior into the exterior.

But this realization, this concession of consideration, this integration, remain in the final analysis decisions of the ego and depend finally only on the good will of the ego: the transcendent function itself can only propose to the ego its own broadening; the last word rests with the ego, an ego for which it has been clearly established that it will have to renounce none of its fundamental privileges. What it knows is acquired; it has then only to acclimate what it does not yet know. Of course, it will have to rid itself of ballast as it goes: and this ballast is the belief of the ego that it knows everything.

Without going to extremes, in order to know if it might not be wishful thinking to imagine that we can receive from our privileges something contradictory and at the same time refuse to abandon them, except in a precarious and politic attitude of compromise, excluding all hope of synthesis—since one of the interlocutors is simultaneously judge and party—it must be admitted that such a position risks bringing with it a perfectionist and righteous attitude on the part of the ego, the ultimate reference point for decision. In fact, the self might well remain my *self*, "my enigma" (Scott, 1949, p. 143), and the net result of the operation will be a fixation in an attitude of ego-ideal.

The paradoxical conclusion of all this is an infatuation of the ego, with the best possible intentions, an identification of the ego-for-itself, if not with absolute and universal truth, at least with the possibility of knowing and living it by dint of its own progress. This is, it seems to me, the fundamental trait of the attitude of the righteous.

And this is why I think we could call this moment of psychic promotion which Jung describes under the name of individuation, where the choice between the broadening and the transcending of the ego is posed, and the final option for its broadening, the *Nicodemus complex*.

THE DISPLACEMENT OF THE
CENTER OF CONSCIOUSNESS

But the goal of the enterprise is not the perfection of the ego. My ego does not have to be perfect if, in its imperfection, it has gone far enough to become conscious of its own contingency.

Should not the ego that is now aware of its own limits realize at the same time that its role is not to restrict itself to pushing them back? For no matter how vast a domain might be, while it remains bordered by frontiers it is still a limited enclosure.

Is it not fitting that the ego realizes that its limits are not only present limits but also functional limits and that its function has precisely been to limit, to prefer, and to deny, and that such has been the price exacted for the conquest of consciousness?

Is it not time for the ego to accept losing its forms and its modes along with its sovereignty, to enable consciousness to bloom on a deeper level which the ego itself will never attain?

But how to convince the ego of this?

There is no convincing it. And that is, precisely, the role of intuition, the irrational prospective function; to tear the ego away from the feeling of its legitimacy and, temporarily, to depose it. Thus the transcendent function can accomplish its task of promotion to another level.

And if the ego can then realize that this temporary deposing was necessary and that, for a while, it will no longer be the judge of what is right, then "joy shall be in heaven over one sinner that repenteth, more than over ninety and nine just persons, which need no repentence" (Luke 15:7).

To be sure, all of this assumes that consciousness can exist without the forms and the modes of the ego, going beyond them. In other words, the ego is not the unmovable center of consciousness; and I promise a great time of it to anyone who would try to show a Westerner that obvious fact, which he refuses and denies with passion. For the identity of the ego and of consciousness is part and parcel of the conventions implicit in the Western consensus to the point that all our psychology is an "Ego Psychology."

At least we are in a position to know that another tradition with several thousand years behind it is based on the fact, the evidence, that consciousness exists without the help of the ego, and we can at least try to understand what that tradition means and even endeavor to bring to bear what it says to our present Western knowledge.

Jung is ambiguous on this point: does he not say, for instance, that the experience of *samādhi* is a return to unconsciousness? (1969b, par. 775.) But does he not also attempt to identify his process of individuation with the union with the *unus mundus* described by Dorn and also with the experience of Zen *satori*? (1970, pars. 770–1).

This ambition of his does not appear legitimate to me, since the essence of the state of *satori* or *samādhi* is precisely one of consciousness but liberated from the fragmentary qualities of the ego, whereas Jung emphasizes an increased responsibility of consciousness related to the ego: "Above all, consciousness experiences a widening of its horizon . . . and . . . the previously unconscious conflict is brought to the surface instead and imposes on consciousness a heavy responsibility, as *it* is now expected to solve the conflict" (ibid., par. 779).

Being myself a Westerner and, consequently, a victim of my prejudices, I tend to ask myself the question, "But a consciousness of what?"

I think we can answer that this consciousness is precisely the consciousness of what Jung calls the "subjective factor," reputedly unconscious and the consciousness of which can be acquired only at the price of abandoning the ego. It is an aura of consciousness of the collective unconscious itself, without dreams, without images, and without symbols, what Zen calls the consciousness of the Void, a notion which, in fact, is taken from Taoism.

The problem consists thus in knowing whether this consciousness of the collective unconscious is a regression of an ego which has not known how, or has not been able, to conquer itself, or the accession to an ulterior consciousness.

In the first instance, the unfinished forms of the ego will not fail to be projected, like flashbacks, into this regressive experience of submersion of consciousness connected to the ego, by autonomous systems: this is the pathological domain of schizophrenia.

It is also the case of certain mystics for whom the experience appears as a brutal projection of consciousness onto autonomous systems and an identification with them. This is what reports of the experience of being face to face with God bring to my mind.

Again, it is the experience of a return to the primitive, primordial mother, being swallowed up by the navel, as Jung puts it. And if a return to clear consciousness centered on the ego does not occur, there is the promise of psychotic dereliction.

But this experience can also be that of the accession to an ulterior consciousness of the archetypes, the archetypes as such, beyond an ego which has learned to construct itself and then to transcend itself. This is what Zen calls the consciousness of *satori*.

We can of course ask ourselves what the expression "archetypes as such" signifies. It is in order to answer this question that I have deemed it useful to introduce the notions of *homo-* and *hetero-polarity*. This is not the place to consider this aspect of things: let us simply say that, in my mind, these two realities constitute the fundamental archetypes of the fact of life, which are its basis and which connect it to its cosmic sources.

Jungian extra- and introversion are the translation of these two archetypes at the level of existential attitudes. It is in starting from them that consciousness and the preferential ego are conquered, and it is the consciousness of them that, in the end, enables accession to the experience of *satori*.

Naturally, just as in the experience of individuation, we will not easily escape the temptation of taking this state of *satori* for an end-in-itself. It is thus difficult for those who have known it to see it as only (!) a new, temporary stage, prelude to a new actualization of the ego at a higher level, enabling new integrations which would have been impossible for the previous ego. But these integrations are equally destined to be transcended.

In sum, this is an amplification of what Fordham has described on another plane as the process of integration-deintegration (Fordham, 1957, pp. 117ff.).

To be sure, this assumes that we might be able some day to leave the known shores without being torn asunder or, to employ the terms of Jungian humor, Mayfair, our telephone, and our J & B.

If the ego revolves around the self like the earth around the sun, we are faced with the problem of knowing whether, aware that the sun is the center of the system, we are going to want to remain on earth—and thus retain the ego as the center of consciousness—or accede to solar consciousness, consciousness centered on the self.

But then, of course, it will no longer be the ego which accedes to this consciousness.

We are perfectly entitled to prefer to remain on earth and content ourselves with the consciousness that our ego has of the totality. The wisdom of nations, which has not hesitated to attribute an ego to God, invites us to make that choice. We shall thereby become fearsome experts of symbolic representation, of the symbol whose function it is, precisely, to suggest to us that the symbol itself is not the reality but the representation of another reality in the form of the world of senses.

But if our demand pushes us irremediably towards the other side of the veil, we will have to decide to abandon the security of known signs and accept losing, with faith in becoming, in being, and in re-becoming.

"Man already is what he will become" (Jung, 1969b, par. 390).

Contrary to Jungian fears, I think that we are not risking much—on the condition that we are not disciplined, forced, prematurely—in this undertaking of aseptic schizophrenia. For we are made of sun as much as of earth; and, by displacing the center of consciousness from one to the other, there will be unveiled only truth and the more profound meaning of life.

*   *   *

We can readily measure the importance of the Jungian relativization of the ego, at this time when two worlds are in confrontation and greet each other after such a long separation; a time when the West is confronted with the necessity of disidentifying itself from an ego which it has learnt, collectively, to construct so masterfully and upon which it has built all its psychology, a time when the East discovers the need to affirm its own ego which, in the euphoria of a premature transcendence, it had somewhat neglected to construct. And that is perhaps one of the meanings of the Cultural Revolution.

But for us Western analysts the first task appears to be learning to recognize the demand of our interlocutor.

In this sense, the structuring of an ego can perfectly well represent an analytical success. And it would be indeed regrettable to use the dream material which will not fail to appear—since each stage is subtended and made possibe by the prospect of the one which will follow—in order to drag, more or less by force, an ego which had not yet constructed itself towards the adventure of relativization.

Moreover, what Jung calls individuation also represents a successful analysis, at a deeper level, if the demand of the analysand were, or were to become, that of discovering the meaning of the reconnection of his ego to the totality.

But further still, if the project of the analysand reveals itself to be the transcendence of the ego, we will then have to avoid the temptation of reducing it to that of a relativization. We will thus have the opportunity of learning whether we are ready to accept the temporary death of our first hero—if he is already relativized.

But is this still analysis? Just as silence was born from language, would not analysis, having arrived at this point, be the springboard to still another adventure?

Translated from the French by David Safier

REFERENCES

FORDHAM, M. (1957). "Ego, self and mental health," *Brit. J. Med. Psychol.*
  33, 4.
—— (1960). *New developments in analytical psychology.* London, Routledge.
JUNG, C. G. (1959). *The archetypes and the collective unconscious, C.W.* 9, I.
—— (1966a). *Two essays on analytical psychology.* 2nd ed. *C.W.* 7.
—— (1966b). *The spirit in man, art, and literature. C.W.* 15.
—— (1967a). *Symbols of transformation.* 2nd ed. *C.W.* 5.
—— (1967b). *Alchemical studies. C.W.* 13.
—— (1969a). *The structure and dynamics of the psyche.* 2nd ed. *C.W.* 8.
—— (1969b). *Psychology and religion: west and east.* 2nd ed. *C.W.* 11.
—— (1970). *Mysterium coniunctionis.* 2nd ed. *C.W.* 14.
NACHT, S. (1964). *Le masochisme.* Paris, Payot.
SCOTT, W. C. (1949). "The 'body scheme' in psychotherapy," *Brit. J. Med.
  Psychol.* **22**, 3/4.

Other Books Published by the Foundation:

The Old Wise Woman
  Rix Weaver $7.50

The Child
  Erich Neumann $7.50

Knowing Woman
  Irene Claremont de Castillejo $7.50

Ego and Archetype
  Edward F. Edinger $12.50

Woman's Mysteries
  M. Esther Harding $7.50

The Grail Legend
  Emma Jung and M.-L. von Franz $10.00

The Well-Tended Tree
  Hilde Kirsch, Ed. $12.00

Striving Towards Wholeness
  Barbara Hannah $7.00

The Analytic Process
  Joseph B. Wheelwright, Ed. $10.00

The Myth of Meaning
  Aniela Jaffé $7.00

The Unholy Bible
  June K. Singer $10.00

Children As Individuals
  Michael Fordham $7.50

The Way of All Women
    M. Esther Harding $7.00

Depth Psychology and a New Ethic
    Erich Neumann $7.00

The Symbolic Quest
    Edward C. Whitmont $9.00

The Reality of the Psyche
    Joseph B. Wheelwright, Ed. $8.00

Jung's Contribution to Our Time
    Eleanor Bertine $6.50

Studies in Analytical Psychology
    Gerhard Adler $7.00

The Psychotherapy of C. G. Jung
    Wolfgang Hochheimer $5.00

Psyche and Death
    Edgar Herzog $6.50

Shakespeare's Royal Self
    James Kirsch $7.95

The Parental Image
    M. Esther Harding $6.50